Asheville-Buncombe
Technical Community College
Learning Resources Center
340 Victoria Rd.
Asheville, NC 28801

DISCARDED

AUG 6 2025

The *Book of Chivalry*
of Geoffroi de Charny

University of Pennsylvania Press
MIDDLE AGES SERIES

Series Editor
Ruth Mazo Karras,
Temple University

Founding Editor
Edward Peters,
University of Pennsylvania

A listing of the available books in the series can be obtained from the publisher.

The *Book of Chivalry* of Geoffroi de Charny

Text, Context, and Translation

RICHARD W. KAEUPER and
ELSPETH KENNEDY

PENN

University of Pennsylvania Press

Philadelphia

Copyright © 1996 by the University of Pennsylvania Press
All rights reserved
Printed in the United States of America

Library of Congress Cataloging-in-Publication Data

Kaeuper, Richard W.
    The book of chivalry of Geoffroi de Charny : text, context, and translation / Richard W. Kaeuper and Elspeth Kennedy.
        p.   cm. — (Middle Ages series)
    Includes English and French text of Livre de chevalerie by G. de Charny.
    Includes bibliographical references and index.
    ISBN 0-8122-3348-4 (cloth: alk. paper). — ISBN 0-8122-1579-6 (pbk. : alk. paper)
    1. Charny, Geoffroi de, d. 1356. Livre de chevalerie. 2. Charny, Geoffroi de, d. 1356. 3. Chivalry. 4. Knights and knighthood. 5. Civilization, Medieval. 6. Courtly love. I. Kennedy, Elspeth. II. Carny, Geoffroi de, d. 1356. Livre de chevalerie. III. Title. IV. Series.
CR4513.K34   1996
940.1—dc20   96-26679
                                                                                                 CIP

Contents

Preface	vii
Acknowledgments	ix

Part One: Geoffroi de Charny and His Book
Richard W. Kaeuper

Charny's Career	3
Charny's Books and Ideals	18
The Practicality of Charny's Book	29
Piety and Lay Independence	35
Charny and Chivalric Reform	48

Part Two: The Book of Chivalry
Elspeth Kennedy

Editorial Introduction	67
Text and Translation	84
Notes to the Text and Translation	201
Bibliography	227
Index	235

Preface

THE LIFE AND THE BOOKS of Geoffroi de Charny have much to tell anyone interested in the Middle Ages. Charny is an important witness on all matters relating to chivalry, in particular, because he lived the life of knighthood in a manner thought ideal by his contemporaries. He played out this role in nearly two decades of Anglo-French warfare, dying appropriately in the swirl of battle at Poitiers (1356), one of the most famous fields of the Hundred Years War. He was the bearer of the sacred banner of the kings of France, the owner of the Shroud of Turin. His several books discuss chivalry not from the perspective of a clerical outsider, but out of the experience of a practicing knight of intense piety.

Yet even his longest, most thorough, and most informative work, the *Livre de chevalerie*, reproduced here, has been known only to specialists; the text has been accessible only in the original Middle French, rather inadequately edited, as an appendix to a set of volumes available only in the most specialized libraries.

The goal of our book is to present Charny to a wide range of readers. In the formal themes that give his *Book of Chivalry* structure and in his many tangential comments and asides, Charny proves a rich source for investigating questions about the political, military, religious, and social history of the later Middle Ages. He can tell us about the prowess and piety of knights, their capacity to express themselves, their common assumptions, their views on masculine virtue, women, and love. For students of the French language and Medieval French literature, of course, the text and translation will provide yet another range of benefits. Readers fascinated by the Shroud of Turin will have their own interests in Charny, the first historically documented owner of the Shroud.

Part One of this book establishes what we might call, in the broadest sense, the cultural context for Charny. It provides a career biography and analyzes the main themes of Charny's book in comparison with other major examples of medieval writing about chivalry. Part Two establishes

the French text of Charny's work and provides an English translation, along with full critical apparatus to explain editorial techniques, textual variants, and the literary background to the work.

RWK

Acknowledgments

HAVING ATTEMPTED FOR YEARS to use Charny's *Livre de chevalerie* in my teaching, I finally decided to launch this project to make the man and his work accessible. Finding a scholar willing and able to establish the text and undertake the translation proved to be something of a quest. Thus my greatest debt is to my collaborator, Elspeth Kennedy, whose meticulous text and lively translation appear below. It has been a pleasure to work with her. Thanks go also to James Campbell and Keith Gore (both of Worcester College, Oxford), who kindly put me in touch with Dr. Kennedy when I was looking for a collaborator. My colleague Harry Gove of the University of Rochester provided valuable information on the scientific dating of the Shroud of Turin (having had a hand in the development of the test procedures used); he shared his list of books and articles on the Shroud, and provided copies of articles he wrote himself. W. S. A. Dale (University of Western Ontario) likewise provided copies of his important articles on the interpretation of the Shroud. The patience and professional interest of Edward Peters, Jerome Singerman, and Alison Anderson at the University of Pennsylvania Press are also much appreciated. As always, my wife Margaret did much more than merely listen; she asked such very good questions.

R W K

I would like to thank Dr. Jane Taylor of St. Hilda's College, Oxford for her help and advice on the text, translation, and literary sources, Professor Carleton Carroll of Oregon State University (Corvallis) for his advice on textual difficulties, and the staff of the Tower of London for advice about military terminology.

E M K

PART ONE

GEOFFROI DE CHARNY AND HIS BOOK

Charny's Career

To his contemporaries Geoffroi de Charny was the quintessential knight of the age.[1] He enjoyed great honors bestowed by the leading figures in chivalric society; his actions won enthusiastic words of praise from chroniclers on both sides of the Channel. To Froissart, Charny was "the most worthy and valiant of them all."[2] To Geoffrey le Baker, he was "a knight more skilled in military matters than any other Frenchman, so that his fame was widespread and who also, through long practice of arms and by a lively, wise character, was until his death . . . chief counsellor of young French knights."[3] As author of three works on chivalric ideas and practices, Charny could also lay claim to the title of theoretician of chivalry in fourteenth-century France, one of its most congenial homes. As a strenuous knight he clearly practiced his principles, ending his career appropriately with an heroic death on the battlefield of Poitiers in 1356, the sacred banner of the kings of France in his hand.

A career that ended with such renown and unforgettable clarity began more obscurely, for Geoffroi was born a younger son in a family that was itself only tangentially linked to the great houses of his native Burgundy through a relationship to the lords of Mont-Saint-Jean. Charny, Philippe Contamine concisely says, was a cadet of a cadet family. Geoffroi's father, Jean de Charny, was Lord of Lirey. His mother, Marguerite de Joinville, connected the Charny family to her father, Jean, Sire de Joinville, who had

---

1. For overviews of his life see Maurice Keen, *Chivalry* (New Haven, CT, 1984), 12; Philippe Contamine, "Geoffroy de Charny (début du XIVe siècle–1356), 'Le plus prudhomme et le plus vaillant de tous les autres,'" *Histoire et société: Mélanges Georges Duby, II, Le tenancier, le fidèle et le citoyen* (Aix-en-Provence, 1992), 107–21; "Les Demandes pour la Jouste, le Tournois et la Guerre de Geoffroi de Charny (XIVème siècle)", ed. Jean Rossbach (dissertation, University of Brussels, 1961–62), 8–15; Arthur Piaget, "Le Livre Messire Geoffroi de Charny," *Romania* 26 (1897); D'Arcy Dacre Jonathan Boulton, *The Knights of the Crown: The Monarchical Orders of Knighthood in Later Medieval Europe, 1325–1520* (New York, 1987), 186.
2. *Oeuvres complètes de Froissart*, ed. Kervyn de Lettenhove (Brussels, 1867–77), V, 412: "le plus preudomme et le plus vailant de tous les autres."
3. Geoffrey le Baker, *Chronicon Galfridi le Baker de Swynebroke*, ed. Edward M. Thompson (Oxford, 1889), 103: "miles plus quam aliquis Gallicus, ut fama ventilavit, in re militari exercitatus atque, cum longa experiencia armorum, nature vivacis sagacitate excellenter dotatus, et ideo Francie tirannorum, usque ad suum interitum et coronati Francorum capcionem in prelio Pictavensi, conciliarius principalis."

been the famous friend of Louis IX and chronicler of that king's initial crusade.[4]

Yet in early adulthood Charny can have held little land. Through the reign of Philip VI (1328–50) he was known by his patronymic, not by some title drawn from a major fief. In these years he most regularly resided at the castle of Pierre-Perthuis, an estate that came to him with his first marriage. Even the battle cry with which he ends his major treatise on chivalry—"Charny! Charny!"—evokes his family, not a fief. By the end of his life, likely as a result of his second marriage, he was lord not only of Pierre-Perthuis and Lirey but of Montfort and Savoisy.[5] Shortly before his death he also came into possession of two houses, one in Paris, through the gift of his sovereign, Jean le Bon.[6]

Though the date of his birth is unknown, Charny comes into prominence in 1337, suggesting a birth date during the opening decade of the fourteenth century; we know, in fact, that his mother had died before the end of 1306. He first married Jeanne de Toucy, who died after 1341; his second marriage was to Jeanne de Vergy, Lady of Montfort and Savoisy; their two children were Geoffroy, who became his heir, and Charlotte.[7]

More significant for our interests than these details of his private life, the span of his adult public life, from his first major campaign in 1337 to his heroic death at his sovereign's side in 1356, coincides almost exactly with the first phase of the Hundred Years War as it is traditionally reckoned (from Edward III's claiming the French throne in 1337 to the Treaty of Brétigny in 1360). Thus the great conflict between the Valois kings of France and the Plantagenet kings of England provided the frame, the given, in Charny's life. War was a setting in which he worked well, for, as Raymond Cazelles

---

4. Contamine traces the family from the late eleventh century, "Geoffroy de Charny," 107–8; cf. André Perrett, "Essai sur l'histoire du Saint Suaire du XIVe au XVIe siècle," *Académie des Sciences, Belles-Lettres, et Arts de Savoie, Memoires,* ser. 6, IV (1960), 54, and the sources cited therein.

5. The best discussion on these points is in Contamine, "Geoffroy de Charny," 107–9. Not far from these seigneuries is the site of the castle called Charny, which had been held by the family since the thirteenth century. See Charles-Laurent Salch, Joelle Burnouf, and J.-F. Fino, eds., *L'Atlas des châteaux forts en France* (Strasbourg, 1977), 210–20. Joinville had himself been Lord of Lirey, as Perrett notes, "Essai sur l'histoire du Saint Suaire," 54.

6. *Chroniques de Jean Froissart,* ed. Siméon Luce (Paris, 1869–99), IV, xxxi, n. 2, citing Archives Nationales JJ 84, 671.

7. "Les Demandes," ed. Rossbach, 15, suggests that he later married Agnes de Durnay, but this is a misreading of information provided by Père F. Anselme, *Histoire généalogique de la maison royale de France* (1733), VIII, 203. Anselme states that Agnes de Durnay was in fact Charny's mother-in-law.

has wisely observed, to live without an enemy to fight would be contrary to the spirit of chivalry Charny embodied.[8]

Any account of Charny's public actions, however brief, shows that throughout the two decades of his active military career he had no difficulties in finding enemies to fight. Leading a small troop of five squires (*ecuyers*), he appeared in the southwest of the realm between July and October 1337, campaigning in Gascony under the Constable of France, Raoul, count of Eu (who seems to have been Charny's patron and whose wife was related to Charny's wife). He was then a new bachelor (*bachelier*), a young nobleman serving under a military captain, a banneret, because he lacked the means to supply his own sizable force for war.[9]

As Edward III constructed a coalition of allies in the Low Countries, Charny's field of action shifted northward, to Flanders and Hainault. Again Charny regularly served under the Constable of France. In 1340 Edward and his allies marched against Tournai, "the first outpost of the royal domain on the banks of the Scheldt."[10] On royal orders, Charny joined in the defense of Tournai. All the defenders won praise for their valor in saving the town, but Charny may well have felt disappointed that the French king refused to fight the pitched battle which the English seemed willing to hazard.[11]

If so, his was not the only dashed hope. The entire campaign was a disappointment to the English, who after a brief truce turned their attention to Brittany where a dynastic quarrel offered new opportunities. Edward III backed one claimant, Jean de Montfort; Philippe VI backed the other, Charles de Blois.[12] It comes as no surprise, then, to find Charny on the frontiers of Brittany in 1341, leading three *ecuyers* in the service of the Duke of Normandy, the future King Jean II of France. Charny's knightly qualities were already bringing him honor. When Charles of Blois came in September of 1342 to relieve Morlaix, besieged by the English under the Earl of Northampton, he gave Charny command of the first line of attacking cavalry. Honor, unfortunately for Charny, did not always mean success.

---

8. Raymond Cazelles, *Société politique, noblesse et couronne sous Jean le Bon et Charles V* (Paris, 1982), 13.

9. Contamine, "Geoffroy de Charny," 109; Anselme, *Histoire généalogique*, VIII, 201; Piaget, "Le Livre," 140–41, 147–48.

10. Edouard Perroy, *Hundred Years War* (New York, 1965), 106.

11. *Oeuvres de Froissart*, ed. Lettenhove, III, 218–19, XVII, 97, XX, 543.

12. Perroy, *Hundred Years War*, 114–18; Jean Favier, *La Guerre de Cent ans* (Paris, 1980), 130–40.

His frontal charge, the classic French tactic, was thrown back and the second French wave rode straight into a defensive line of pits disguised by greenery. Some fifty French knights died and three times that number were captured, Charny among them. Richard Talbot, his captor, sent Charny for honorable safe-keeping to his principal residence, Goodrich castle in Herefordshire.[13] Perhaps Charny's military eye could appreciate the details of his captor's castle: the rock-cut ditch, the reddish stone walls and towers set with massive spurs; perhaps his eye could only look beyond the castle across green countryside stretching toward the distant Channel.

Charny did not pine long in captivity. He was evidently soon acquired as a prisoner by an even more powerful victor from the field of Morlaix, William de Bohun, earl of Northampton, who quickly ransomed him — or at least released him from captivity to seek the money to pay his ransom.[14] His reputation had suffered not one whit. We know that by 1343 he had been knighted; he is termed a knight in both English and French governmental documents in this year. We would like to know by whom he was knighted and on what occasion, but the evidence provides only the rough date for what must have been one of the most significant days in his life.[15]

In the closing months of 1342, after Edward III crossed the Channel in October to take personal command in the Breton theater, Charny was back in harness serving with the French forces; joining the Sire de Castiel-Villain he acted as one of the marshals of the army coming to raise the siege of Vannes. Edward's army by this time had pillaged its way up to the town walls. Once again, however, the great open confrontation of armies failed to happen; in mid-January 1343 papal legates prevented an immediate and

13. A brief description of the battle and a full set of sources appear in Jonathon Sumption, *The Hundred Years War: Trial by Battle* (Philadelphia, 1990), 402. That Talbot was Charny's battlefield captor appears in Adam Murimuth's chronicle: *Adae Murimuth, continuatio Chronicarum Robertus de Avesbury, De Gestis Mirabilibus Regis Edwardi Tertii*, ed. Edward M. Thompson, Rolls Series 93 (London, 1889), 129.

14. By October 1343 an English letter patent refers to "Geoffrey de Charniz, knight, lately taken prisoner in Brittany," who has "gone to France to find the money for his ransom." At this point Charny is expected back in England; in this document William de Bohun names attorneys to receive Charny back into captivity. *Calendar of Patent Rolls, 1343–45*, 130 (hereafter *CPR*). Evidently Charny found and paid the money and did not return.

15. Siméon Luce states that he was knighted at the siege of Aiguillon, in August of 1346, *Chroniques de Jean Froissart*, IV, xxxi, n. 2, an opinion followed by Piaget, "Le Livre," 394; but P. Savio cites a document of June, 1343, in which Philip VI writes to his "ame et feal Gieffroy de Charny, chevalier." Archives Nationales JJ 1174, no. 357, cited in his "Ricerche sopra la Santa Sindone," *Pontificium Athenaeum Salesianum* 1 (1955), 120–41. Likewise an English entry on the patent roll in October, 1343, refers to "Geoffrey de Charniz, knight." *CPR 1343–45*, 130.

epic Anglo-French pitched battle and produced a truce not broken for a year and a half.[16]

Evidently dissatisfied with this period of military inactivity, Charny soon sought out enemies in another field altogether. In 1345 he joined the crusade of Humbert II, Dauphin of Viennois.[17] After consultations with the pope, Humbert had given up his plan for a Spanish crusade and instead led his forces to Smyrna in Anatolia, "the finest of the Turkish ports,"[18] which had recently been captured by Christian forces; this victory had produced a new wave of crusading interest in the west. Humbert's own force sailed from Marseilles in September 1345, landed at Genoa, crossed the Italian peninsula, sailed to Venice, and only after lengthy negotiations set sail again, arriving in Smyrna—delayed by quarrels with Italian allies—in June 1346. But if Humbert was, in Sir Steven Runciman's words, "genuinely pious and without personal ambition," he was also "a weak, vain man." In the end the entire effort, Runciman concluded, "had been singularly futile."[19] What Charny thought of battling the Turks we can guess; what he thought of the trials, perils, and inconveniences of a crusade shows up unmistakably in one of his books, in which crusading appears as a form of quasi-martyrdom.[20]

Exactly when Charny and his men returned to France is uncertain, although it seems to have been in the summer of 1346, well before their leader Humbert returned in 1347.[21] Had he learned of the active reopening of the Anglo-French war? Humbert on his return to France gave up worldly

---

16. *Oeuvres de Froissart*, ed. Lettenhove, IV, 189–90; Perroy, *Hundred Years War*, 115.

17. Piaget, "Le Livre," 394. Jonathan Riley-Smith provides an overview and excellent maps in *The Atlas of the Crusades* (New York, 1991), 140–41. Details regarding this crusade come from the following authors and chapters of Harry W. Hazard, ed., *The Fourteenth and Fifteenth Centuries*, vol. 3 of *A History of the Crusades*, gen. ed. Kenneth M. Setton, 4 vols. (Madison, WI, 1969–89); Aziz S. Atiya, "The Crusade in the Fourteenth Century," 12; Deno Geanakoplos, "Byzantium and the Crusades, 1354–1453," 61–62; Peter Topping, "The Morea, 1311–1364," 133. Philippe Contamine suggests two additional factors possibly influencing Charny: the death (in a tournament) of his patron, the Count of Eu, and the association of his family with previous crusading ventures. "Geoffroy de Charny," 109–10.

18. Riley-Smith, *Atlas of the Crusades*, 140–41.

19. Steven Runciman, *A History of the Crusades, III: The Kingdom of Acre* (Cambridge, 1951–54), 452. This judgment is echoed by the several authors who comment on this crusade in Hazard, *The Fourteenth and Fifteenth Centuries*.

20. *Livre Charny*, ll. 594–845, printed in "A Critical Edition of Geoffroy de Charny's 'Livre Charny' and the 'Demandes pour la joute, le tournois et la guerre,'" ed. Michael Anthony Taylor (unpublished Ph.D. dissertation, University of North Carolina at Chapel Hill, 1977), 24–34.

21. See sources cited in Contamine, "Geoffroy de Charny," 110; "Les Demandes," ed. Rossbach, 9; Perrett, "Essai sur l'histoire du Saint Suaire," 55.

struggle and entered a Dominican convent;[22] Charny lost no time in reentering the Anglo-French warfare.

Charny missed the great set-piece battle of Crécy because he was engaged in other missions for the French war effort. Under the Duke of Normandy he was part of the force in the southwest trying to blunt the Anglo-Gascon initiative, which had already taken the town of Aiguillon, a strategically crucial spot at the confluence of two rivers, the Lot and Garonne. The French siege had to be lifted, however, as news came that the army of Edward III had landed on the coast of Normandy, launching the campaign that would bring the great English victory at Crécy. At the time of this battle Froissart places Charny among the heroic defenders of the town of Béthune, besieged by a Flemish army.[23] Charny's reputation perhaps benefited from being associated with a successful defense at just the time when the host representing French chivalry in general had suffered a humiliating defeat.

Following their triumph on the field of Crécy, the English went on to besiege the important port of Calais. The French king was vainly trying to find a way to pry open the English stranglehold on this strongly fortified town. His efforts were frustrated by the topography of the region (seacoast dunes exposed to fire from the English fleet, swampy land cut by frequent canals), as well as by the fortifications the English had built at vulnerable points.[24] Philippe decided to send Edward a challenge to come out and fight. Charny's growing reputation led Philippe to choose him as one of two emissaries to convey the challenge to the English king. Charny and his colleague, the Lord of Montmorency, took mental notes on all the defenses they passed in reaching Edward III, but once they talked with the king they could only take back a disappointing answer. Edward told them that Calais was his in right and would soon, after an expensive siege, be his in fact; if the king of France wanted to come to him he would have to find a way. Philippe, in fact, had no desire for a frontal assault encountering the dif-

---

22. Humbert ceded the Dauphiné to the future Charles V in 1349. He was formally created Latin Patriarch of Alexandria in 1351, and (despite his clerical orders) was named a member of the royal Company of the Star. Aziz S. Atiya tells the story of his crusade and his subsequent life in *The Crusade in the Later Middle Ages* (London, 1938), 301–18.

23. Froissart specifically names Charny among the heroic defenders of Béthune along with three other prominent knights and a force of 200 lances. After they held the town for six weeks, the discouraged Flemish army gave up the siege. This sturdy defense, Froissart says, won great renown for Charny and the other lords. *Oeuvres de Froissart*, ed. Lettenhove, V, 148–49. For the siege, see Sumption, *Hundred Years War*, 524.

24. For what follows, see Favier, *La Guerre de Cent ans*, 120–27, *Oeuvres de Froissart*, ed. Lettenhove, XVII, 250–52; V, 501; XX, 540.

ficult terrain and daunting fortifications seen first hand by Charny and Montmorency. The French army withdrew and Calais, its citizens starving, heroically held out six more weeks before the town surrendered in early August. It would be the English beachhead in France for the next two centuries.

The more immediate effect was to precipitate a political crisis in France. Philippe VI and his chief vassals had repeatedly failed to carry out the most elementary function of knights and feudal lords, the defense of their land. When, at the end of November 1347, Philippe of necessity summoned the Estates to refill his war coffers, he had to listen to trenchant criticisms: the King had raised hosts of men at great cost and suffered humiliating defeat; he had been reduced to making truces with enemies still within his realm; he had been badly counseled. Such criticisms helped generate the current of reform that swept new men into the royal council, men who might bring about political and military success, men who might even be able to provide the new moral tone so necessary since God was obviously punishing the kingdom for sin.

Geoffroi de Charny figured among the several virtuous knights added to the council in this time of crisis and uncertainty; the king even arranged a residence in Paris for Charny as a convenient base for his new councilor and as a reward for his good and loyal services in the king's wars and other affairs.[25] Charny had, in fact, for some time been as busy with diplomacy as with war. He had served, for example, as one of the group of French negotiators who secured a peace between Humbert II, Dauphin of Viennois, and the Count of Savoy. He had also helped to negotiate an Anglo-French truce in September 1347.[26]

Yet he may well have likewise helped to formulate ambitious plans for a bold counterstroke, an invasion of England.[27] Such military work would have undoubtedly been more congenial to him than rounds of diplomatic conversation. These plans for invasion soon dissolved, however, as France suffered an invader much more deadly than anything either Valois or Plantagenet could muster. The Plague devastated France in 1348, killing on a scale beyond the capacity of warriors' weapons, utterly disrupting the finan-

25. He sat on the king's council from January of 1348. *Les Journaux du trésor de Philippe VI de Valois, suivis de l'Ordinarium thesaurii de 1338–1339*, ed. Jules Viard, Collection des Documents Inédits de l'Histoire de France (Paris, 1899), 799, 838–39; *Documents parisiens du règne de Philippe VI de Valois*, Vol. I, *(1328–1338)*, ed. J. Viard (Paris, 1899), 295–96.
26. Contamine, "Geoffroy de Charny," 111; "Les Demandes," ed. Rossbach, 10.
27. Raymond Cazelles, *Société politique*, 121–25; Favier, *La Guerre de Cent ans*, 127; Perroy, *Hundred Years War*, 121.

cial scheme designed to amass the needed war fund of more than three million livres.[28]

The war went on nonetheless, and Charny rode by order of Philippe VI to watch the military frontier from a base at St. Omer. Froissart says that for the business of war Charny functioned "like a king."[29]

Certainly he was second to none in his obsession to recover the great prize of Calais.[30] He conceived a plan to regain the town by bribing a Lombard named Aimery de Pavia, who was apparently a captain of its citadel (though Froissart inflates his position to that of governor of the town).[31] Froissart says Charny reasoned that Aimery was not a man of high status, that he was not a native Englishman, and that (being a Lombard) he was greedy. Since it was a time of truce, contacts were easily established and negotiations begun.

Though Aimery had served Edward III loyally as a naval commander,[32] he may have been tempted by Charny's offer of 20,000 écus. But he was also prudent. Called suddenly to London by King Edward, who had heard disturbing rumors—so Froissart relates in one version of his chronicle—Aimery saved himself by telling all (from a suitable kneeling position) and by cooperating with Edward in setting a trap.[33] In another version of his chronicle Froissart asserts that Aimery only pretended to negotiate with

---

28. John Bell Henneman, *Royal Taxation in Medieval France: the Development of War Financing (1322–1356)* (Princeton, NJ, 1971), 227–38; Cazelles, *Société politique*, 125–26.

29. *Oeuvres de Froissart*, ed. Lettenhove, V, 229–30: "et y estoit et usoit de toutes coses touchans as armes, comme rois."

30. Lettenhove, *Oeuvres de Froissart*, ed. Lettenhove, V, 230: "Cils messires Jeffrois estoit en coer trop durement couroucies de le prise et dou conques de Calais, et l'en desplaisoit, par samblant, plus c'a nul autre chevalier de Pikardie. Si metoit toutes ses ententes et imaginations au regarder comment il le peuist ravoir." The account that follows draws on Froissart's several accounts and on the information in Contamine, "Geoffroy de Charny," 112.

31. Geoffrey le Baker writes of the "turrim cui Emericus preficiebatur." *Chronicon*, ed. Thompson, 103. Aimery could not have commanded Calais, town and castle. John de Beauchamp became captain of the castle 29 July 1349, captain of the town 1 January 1349. His appointment was renewed 12 July 1349, and his functioning in office is mentioned in August 1349. By 26 September 1349, Robert de Herle was "locum tenentis capitanei villae nostrae Calesiae" and on 9 March 1350 Herle was commissioned captain of the town, to take effect 1 April. Thomas Rymer, *Foedera, Conventiones, Literae*, ed. Adam Clarke and Frederick Holbrooke (London, 1856), III, pt. 1, 165, 181, 185–88, 189, 193. Administrative orders refer only to Beauchamp and Herle, and sometimes to John de Chevereston in charge of the town or castle of Calais through this period: *CPR 1348–50*, 172, 590; *CPR 1350–54*, 326; *Calendar of Fine Rolls, 1347–56*, 92; *Calendar of Close Rolls, 1349–54*, 274, 424.

32. Rymer, *Foedera*, III, pt. 1, 159.

33. *Oeuvres de Froissart*, ed. Lettenhove, V, 229–51 provides the several versions of this entire story. For earlier accounts see Geoffrey le Baker, *Chronicon*, ed. Thompson, 103–8; Thompson, *Adae Murimuth*, 408–10. Details of Aimery's motives and the clever plans by which Edward III captured the French force vary with the teller, but in broad outline the story is clear.

Charny and, at the right time, loyally informed Edward of the attempt to regain Calais by a bribe. In any event he soon returned to his negotiations with Charny. The exchange of castle and town for money was to take place in the waning hours of the last day of 1349.

Charny came prepared with the money and a sufficient force to hold Calais. Froissart pictures Charny and his close companions joking to ease their impatience while a few men carried in at least a large part of the money and saw to the opening of the gates.[34] "That Lombard takes a long time," Charny is made to say, "He'll kill us with the cold." Charny insisted that he would ride, preceded by his banner, through the high gate before him, as soon as it was opened; he would not enter the low wicket-gate through which the small party passed in making the final arrangements. But while he and his men shivered in their cold armor, Aimery (who had securely stashed away his bribe) alerted a hidden but overpowering English force.

Edward III had secretly reinforced the garrison at Calais and had then brought his son and a few trusted companions to join in springing the trap, the exact nature of which much exercised the chroniclers' creative powers. Geoffroy le Baker pictures the English, hidden behind a false wall cleverly joined to the solid stonework, suddenly bursting out on their enemies while a trusted man hurled a huge stone to smash the beams of the turning bridge, already cut nearly in two, thus trapping the French within the walls. While such details seem invented, the outcome is clear. Once this small French party within the castle was captured, the English swung open the outer gates and rushed the surprised force outside. Charny apparently shouted to his companions that they were betrayed and must stand and fight bravely. Most of the French force in fact fled, pursued rashly by Edward III leading what seems to have been a smaller force of knights and archers than those they pursued. A sharp fight ensued on a causeway leading through marshy ground; the herald of Sir John Chandos claimed that this was one of the king's hardest fights, and that the day was won for the English only by the entry into the combat of Edward the Black Prince and his men.[35] When the king's son arrived with English reinforcements, the French broke again and the fight was finished. Charny, who had apparently stood his ground, fell captive, suffering a head wound. The knight to whom he actually surrendered, John de Potenhale, would receive 100 marks from

---

34. As Contamine observes, Froissart has a keen sense of dialogue. "Froissart: Art militaire, pratique et conception de la guerre," 142.
35. Chandos Herald, *Life of the Black Prince by the Herald of Sir John Chandos*, ed. Mildred K. Pope and Eleanor C. Lodge (Oxford, 1910), ll. 415–75.

Edward III "for the good services by him performed for the said Lord the King, and especially for taking Geoffrey de Charny." Potenhale later personally conducted Charny to London at the king's expense,[36] taking him into a second period of captivity that can only have been as honorable in its conditions as it was frustrating in its enforced inactivity.

On the very night after the battle the survivors were treated to a classic chivalric display. They learned for the first time that they had fought Edward III in person; the English king had in fact fought in plain armor under the banner of Walter Mauny. Now he personally waited on his prisoners at the supper table. After the meal he mingled with his captive guests in friendly conversation. But his demeanor changed somewhat when he came to Charny. Froissart gives him a reproving speech:

Messire Geoffroy, Messire Geoffroy, I rightly owe you very little love since you wanted to take from me by night what I have won and what has cost me much money: so I am very pleased to have put you to the test. You wanted to get it more cheaply than I, for 20,000 écus; but God aided me so that you failed in your intent. He will yet aid me, if it pleases Him, in my greater endeavor.[37]

Edward's comments apparently left Charny little to say, so he stood in silence, listening with what one of the Froissart manuscripts describes as feelings of shame.[38]

Since shame was the feeling or condition most to be feared by an honorable knight, the issue is important. Had Charny violated a truce and reduced his honor by negotiating the seizure of Calais for mere money? Kervyn de Lettenhove, one of the prominent nineteenth-century editors of Froissart, provided a legalistic defense. Charny had not violated a truce because he had not personally negotiated it nor sworn to uphold it. After his release, he was careful to swear to uphold the current truce.[39] This argument may have some force, but of course the issue transcends legal niceties to touch Charny's general reputation as a knight.

A more significant argument could rest on the attitude of the French king, in whose eyes Charny, far from being compromised, was evidently

---

36. Frederick Devon, ed., *Issues of the Exchequer* (London, 1837), 156, 157.
37. *Oeuvres de Froissart*, ed. Lettenhove, V, 246–47: "Messire Joffroi, messire Joffroi, je vous doi par raison petit amer quant vous volies par nuit embler ce que j'ay si comparet et qui m'a coustet tant de deniers: si sui moult lies quant je vous ay mis a l'espreuve. Vous en volies avoir milleur marchiet que je n'en ay eu, qui le cuidies avoir pour XXm escus; mes Diex m'a aidiet que vous aves falli a vostre entente. Encores m'aiderail, se il le plaist, a ma plus grant entente."
38. *Oeuvres de Froissart*, ed. Lettenhove, V, 250: Froissart says Charny was "tous honteus et ne respondi mot."
39. *Oeuvres de Froissart*, ed. Lettenhove, XX, 544.

considered ever more worthy.[40] Philippe VI died while Charny was a captive in London, but his successor, Jean II, contributed 12,000 écus toward Charny's ransom in July 1351.[41] As we will see, he also chose Charny unhesitatingly as a member of the new chivalric order he founded in the following year and apparently even commissioned him to write the series of works intended to set the moral tone of this new royal order. Charny was scarcely under a cloud in France. Perhaps most fighting men of the time would simply have thought that Charny played the game by a hard set of rules, and when he lost temporarily, endured Edward's taunting rebuke in silence as the only practical response.

In the summer of 1351 Charny was back in harness. He fought at Ardres in June; in July he took part in negotiations between the King of France and the Count of Flanders; in September he attended the negotiations that prolonged the Anglo-French truce.[42]

His new responsibilities, indicated by the sonorous title of "Captain General of the Wars of Picardie and the Frontiers of Normandy,"[43] did not deter him from settling a personal score. Whether or not he suffered any pangs of conscience about his attempt at Calais, he had no doubts that Aimery had betrayed him and should be dealt with accordingly. Aimery was now living in a fortified dwelling given to him by Edward III, who had nonetheless removed him from any position at Calais. Good service must be rewarded, but trust apparently went only so far. Aimery, if we can believe Froissart, was living a joyful life with an English mistress named Marguerite. Charny decided on a night raid, which this time was a complete success. He surprised Aimery—Froissart insists he was in bed with Marguerite, who with distressing pragmatism soon took up with a French squire—and led him back to his base at St. Omer. There he decapitated the Lombard, quartered his body, and displayed it at the town gates. To show that all this was a private matter and not a part of the business of war,

---

40. Contamine argues, plausibly, that the king must have approved the plan in the first place. "Geoffroy de Charny," 112. Cazelles notes that the truce was being broken even before the death of Philip VI. Since the English captains did not respect it, Jean II, he argues, was not eager to have it renewed unless secured by better guarantees. *Société politique*, 140.

41. According to Lettenhove the ransom was 1000 écus. *Oeuvres de Froissart*, XX, 543; Anselme states that it was 12,000 écus. *Histoire généalogique*, 201.

42. Contamine, "Geoffroy de Charny," 112 and sources given there.

43. Anselme, *Histoire généalogique*, 201–2, says the French king paid a part of the ransom in July 1351, but then adds that Charny held the command noted from 29 August 1350 (presumably an error for 1351). The *Chronique normande du XIVe siècle*, ed. Auguste Molinier and Emile Molinier (Paris, 1882), 101, places Charny in June 1351 in an attack on an English party of seven hundred; this force, moving out from Calais, was attacked near Ardres and all were killed or captured.

prohibited for a time by the current truce, Charny took possession only of Aimery himself, not his castle.[44]

Aimery de Pavia was, in Charny's eyes, a traitor in the broad contemporary sense (encountered often in medieval literature) of faithlessness to sworn word. But Charny came to the same judgment in the case of Hugues de Belconroy, the French commander of the castle of Guines, who had delivered his fortress to the English for a sum of money. Here was a traitor in the emerging political sense of disloyalty to the king of France. When Belconroy was turned over to Charny at St. Omer, Charny had the man put to death, although he had done precisely what Charny had expected Aimery to do.[45] Perhaps he would not have objected had the English king similarly executed Aimery, if he had kept to his bargain, delivered Calais to the French, and later had the misfortune of being captured by his English lords. Unfaithful to his sworn agreement with Charny, Aimery deserved death; Belconroy, unfaithful to his king, likewise deserved death. Charny might have felt surprise at any sense of moral ambiguity on our part. Did not both the castle of Guines and the castle and town of Calais rightfully belong to the king of France?

In January 1352, this king was breathing life into a plan that had lived only in his imagination since 1344, when he was simply duke of Normandy and heir to the throne. Jean II wanted to create a company of knights that could stand as the premier order of chivalry in the Christian West, a noble Company of the Star that could outshine even Edward's royal chivalric order announced only a few months previous (the order that would later result in the Garter).[46] The French royal order, dedicated to the Blessed Virgin, was to be served by an ecclesiastical college that would provide divine service and pray for the knightly conduct of the members. The company was to meet twice annually in the royal manor of Saint-Ouen, embellished for its new role with significant renovations as well as the new name of the Noble Maison. If he could have enrolled 500 members as planned, this order would have encompassed between an eighth and a fifth of all the knights in the realm.

In fact, far from dominating the world of fourteenth-century chivalry,

---

44. *Oeuvres de Froissart*, ed. Lettenhove, V, 271–74. Cf. *Chronique normande du XIVe siècle*, ed. Molinier and Molinier, 103–4 and *Chronique des quatre premiers Valois*, ed. Siméon Luce (Paris, 1862), 29–30.
45. *Oeuvres de Froissart*, ed. Lettenhove, XVII, 293–94.
46. What follows is based on Boulton, *Knights of the Crown*, 167–210.

the Company of the Star crumbled swiftly and completely under the hammer blows of defeat on the battlefield and corrosion of internescine strife. Perhaps more than eighty members died in a battle described by Froissart (apparently the battle of Mauron in Brittany in August 1352); the casualty rate may well result from an oath taken by the members that they would not flee a battle.[47] After the yet more disastrous defeat of French chivalry and the capture of King Jean himself at Poitiers in 1356, the order was virtually dead.

But in the heady days of its founding the Company of the Star must have seemed truly grand. Charny, like the other initial members, could consider themselves near the pinnacle of the chivalric world. Indeed, as Jonathon Bolton suggests, "Charny seems to have been the very model of the sort of knighthood that Jean was attempting to promote when he founded the Company of the Star, and it is very probable that Charny composed all three of his works on chivalry at Jean's request."[48]

The ultimate chivalric honor for Charny, however, has yet to be mentioned. In March 1347, and again in June 1355, Jean II named him the bearer or keeper of the oriflamme,[49] the sacred banner of the king of France, which was raised boldly in the front ranks of his major battles. Contemporary opinion held that the keeper must be "the most worthy and the most adept warrior" (le plus preudomme et plus preux es armes), that the king's choice must fall on "a knight noble in intention and deed, unwavering, virtuous, loyal, adept, and chivalrous, one who fears and loves God" (ung chevalier noble en couraige et en fais, constant et vertueulx, loyal, preux, et chevalereux et qui doubte et ayme Dieu).[50] The oriflamme, a tassled square or rectangle of red silk ending in a number of small streamers, was attached in battle to a gilded lance. In peacetime it was deposited in the monastery at St. Denis. Periodically the kings of France brought it forth for war in an elaborate liturgy of masses, relics, and benedictions. Immersed in this atmosphere of candlelight and incense, the guardian of the oriflamme, kneeling with head bared, took the following oath, said out to him by the Abbot of St. Denis:

---

47. Boulton, *Knights of the Crown*, 36.
48. Boulton, *Knights of the Crown*, 186.
49. For what follows see Philippe Contamine, "L'Oriflamme de Saint-Denis aux XIVe et XVe siècles," *Annales de l'Est* 7 (1973), 179–244. Anselme gives the 1355 date, but cites other sources that indicate 1347. *Histoire généalogique*, 202.
50. Contamine, "L'Oriflamme de Saint Denis," 225, n. 5, quoting Jean Golein and Philippe de Villette.

You swear and promise on the precious, sacred body of Jesus Christ present here and on the bodies of Monsigneur Saint Denis and his fellows which are here, that you will loyally in person hold and keep the oriflamme of our lord king, who is here, to his honor and profit and that of his realm, and not abandon it for fear of death or whatever else may happen, and you will do your duty everywhere as a good and loyal knight must toward his sovereign and proper lord.[51]

After this oath the king raised the bearer to his feet and kissed him on the mouth. The bearer then genuflected before the sacred relics and took the sacred banner in his joined hands; he raised it aloft for all to see. The lords and barons present were permitted to kiss (*embrasser*) the oriflamme "as a relic and worthy thing." If the banner was not already attached to its lance, the king draped it dramatically around the shoulders of its bearer for the recessional.

Charny was occupied with numerous diplomatic missions in 1353 and 1354, but he was once again entrusted with the oriflamme as hostilities reopened in 1355.[52] On the battlefield at Poitiers in the early autumn of 1356, Geoffroy de Charny unfailingly met the conditions of his oath as keeper of the oriflamme.

The climactic battle was provoked by a renewed English invasion.[53] As part of an ambitious three-pronged attack, Edward the Black Prince had led an Anglo-Gascon force from Bordeaux into central France. In fact, the Black Prince soon found himself pursued (slowed down by dragging along a vast load of booty) by a much larger French host commanded by Jean II. So certain of victory was the French king that he brushed aside the peace negotiations of two cardinals and insisted on battle. The English likewise brushed aside the classic chivalric suggestion of Charny that the conflict be settled by one hundred chosen champions on each side, to limit the bloodshed.[54]

On September 19 near Poitiers the French suffered one of their worst military disasters of the Middle Ages. A charge of elite French knights failed

---

51. "Vous jurez et promettez sur le precieux corps Jesus Crist sacre cy present et sur le corps de monseigneur saint Denis et ses compaignons qui cy sont, que vous loialment en vostre personne tendrez et gouvernerez l'oriflambe du roy nostre sire, qui cy est, a l'onneur et profit de lui et de son royaume, et pour doubte de mort ne d'autre aventure qui puisse avenir ne la delairez, et ferez partout vostre devoir comme bon et loyal chevalier doit faire envers son souverain et droiturier seigneur." Quoted in Contamine, "L'Oriflamme de Saint Denis," 211.

52. Contamine notes these. "Geoffroy de Charny," 113.

53. For the campaign, see Perroy, *Hundred Years War*, 125–31; Favier, *La Guerre de Cent ans*, 181–225; H. J. Hewitt, *The Black Prince's Expedition of 1355–1357* (Manchester, 1958).

54. See R. Delachenal, *Histoire de Charles V* (Paris, 1909), 226, and the sources cited there. In his *Life of the Black Prince*, ed. Pope and Lodge, the Chandos Herald quotes Charny's speech.

to break through improvised English defense lines, and the battle became a confused series of piecemeal actions. King Jean took his stand at the center of the most desperate fighting, with Charny close at hand. Froissart's words picture the action vividly:

There Sir Geoffroy de Charny fought gallantly near the King. The whole press and cry of battle were upon him because he was carrying the King's sovereign banner [the oriflamme]. He also had before him on the field his own banner, gules, three escutcheons argent. So many English and Gascons came around him from all sides that they cracked open the King's battle formation and smashed it; there were so many English and Gascons that at least five of these men-at-arms attacked one [French] gentleman. Sir Geoffroy de Charny was killed with the banner of France in his hands, and the French banners fell to the earth.[55]

Before he was killed, Charny had cut down the first man to lay a hand on the bridle of Jean's horse, but now the king was forced to yield to enemies who surrounded him shouting, "Give yourself up! Give yourself up!"[56]

The consequences of this battle can be read at length in the tumultuous history of France in the later fourteenth century. But the conclusion to Charny's own story is quickly told. His body was first buried at Poitiers, at the house of the Grey Friars,[57] but was taken from Poitiers to Paris at royal expense and given formal reburial in 1370 in the church of the Celestines, a site frequently used by the crown for the burials of royal servants. This latter ceremony was double: Charny and the marshal Arnould d'Audrehen, both

---

55. Combining into one narrative Froissart's two slightly differing accounts: "La se combattoit vassaument messires Joffrois de Chargny. Et estoit toutte li priesse et li huee sour lui pour tant qu'il portoit le souverainne banniere dou roy, et il-meysmes avoit sa banniere devant lui, qui estoit de gueulles a trois escuchons d'argent. Tant y sourvinrent autour de lui d'Engles et de Gascons, et si s'efforchierent que par forche il ouvrirent et rompirent le bataille dou roy; et fu si plainne d'Engles et de Gascons qu'il y avoit bien V hommes d'armes sour ung gentil homme prissonier, voirs s'il n estoit pris en le cache, et la fu mors et ochis messires Joffroys de Chargny, et les bannieres de Franche gettees par terre...." *Oeuvres de Froissart*, ed. Lettenhove, V, 453. "La se combatoit vaillament et asses pries dou roy messires Joffrois de Cargni, et estoit toute la presse et la huee sur lui, pour tant qu'il portoit la souveraine baniere dou roy, et il-meismes avoit la sienne sus les camps, qui estoit de geules a III escucons d'argent. Tant y sourvinrent Engles et Gascons, de toutes pars, que par force il ouvrirent et rompirent le priesse de le bataille le roy de France, et furent li Francois si entouelliet entre leurs ennemies que il y avoit bien, en tel lieu estoit et tels fois fu, V hommes d'armes sus un gentil homme... et fu occis messires Joffrois de Cargni, la baniere de France entre ses mains." *Oeuvres de Froissart*, ed. Lettenhove, V, 433.

56. Lettenhove mentions Charny's rescue of the king in *Oeuvres de Froissart*, V, 543. Alfred Coville likewise mentions this incident. *Les premiers Valois et la Guerre de cent ans (1328–1422)*, vol. 4 of *Histoire de France depuis les origines jusqu' à la Révolution*, ed. Ernest Lavisse (Paris, 1901–1910, reprint New York, 1969), 107. Froissart's description of the capture of Jean II appears in *Oeuvres de Froissart*, ed. Lettenhove, V, 433–34, 453–54.

57. Contamine, "Geoffroy de Charny," 114.

former keepers of the oriflamme, were interred on the same day.[58] Charny's son, the second Geoffroi, died without heirs in 1398, thus ending the line.[59]

Told in this way, the story of Charny's life takes on a bleak cast. Vigorous and valiant as he may have been, he was captured twice, went on a useless crusade, failed to secure Calais for his king, and was hacked to death in the great set-piece battle for which he had presumably longed all his life. Yet he was vastly admired by his contemporaries, and when we turn to the ideals he presents in his writing we find that he lived the sort of life he most valued, dying in the manner most fitting his strong sense of vocation. Moreover, through the window of his words, we modern readers can get a new glimpse into the lay aristocratic mind of his age.

Charny's Books and Ideals

That Geoffroi de Charny was a man of words as well as a man of war need cause no great surprise. Historical studies have for some time emphasized the rising literacy of medieval lay people in general and the level of education among the nobility in particular.[60] For example, at about the same time Charny composed his three works, across the Channel in England another great warlord, Henry of Lancaster, wrote *Le livre de seyntz medicines*, an intensely pious devotional treatise.[61]

In neither case does authorship necessarily imply penmanship. Lancas-

---

58. *Oeuvres de Froissart*, ed. Lettenhove, XX, 543; Contamine, "Geoffroy de Charny," 114; Anselme, *Histoire généalogique*, 201; "Les Demandes," ed. Rossbach, 137; Cazelles, *Société politique*, 527–28.

59. *Oeuvres de Froissart*, ed. Lettenhove, XX, 525.

60. H. G. Richardson and G. O. Sayles, *The Governance of Medieval England from the Conquest to Magna Carta* (Edinburgh, 1963), chap. XV; K. B. McFarlane, "The Education of the Nobility in Later Medieval England," *The English Nobility in the Later Middle Ages* (Oxford, 1973), 228–48; Malcolm Parkes, "The Literacy of the Laity," *The Medieval World* (London, 1973); Bernard Guenée, "La culture historique des nobles: le succes des *Faits des Romains* (XIIIe–XVe siecles)," *La noblesse au Moyen Age*, ed. Philippe Contamine (Paris, 1976), 261–88; Ralph V. Turner, "The *Miles Literatus* in Twelfth-Century England: How Rare a Phenomenon?" *American Historical Review* 83 (1978), 928–45; Janet Coleman, *Medieval Readers and Writers, 1350–1400* (New York, 1981), chapter 2; Keen, *Chivalry*, 102–24; Michael Clanchy, *From Memory to Written Record: England, 1066–1307*, 2nd ed. (London, 1993).

61. *Le Livre de seyntz medicines: The Unpublished Devotional Treatise of Henry of Lancaster*, ed. S. J. Arnould, Anglo-Norman Text Society (Oxford, 1940). Lancaster was one of the original knights of the Garter. For comments on this text, see S. J. Arnould, "Henry of Lancaster and His Livre de Seyntes Medicines," *Bulletin of the John Rylands Library* 21 (1937), 352–86, and W. A. Pantin, *The English Church in the Fourteenth Century* (Notre Dame, IN, 1962), 231–33.

ter could, in fact, write, as his autograph on one copy of his work testifies.[62] But K. B. McFarlane directs our attention to the "ever-available secretaries" used by everybody from king to gentry. "The only safe rule," he suggests, "is to assume that letters, memoranda, and other documents were the work of professional scribes of some sort unless there is definite evidence to the contrary." We must remember that "like the busy men of today the busy men of the fourteenth century preferred to dictate."[63] With this opinion in mind we might justly picture Charny dictating to a scribe, perhaps pacing to put his characteristic vigor to work in the service of composition, certainly exclaiming an occasional "He! Dieu!" to emphasize a point he felt with particular keenness.

The issue is thus not whether Charny could write, pen in hand, but how well he could organize his thoughts and express his ideas in written form. Three texts stand in evidence.[64]

The *Demandes pour la joute, les tournois et la guerre* (Questions concerning the joust, tournament, and war) poses a long series of intricate questions on chivalric practice; 20 questions consider the individual encounter of the joust; another 21 questions consider the group encounter of *mêlée* or *tournois*; the final 93 questions move from the tournament field to consider the yet graver business of knights on the battlefield. Unfortunately, these detailed questions all appear without answers. In modern typescript this treatise fills 61 pages.[65] A second treatise, the *Livre Charny*, a verse work on the manner of life and the qualities demanded by chivalry, fills 76 pages of typescript.[66]

A longer and more complete statement on chivalry appears in prose in his *Livre de chevalerie*, the text and English translation for which appear in this volume. This is the book that provides Charny's most thoughtful and comprehensive statement on chivalry. We will occasionally draw on the other two treatises, however, to qualify or amplify the views expressed in the major work, the *Book of Chivalry*.

With what skill does this great knight write his books? Charny's ver-

---

62. See Arnould, "Henry of Lancaster," 353. The hand of the text and the hand of the autograph, however, appear to be quite distinct.
63. McFarlane, *Nobility*, pp. 239, 241. Even Ramon Llull, in his treatise on chivalry, "recounted and allowed to be put down in writing what follows." *Selected Works of Ramon Llull (1232–1316)*, ed. Anthony Bonner (Princeton, NJ, 1985), 13.
64. For a general discussion see Keen, *Chivalry*, 12–15, and the same author's "Chivalry, Nobility, and the Man-at-Arms," *War, Literature and Politics in the Later Middle Ages*, ed. C. T. Allmand (Liverpool, 1976), 36–40.
65. "Critical Edition," ed. Taylor. See also "Les Demandes," ed. Rossbach.
66. "Critical Edition," ed. Taylor.

sification in the *Demandes* has won few admirers and even his prose can ramble and cross its own tracks.[67] He cannot rival the romance writers (in either verse or prose); he does not have the gifts of Froissart, who could write both colorful chronicle and romance. But coming from a layman who necessarily devoted most of his life to knightly training and military campaign, the treatises of Charny are impressive. His program of writing was ambitious and timely; in an age of acute crisis he took as his subject both the broad ethos and particular practices of chivalry, the dominant force in the lives of men in the dominant layers of his society; he wrote with conviction and, at his best, with powerful effect. Thus his works have great interest beyond their modest aesthetic merits.

The value of Charny's ideas, moreover, extends far beyond the issue of his skill or originality as a writer. In fact, much of the interest for the modern reader who wants to understand the phenomenon of medieval chivalry lies precisely in Charny's lack of originality. We can read in Charny's pages the essential commonplaces, the self-conception of his calling presented by a vigorous knight in the mid-fourteenth century, after more than two centuries of learned discussion, praise, valorization, and criticism directed at chivalry from all sides. From this book we can gain a fair idea of what a knight has absorbed out of the vigorous medieval world of ideas all around him, what he has rejected or ignored, what he has added from the yet more vigorous world of his own experience in camp, court, and campaign.

To read any of Charny's treatises with full understanding we clearly need to consider when and for whom he wrote. The determining factor in making a writer of this knight seems to be Jean II's founding of the Company of the Star. The opening to the *Demandes pour la joute, les tournois et la guerre* specifies that this treatise is intended for the king's chivalric order:

---

67. Philippe Contamine calls Charny's work "oeuvre littérairement assez médiocre mais historiquement suggestive." "Froissart: art militaire, pratique et conception de la guerre," *Froissart, Historian*, ed. J. J. N. Palmer (Bury St. Edmunds, 1981), 143. Contamine complains that in Charny's *Demandes* "la pauvreté de son vocabulaire, la maladresse de sa syntaxe obscurcissent souvent sa pensée." *Guerre, état et société à la fin du Moyen Age* (Paris, 1972), 190, n. 37. Piaget found in the *Livre Charny* a "manqué d'art" and a "défaute de mérites littéraires," which, however, "n'enlève rien a l'intérêt du poème." "Le Livre," 410. Jean Rossbach says of the *Livre Charny* that it is "poésie médiocre, qui témoigne plus de la bonne volonté du chevalier que de son talent." Analyzing the *Demandes*, Rossbach writes, "Nous n'avons pas affaire à un écrivain de talent mais simplement à un chevalier qui aime son état, connait les difficultés et les problèmes de sa profession et veut les faire apparaître." "Les Demandes," 28, 31. Michael Taylor defends both the art and the structure of two of Charny's works in "Critical Edition," xxi–xxxii.

These are the questions regarding the joust which I, Geoffroy de Charny, present to the high and powerful prince of the knights of Our Lady of the Noble Maison, to be judged by you and the knights of our noble company.[68]

In fact, it seems likely that all three of Charny's works were written for Jean le Bon and the Company of the Star.[69] Although the *Demandes pour la joute, les tournois et la guerre* alone states this purpose explicitly, the other two treatises fit the objectives of the royal reform program perfectly, as we will see. Even the costume Charny suggests for a squire's knighting ceremony (which he borrowed from an earlier work, the anonymous *Ordene de chevalerie*) looks very similar in basic form and colors to the habit chosen for the knights of the Star.[70]

It is also worth noting that the order was involved with books from its inception: according to the chronicler Jean le Bel, who wrote shortly after the founding of the Company of the Star, in the great assemblies of the order,

each one [of the companions] should recount all his adventures, the shameful as well as the glorious, which happened to him during the time since he spent away from the noble court, and the king should order two or three clerks to listen to all these adventures and put them in a book so that they would be reported each year in front of the companions, so that the most valiant should be known and those honoured who most deserve it.[71]

The French king could easily have borrowed this idea from widely read works of French Arthurian romance. *Lancelot do Lac*, a popular prose ro-

---

68. This statement of purpose and patronage appears at the head of each of the three sections of Charny's treatise, that is, for the questions regarding joust, tourney, and war.
69. Boulton, *Knights of the Crown*, 185–86, 208–9; Contamine, *Guerre, état et société*, 184. The seventeenth-century antiquarian François Menestrier suggested that the manuscript today preserved in the Bibliothèque Royale Albert Ier, Brussels (ms 11124–11126), containing all three of Charny's works written in the same hand, is the original text presented to the French king. *De la Chevalerie ancienne et moderne* (Paris, 1683), 179–80. Some modern scholars identify the Brussels ms as dating from the early fifteenth century since it is decorated with a leafy border in which the arms of John the Fearless, Duke of Burgundy (1404–1419) appear prominently; they argue that the character of the hand in which the manuscript is written confirms this date. See "Les Demandes," ed. Rossbach, 34–40. Rossbach discusses the manuscripts, as does Michael Taylor, "Critical Edition," viii–xiv. As Elspeth Kennedy notes, however, the modern Belgian experts who wrote the subject catalogues for the Bibliothèque Royale, Brussels, consider the arms of John the Fearless a later addition to a manuscript written in the late fourteenth century. Kennedy prefers this dating, after examining the manuscript personally.
70. See Boulton's comment in *Knights of the Crown*, 205.
71. Translation by Elspeth Kennedy. See the discussion in Boulton, *Knights of the Crown*, 180.

mance written in the early thirteenth century, provides the first known outline of the scheme: it attributes to the Arthurian court a system of reporting and recording of deeds very similar to that for King Jean's chivalric order. Two works of slightly later date, the *Mort Artu* and the *Queste del sainte graal*, likewise portray King Arthur ordering that all the adventures of the companions of the quest for the Holy Grail be set down in writing.[72]

Although Jean II had been thinking about founding a great chivalric order since 1344, conditions in France prevented him from transposing his ideas into reality before January 1352. We can therefore argue, as a first approximation, that Charny would likely have written between these two dates. His own words provide further, if indirect, clues to dating. His vivid description of the perils of crusading ventures in the *Livre Charny* suggests a date after his return from Humbert of Vienne's crusade in 1346. His strict advice in the *Livre de chevalerie* to have no dealings whatsoever with the enemy suggests a date after his disastrous involvement with Aimery de Pavia at the very end of 1349. It seems likely that Charny took advantage of his enforced inactivity while a captive in London in 1350–1351 to outline and begin composing works for the chivalric order for which plans were then being finalized at the French court.[73] We would probably not go far wrong in suggesting that the treatises were written more or less as a group about the time the Company of the Star was founded.

If knowing Charny's intended audience is helpful, we likewise want to know what literary company his book kept, to what comparable works on chivalry his book relates. Any attempt to reconstruct the exact contents of whatever library he owned is of course fruitless. Rather, it would be useful to set his book in the context of previous vernacular writing on chivalry, in

---

72. *Lancelot do Lac: The Non-Cyclic Old French Prose Romance*, ed. Elspeth Kennedy (Oxford, 1980), I, 298, 406, 571; *La Mort le Roi Artu*, ed. Jean Frappier (Paris, 1964), 1–2; *La Queste del Saint Graal*, ed. Albert Pauphilet, (Paris, 1923) 279–80. In the *Lancelot do Lac*, a kneeling Hector, followed by all the Companions of the Quest, promises "that he would not lie about anything that happened in his quest, whether to hide his shame or to increase his honour." Kennedy, *Lancelot do Lac*, I, 406. See Kennedy's discussion of this point in her Editorial Introduction below.

73. From honorable captivity he could easily have maintained connections with Jean II's court. In December 1350, for example, by the license and with the safe-conduct of Edward III, he sent his servant with two subordinates to France to procure money "and other necessaries." Rymer, *Foedera*, III, part 1, 212. Mr. Ian Wilson has noticed and kindly brought to my attention what seems to be a fair copy of Charny's *Demandes* among the Holkham Hall mss now in the Bodleian Library (MS Holkham 43). He described this manuscript in personal correspondence and wrote about it (providing a copy of a part of the initial page) in the *Newsletter* of the British Society for the Turin Shroud 32 (September 1992), 3–6. He suggests the ms could have been obtained by Thomas Coke (d. 1759) while on a continental tour.

other words, to compare it to the sorts of books written for knights in their own language rather than in more esoteric and ecclesiastical Latin. Works written in the vernacular will likely have less of the idealistic coloration, less of the set of "priestly priorities" Maurice Keen notes in ecclesiastical treatises. Keen thinks that the vernacular treatises by contrast are much more useful to the student of chivalry; being "written specifically for the instruction of knighthood" they "do make an attempt to treat of chivalry as a way of life in its own right."[74]

Since Charny's text is one of the vernacular manuals of chivalry, our primary comparison must be between his book and the other examples of this sort written openly to instruct and instill chivalric values. Three outstanding examples of this type demand our consideration: the *Roman des eles* by Raoul de Hodenc; the anonymous *Ordene de chevalerie*, and Ramon Llull's *Libre que es de l'ordre de cavalleria*.

We can occasionally supplement the views of these treatises with an informative work of a somewhat different sort, the *Histoire de Guillaume le Marechal*, a biography of William Marshal commissioned by his son, which instructs—however indirectly—while it tells the life of the great English knight.

Finally, there is the vast realm of imaginative literature, of chivalric romance, likewise written in the vernacular and likewise an indirect source of much instruction to knights. Given the sheer volume of this literature, we must limit our comparison to a few examples. To illustrate ideas useful to Charny we have already found the prose work *Lancelot do Lac* a particularly helpful and important source.

The first of our three vernacular treatises appeared early in the thirteenth century, possibly in 1210. Raoul de Hodenc's *Roman des eles* (The Romance of the Wings) explains that knights can rise through prowess only if that prowess is borne aloft on the two wings of liberality and courtesy. Seven feathers compose the right wing, each a specific aspect of *largesse* or liberality. The knight must be courageous in liberality; give to rich and poor alike; spend without care for landed wealth; give what is promised; give promptly; give liberally; give fine feasts. Seven feathers again compose the left wing, each a specific component of courtesy. The knight must honor and guard Holy Church; avoid pride; refrain from boasting; enjoy good entertainment; avoid envy; avoid slander; be a lover.

74. Keen, *Chivalry*, 2–6, with quotations from the last page.

The author may have been a knight, although scholars have debated whether he was a minstrel. As we have seen, he certainly praises largesse and condemns miserliness with a fervor traditional with minstrels. He likewise devotes much attention to love—earthly, human love—of which he thoroughly approves. As Keith Busby has suggested, his message "is largely social, and it concentrates on telling knights how to behave rather than elaborating on the symbolic significance of knighthood." Though the poem makes its case in religious and moral terms, it "could not be called essentially religious."[75]

The anonymous *Ordene de chevalerie* (The Order of Knighthood), written about a decade later, is a quite different vernacular treatise.[76] It presents the qualities of the model knight by telling the fictional story of Hue of Tabarie, a crusader captured by Saladin; Hue can only win his release by showing the famous Muslim conqueror the manner in which knights are made in Christian Europe. Hue takes Saladin and the reader step by step through an ideal knighting ceremony, explaining the meaning of each symbolic act; in the process he compiles his list of the desirable knightly attributes. The knight should be freed from wickedness so that he will win a place in paradise; he must be willing to shed his own blood in defense of God and can avoid pride if he thinks often of his own death. He must keep his body pure and avoid all sexual sin. He must hasten into action with the love of God in his heart. He must preserve the inseparable pair of virtues, justice and loyalty. He must be ready to return his soul to God. Appended to this daunting and somewhat overlapping set of qualities is a list of four special virtues in a new knight: he must not witness false judgment or be involved with treason; he must protect ladies; he must fast on Fridays; he must hear mass every day.

It comes as no surprise to learn that the author of this treatise was a cleric. In the fine phrase of Jean Flori, he sees the making of a knight as "un véritable sacrement quasi ésotérique."[77]

In the last quarter of the thirteenth century Ramon Llull wrote his important *Book of the Order of Chivalry* (the *Libre que es de l'ordre de cavalleria* in the original Catalan, soon translated into French as *Livre de l'ordre de*

---

75. Raoul de Houdenc, *Le Roman des Eles, The Anonymous Ordene de Chevalerie*, ed. Keith Busby (Amsterdam, 1983), 14–21; quotations at 18. The text is printed 31–49.
76. Raoul de Houdenc, *Roman des eles*, ed. Busby, 105–19. Keen discusses this text, *Chivalry*, 6–8.
77. Quoted by Busby, *Roman des eles*, 91.

chevalerie).⁷⁸ Llull, who had spent his youth in chivalric pursuits, experienced a dramatic religious conversion in 1263, after which he "became very close to the Franciscans in thought and spirit" and decided to dedicate his life to missionary work, refuting unbelievers and teaching them Christian truth. Llull is a man of astonishing range and ambition, a mystic, a philosopher, a missionary, a writer of both treatises and romance, able to compose in Latin, Arabic, and Catalan. He showed a concern for ideal knighthood all his life; his *Book of Chivalry*, which he wrote perhaps between 1279 and 1283, was undoubtedly the most popular medieval vernacular manual for knights.⁷⁹ This book employs the story frame of a wise old hermit, a former knight, giving advice to a young squire who seeks knighthood. This device allows Llull to explain the duties of a knight, the proper questions to be asked of any aspiring squire, the elaborate symbolism in the ceremony for making a knight, the seven virtues (theological and cardinal) constituting the proper customs of a knight, and the honor owed to a knight.

From Llull's treatment of these several categories we can extract two themes that seem particularly significant for our interests. In the first place, Llull, the former knight become scholastic and quasi-friar, balances a clerical and a lay point of view. Knighthood and the priesthood are the two pillars that support the world; only the priests are higher than the knights and each should support and love the other. Each vocation should likewise be taught as a science in the schools.

Llull's view of knighthood as an ideal could scarcely be higher. In the opening pages of his work, for example, he presents a myth of chivalric origins in which the fall of human society has been redeemed by the creation of knighthood: in the misty past the best man out of each thousand people was selected to be a knight; only then could justice return and proper hierarchy at last be observed and enforced.⁸⁰

---

78. Ramon Llull, *Libre que es de l'ordre de cavalleria*, *Obres essencials*, I, ed. Pere Bohigas (Barcelona, 1957), 515–45. For the French text, see *Livre de l'ordre de chevalerie*, ed. Vincenzo Minervini (Bari, 1972). William Caxton printed an English version: *The Book of the Ordre of Chyvalry*, ed. Alfred T. P. Byles, EETS (London, 1926). For a general discussion of Llull's life and work, see *Selected Works of Ramon Llull*, (1232–1316), ed. Anthony Bonner (Princeton, NJ, 1985), Introduction.

79. *Selected Works*, ed. Bonner, I, 32; II, 1262.

80. The importance of so positive a myth about the origins of privileged governors (covering kingship, lordship, and knighthood) — which will appear again in Charny's work — is underscored by the existence of a directly contrary view. The popular *Romance of the Rose*, trans. Charles Dahlberg (Princeton, NJ, 1971), 172, pictures another sort of beginning: "They elected a great scoundrel among them, the one who was largest, with the strongest back and limbs, and made him their prince and lord. He swore that he would maintain justice for them

If clerics are conspicuously absent from the myth of origins, they soon appear and take their place beside the knights, the two orders together ensuring a world freed from error. Knightly swords and priestly scripture and reason work in parallel toward this high goal.

We can recognize the clerical impulse in Llull's elaborate explanation of the symbolism involved in the making of a knight. The rite is preceded by prayers and a mass: it takes place in a church, before an altar, after a sermon, and with a priest attending the "blameless" knight who actually confers the accolade. Llull's explanation of the symbolic significance of each part of the new knight's arms and equipment clearly follows ecclesiastical lines. The sword predictably images the cross, the hauberk defense against vice, and so forth. Many links between physical object and ideal chivalric quality, however, are more tenuous: that a dagger stands for trust in God and horse head armor for reason suggests the primacy of a list of virtues that originates in the clerical space in Llull's mind. The list, we should note, explicitly includes chastity. This clerical tenor to his thought is even more apparent in the section of his book called "the customs of a knight." Llull explains these largely in terms of faith, hope, charity, justice, prudence, temperance, and strength against the seven deadly sins.

Yet throughout his work Llull also insists on what we can broadly consider lay knightly prerogatives and qualities. He specifically asserts the knight's right to govern, to hold courts and give justice, to compel ordinary folk to till the soil, to own a castle, to hunt and practice with arms in tournaments, and to accuse and fight traitors. He thinks the knight should be nobly born, rich enough to sustain himself, and certainly not fat, old, or maimed.

A second theme in Llull's work is equally pervasive, but is more subtle and has attracted less scholarly attention. If true knighthood is one of the props of civilization, Llull is nevertheless deeply worried about the actual practice of knighthood in the world. A profound fear of knightly wickedness tempers the extravagant praise he heaps on knighthood as an ideal. His work, in short, is as much a sermon against actual knightly vice as a hymn of praise for knightly perfection. In discussing the office of a knight, for example, he thinks it important to remind his readers that it is against

---

and would protect their dwellings if each one individually were to hand over to him enough goods to enable him to support himself." The myth presented in *Lancelot do Lac* resembles that of Llull and may have influenced his book as well as Charny's. See *Lancelot do Lac*, ed. Kennedy, 142–47.

the order of chivalry to force women and widows, to rob and destroy the feeble, to injure the poor, to destroy castles, cities, and towns, to burn houses, cut down trees, slay beasts, rob people on highways, and so forth. The knights of his day, he thinks, are wolves watching the sheep. Significantly, his ideal knighting ceremony ends with a ride through town so that the new knight will henceforth be known and therefore less inclined to evil.

We will want to think again about both themes—balance between clerical and lay thrusts, and the reform of chivalry as actually practiced—when we examine Charny's treatise. In fact, we will see that some close verbal parallels (as well as these broad themes) connect Charny's work with Llull's.[81] However, before we turn to Charny there are two final sources of ideas about chivalry to consider.

L'Histoire de Guillaume le Marechal,[82] though not actually one of the vernacular manuals on chivalry, functions very much like one. The tone of the *Histoire* is reverentially instructive, as befits a book commissioned by William's son. Yet this quality of "authorized biography" hardly diminishes the work's value for our purposes; to the contrary, it provides the reader with a priceless view of chivalric ideals and practices a century and a half before they were taken up by Geoffroi de Charny. Perhaps we should not be surprised that this earliest surviving biography in the French language[83] tells the life of the knight considered in his day to be the paragon of chivalry.[84] We will often compare this twelfth-century exemplar of knightly qualities with our primary subject in the fourteenth century. William, as revealed through his biographer's pages, and Geoffroi, through the pages of his own treatise, view the world in remarkably similar ways; had they lived in the same generation they would have been mutual admirers.

---

81. The details of the verbal parallels between Llull and Charny appear in Elspeth Kennedy's notes and introduction to the Charny text in this volume.

82. *L'Histoire de Guillaume le Marechal*, ed. Paul Meyer, 3 vols. (Paris, 1891–1901) gives the text in the original language. For modern studies of William see Sidney Painter, *William Marshal* (Baltimore, 1933); Georges Duby, *William Marshal, the Flower of Chivalry*, trans. Richard Howard (New York, 1985); Larry D. Benson, "The Tournament in the Romances of Chretien de Troyes and *L'Histoire de Guillaume Le Marechal*," *Chivalric Literature*, ed. Larry D. Benson and John Leyerle (Toronto, 1980), 1–25; John Gillingham, "War and Chivalry in the *History of William the Marshal*," *Proceedings of the Newcastle Upon Tyne Conference*, 1987, ed. P. R. Cross and S. D. Lloyd, Thirteenth Century England 2 (Bury St. Edmunds, 1988), ll, 1–13.

83. As Duby points out, *William Marshal*, 30.

84. As the poet says, "Ma matire est del plus pre[u]dome / Kui unkes fust a nostre tens." *Histoire*, ll. 16–17. One character after another repeats this evaluation throughout the biography. At his funeral, for example, the Marshal is praised as "Le meillor chevalier del monde" (l. 19072).

Finally, in searching for sources for Charny's ideas we will turn to the influential Arthurian prose romances that began to appear about the time Charny was born. In the *Lancelot do Lac*, the first step toward what became the vast Lancelot-Grail cycle and "one of the . . . most influential of the French prose romances" with "a wide appeal amongst the nobility and gentry,"[85] we can find material of great interest in addition to the first program for recording knightly adventures in writing. Charny's ideas on the high status of chivalry and on the importance of discreet love show, for example, distinct similarities to the *Lancelot do Lac*.[86]

Charny's *Livre de chevalerie*, then, stands in the tradition of these works; as we will see, at times he draws upon them quite specifically. For example when he comes to describe the making of a knight, Charny borrows heavily from the *Ordene de chevalerie*. When Charny talks about the origins of governance, he draws on Llull who has also, it seems, learned from the *Lancelot do Lac*. In his comments on love, we again find echoes of this prose romance. Charny may not have known the *Roman des eles*, but he had clearly read the *Ordene* and it is hard to believe he was unfamiliar with Llull's book or with the *Lancelot do Lac*. Even if he had not read them all, the comparison of views seems as significant for our understanding of chivalry as any particular questions of textual borrowing.

Nevertheless, Charny's *Book of Chivalry* is also striking for its unique features and emphases. Although he draws on a tradition of writing about chivalry that is nearly two centuries old, Charny is not merely a retailer of old advice; he definitely wrote his own book in the context of his own age. Thus his work takes on full meaning when read in the long tradition of vernacular writing on chivalry which we have just noted, and as a work which relates specifically to the context of chivalry in fourteenth-century France.

Considering three linked features in Charny's book will allow us to read his ideas in this desired double context; we will look in turn at the pronounced practical quality in the *Livre de chevalerie*, at its yoking of intense lay piety with strongly felt lay independence, and, finally, at its role as a chivalric reform text.

---

85. *Lancelot do Lac*, ed. Kennedy; *Lancelot of the Lake*, trans. Corin Corley (Oxford, 1989). The quotation is from Kennedy's introduction to the Corley translation, xvii.
86. These influences will be discussed more thoroughly below by Kennedy.

The Practicality of Charny's Book

The visual richness and elaborate ceremonials of chivalry must surely have appealed to Charny as to other contemporary knights. As bearer of the oriflamme, knight of the Company of the Star and (as we will see) owner of the Shroud of Turin, Geoffroi de Charny could scarcely have been indifferent to the more showy and esoteric sides of chivalric practice. Yet, as a belted knight writing for other practitioners of his vocation, Charny produced an eminently practical treatise, probably the most thoroughly practical treatise in the entire tradition of vernacular treatises on chivalry.[87]

Of course the *Livre de chevalerie* is not practical in the most limited sense of instructing warriors how to aim lances or spur chargers.[88] Neither is it practical in the immediate sense of the *Demandes*, another of Charny's works, which presents scores of questions on the fine points of knightly challenges, the taking of prisoners, and the allocation of loot. It is, however, eminently practical in the sense that separates it from the writing on chivalry Keith Busby has called mystico-symbolic.[89] The *Ordene de chevalerie*, and even Llull's book, place more emphasis on mysticism and symbolic interpretation. The *Ordene*, in fact, provides Jean Flori with one of the finest examples of the sort of text that describes the act of dubbing in esoteric and sacramental terms.[90] Within the frame established by its story of Saladin and Hue, this treatise offers an explanation of chivalric symbols in the knighting ceremony. Even Llull, whose book historians reasonably regard as more pragmatic than the *Ordene*,[91] presents the reader with many pages

---

87. The sumptuous *pas d'armes* held at the "Tree of Charlemagne" not far from Dijon, elaborately described by Olivier de la Marche, is incorrectly attributed to the patronage of Geoffroy de Charny by Rossbach, "Les Demandes," 139–40. In fact, its patron was Pierre de Bauffremont, the mid-fifteenth-century lord of Charny, and it took place in July 1443, nearly a century after Geoffroy de Charny's death. See Olivier de la Marche, *Mémoires*, ed. Henri Beaune and J. d'Arbaument, 4 vols. (Paris, 1883–88), I, 290–335.

88. For an example of a more pragmatic treatise, see *The Art of Good Horsemanship*, written by King Duarte of Portugal in the fifteenth century. Large extracts from this treatise appear in English translation in Richard Barber and Juliet Barker, *Tournaments, Jousts, Chivalry, and Pageants in the Middle Ages* (New York, 1989).

89. *Roman des eles*, ed. Busby, 88.

90. *Roman des eles*, ed. Busby, 88; Jean Flori, "Pour une histoire de la chevalerie: L'adoubement dans les romans de Chretien de Troyes," *Romania* 100 (1979), 21–53; 36 in particular.

91. See the comments of Keen, *Chivalry*, 10–11. He regards Llull's book as "somewhat more ecclesiastically oriented than the *Ordene de chevalerie*," but notes that "deeply Christian as it is," the text is "so remarkably free of priestly overtones, so humane and in many ways so secular in its outlines." My argument is that Charny's text stands yet farther along this same scale and that it represents what Americans would be more likely to term laicization than secularization.

of symbolism and, if not mysticism, at least thoroughly theological instruction. The ceremony of making a knight (with its lengthy explanation of the symbolism of each part of the knightly arms) and the discussion of the seven theological and cardinal virtues occupy nearly half of Llull's book.

There is elaborate symbolism at only one spot in Charny's book, a passage that is borrowed and fills only a few pages. When Charny tells how a knight is made, he lifts his description from the *Ordene*, using the same steps and attributing the same meanings to each piece of armor and equipment, and to each step in the ceremony. The rest of the text, by far the largest part of Charny's book, reveals a different spirit. Though he may never have read the *Roman des eles*, Charny's approach is closer in tone to this work, also written by a layman. As Busby notes, the *Roman des eles* prescribes behavior that is largely social and "concentrates on telling knights how to behave rather than elaborating on the symbolic significance of knighthood."[92]

In fact, Charny has an even more clearly lay, non-symbolic, pragmatic emphasis. At times, especially in the section of "Advice for the Young Knight" (beginning at 19.39), the spirit of his book seems almost appropriate to the modern athletic field, with Charny playing the role of coach, giving the lads advice that will serve them for the game of life as well as the game at hand. As you enter the fray, he says, never think of what your opponent can do to you, think rather of what you are going to do to him. Praise others, do not boast of yourself. Guard your own honor "sovereignly," but never let envy keep you from honoring others. Never quarrel with a fool or a drunk. Steer clear of prostitutes. Love the ladies, but never boast of your conquests. Avoid sleeping late in soft beds and eating too much fine food. Time is too important to waste. Sometimes the lesser side in a struggle wins; this happens in the world, but it cannot last, for it is contrary to reason. Perhaps the parent as well as the coach appears when he exclaims that all who survive youth honestly must praise God all their lives for it.

In a broader vein Charny's book is practical because, although it presses knights always to do their best, it never requires the impossible of them. He warns sternly against the vice of gambling, for example; yet he knows his audience and knows that they will be "determined to play" with dice. His admonition therefore shifts to a warning against excess and especially about the risk of anger.

92. *Roman des eles*, ed. Busby, 18.

The touchy issue of sexual morality shows his pragmatic approach even better. In the *Queste del Sainte Graal*, written (under Cistercian influence) around 1225, virginity stands at the head of a prominent list of ideal knightly virtues projected into an imagined golden age of chivalry. Early in his adventures Perceval hears how crucially important his virginity is to his high knightly status:

for had your body been violated by the corruption of sin, you would have forfeited your primacy among the Companions of the Quest, even as Lancelot of the Lake, who through the lusts and fevers of the flesh let slip long since the prospects of attaining what all the rest now strive after.[93]

At times in this work the monastic sexual ethic urged on knights takes on an almost hysterical tone.

Contrary to clerically inspired exhortations about virginity, Charny accepts discreet love affairs. There is a sense of balance here. A love can make a warrior more *preux*, but he will be wise always to think less about his body and more about his soul and his honor.

This balance is all the more striking when we compare Charny's views not only with the monastic ethos of the *Queste*, but with his predecessors among the writers of the vernacular manuals. The anonymous author of the *Ordene de chevalerie* suggests a close connection between knights and ladies; he wants knights to support ladies and never give them bad counsel. However, his ceremony of knighting includes placing around the candidate a white belt of virginity. Charny will say even more about the defense of ladies, as we will discover, and he dutifully borrows the knightly chastity belt along with all the other symbolism of the *Ordene*; but in fact he looks understandingly aside at a well-conducted love affair. Llull, who in later life turned away from his profligate youth, confessed that "the beauty of women, O Lord, has been a plague and a tribulation to my eyes." He wanted the good knight to practice chastity and urged strength against impurity as one stone in the wall of defense provided by the cardinal virtues.[94]

---

93. *The Quest of the Holy Grail*, trans. Pauline M. Matarasso (Harmondsworth, 1969), 102. See *La Queste del Saint Graal*, ed. Pauphilet, 80, for the original French. Statements showing the radical emphasis on virginity appear throughout the sections of this romance devoted to Lancelot and Perceval. Contrasting this sexual ethic with that of the roughly contemporary romance *La Mort le roi Artu*, Jean Frappier comments on "cette obsession monacale de la luxure qui caractérise tant de pages de *La Queste!*" *Étude sur la Mort le Roi Artu*, 2nd ed. (Paris, 1961), 249.

94. The quotation is from his *Libre de contemplacio*, in Keen, *Chivalry*, 8. For the importance of chastity, see Llull's comments in the section on the "Customs That Pertain to a Knight" in his *Book of the Order of Chivalry*.

Raoul de Hodenc occupies the other end of the spectrum in writing about earthly love. In the *Roman des eles*, Raoul states as the seventh feather of the left wing of his image that the knight should be a lover, loving truly for the sake of love and gaining all its benefits. With enthusiasm he elaborates comparisons of love to the rose, to wine, and to the sea. Busby comments on the "strong sense of 'literariness'" that these images produce.[95] The fervor of Raoul's views in fact forces us to relocate Charny, who now occupies a place in the center of this spectrum, with Raoul de Hodenc to his left, waxing enthusiastically in favor of earthly love, and Llull, the *Ordene*, and finally the *Queste del saint graal* to his right, unyieldingly urging virginity. Significantly, Charny is joined in this centrist stance by William Marshal, whose biographer included unforgettable tales not only of William aiding women in distress (Queen Eleanor, who was very grateful; a lady eloping with a monk, who may have been somewhat less grateful), but also tantalizing hints of flirtation or even more (the "liberal and debonair" lady who aids young William while he is a captive; the charges linking him to Margaret, the wife of the Young King, the son of Henry II).[96]

Perhaps Charny's quality of worldly practicality appears most clearly in his untiring emphasis on prowess, the quality that would come as quickly as any into the minds of his contemporaries when they thought of chivalry. For prowess involved the entire cluster of warrior virtues: great skill, strength, and hardiness in using arms on horseback or on foot as well as the courage and determination that must inform success at arms. As Froissart observed, "As firewood cannot burn without flame, neither can a gentleman achieve perfect honor nor worldly renown without prowess" (*Si comme la busce ne poet ardoir sans feu, ne poet li gentilz homs venir a parfait honneur ne a la glore dou monde sans proece*).[97] This emphasis on prowess as the key quality in knighthood sets Charny's treatise apart from the earlier vernacular treatises and their more clerical and symbolic programs. In these earlier manuals prowess does not appear with anything like Charny's primary emphasis or his emotional investment.

Yet as William Marshal's biography shows us, the sentiment was venerable; knights had long virtually equated prowess and chivalry. The author of this biography could describe knights issuing from the besieged town of

---

95. *Roman des eles*, ed. Busby, 18.
96. But, as Duby is at pains to point out, Marshal's world remains masculine with status and worth determined completely by male standards. *William Marshal*, 38–50.
97. Quoted in *Chroniques de Jean Froissart*, ed. Luce, I, 2.

Winchester as riding out "to *do* chivalry" (*por faire chevalerie*),[98] making the link with prowess as complete as his statement is terse. The young hero of *Lancelot do Lac* innocently but tellingly asks his protectress, the Lady of the Lake, what quality other than prowess could possibly produce nobility since the human race arose from a single parentage.[99] Both this biography and this romance (unlike the more theoretical and diffuse treatises on chivalry) read as paeans of praise to prowess. In fact, the virtual identification of chivalry with knightly prowess can be documented in scores of works of chivalric literature; clearly this is the opinion of the knights, reflected in the literature they patronized.

The emphasis appears unmistakably in Charny's work. In the opening pages of his treatise Charny carefully lays out a scale of knightly deeds, drawing on the categories of prowess familiar to his audience through military contracts: the joust, the tournament, and war.[100] All men-at-arms are honorable, he insists, as are all acts of prowess: "I maintain," Charny says tersely, "that there are no small feats of arms" (3.16). But the honor of those who primarily joust (one knight against another) will not match that of the men who engage in the tourney; the tourneyers must, in turn, yield pride of place to those who engage in war. The reason for this scale is the increasing requirement of prowess: the *tournois*, of course, involves jousting, but it also includes the dangerous free-for-all of the *mêlée*. As war encompasses all the forms of combat, it brings the highest honor. War occupies the greatest space in another of Charny's treatises, the *Demandes*, where, as we have already noted, Charny poses 20 questions concerning joust, 21 on *mêlée*, and 93 on war.[101] In effect, Charny moves his reader along an upward scale of prowess from the two types of deeds of arms in peacetime to the more comprehensive, strenuous, and risky deeds of arms in war. Repeatedly Charny states his principle in lapidary form "he who does more is worth more" (*qui plus fait, mieux vault*).

---

98. *Histoire*, l. 176. emphasis added. Describing the later battle of Lincoln the poet says that the French did not have to look far to find chivalry, meaning prowess in battle: ll. 16830–33.

99. *Lancelot of the Lake*, trans. Corley, 44; original French in *Lancelot do Lac*, ed. Kennedy, 110–11. Cf. 71–72 in the Kennedy text for a statement of belief in the superiority of *fiertez* over other chivalric qualities.

100. Noel Denholm-Young, "The Tournament in the 13th Century," *Studies in Medieval History Presented to Frederick Maurice Powicke*, ed. R. W. Hunt, W. H. Pantin, and R. W. Southern (Oxford, 1948), 260 and Malcolm Vale, *War and Chivalry* (Norwich, 1981), 67, note the general use of these categories.

101. The parallel between Charny and William Marshal is, again, interesting. As John Gillingham has noted, the *Histoire* devotes something between two and three times as many lines to war as to tournament. "War and Chivalry in the History of William the Marshal," 2.

A final example of Charny's practicality appears in his attempt to write a book that could reach all layers of power, status, and wealth within the body of knights. He constantly speaks with respect and encouragement even to poor knights. Here he changes the emphasis found in Ramon Llull. The *Libre que es de l' ordre de cavalleria* insists that knights be not only nobly born but wealthy enough to sustain themselves in the proper state; Llull had worried that poor knights would turn to robbery. Charny, however, stands rather with such works as the *Lancelot do Lac* in which the valiant poor knight was recognized.[102] His thoughts could potentially go to all those who lived honorably by the profession of arms, whatever their particular social substratum. He thereby assured the possibility of the widest audience for his treatise.

We have already seen that he wrote specifically for Jean le Bon and the elite members of the Company of the Star. But the king's plan called for membership in the order to reach 500 men, more than 150 of whom were to be simple bachelors; possibly men of this rank were to form the majority. Each year, as the king announced, three princes, three bannerets, and three bachelors would sit at a Table of Honor.[103] If Charny's treatises are read in the context of a great program of reform of French chivalry to be led by the crown, the inclusive aim of the *Livre de chevalerie* is thoroughly practical and quite significant.

We often view the later medieval aristocracy as exclusive and caste conscious, qualities they no doubt exhibited in important ways. But in the face of the crisis examined below, it made sense to close ranks in a manner that included all men who lived by arms.

Ever the conservative and the moralist, Charny soon reveals the limits of his inclusivity. He wanted the most comprehensive audience for his ideas, of course, but he drew the line at the shorter and more form-fitting clothing that was all the rage in the France of his day. As we will see in more detail later, Charny joined with hosts of other moralists who bitterly denounced these styles. The trend had apparently begun among valets and

102. *Lancelot do Lac*, ed. Kennedy, 287: "And when you see the poor *bacheler* whom poverty has in bondage and who has not neglected physical prowess, in his place amongst other poor men, do not forget him because of his poverty or his lowly lineage, for beneath poverty of the body [on the physical level] often lies great riches of the heart [on the moral level], and under great abundance of money and of lands is often disguised poverty of the heart." I draw here on Kennedy's translation in "The Quest for Identity and the Importance of Lineage in Thirteenth-Century Prose Romance," *The Ideals and Practices of Medieval Knighthood II*, ed. Christopher Harper-Bill and Ruth Harvey (Woodbridge, 1988), 70–86.
103. Boulton, *Knights of the Crown*, 190.

artisans and through young serving men made its way up the social hierarchy into noble society. In wearing short suits, Stella Mary Newton observes, the high-born were "making a gesture."[104] Charny was also making a gesture in trying to reach all these social ranks with his ideas on chivalry, but he wanted the entire hierarchy of those living honorably by the practice of arms to listen to his ideas and he wanted them dressed in the good old styles.

Piety and Lay Independence

Charny's text reveals a conservative mind, one not much given to elaborate symbolism or "literariness." Throughout most of his book he approaches his subject as he would a castle to be stormed, directly and with few concessions to aesthetics. He does not give us a story frame of a captive lord in the exotic setting of *outremer* or even a wise old hermit instructing a squire by a fountain; he will surely not send his treatise aloft on a set of symbolic wings. His framework often seems worldly rather than mystical. At the same time his work is fervently religious. Reading even a few pages of Charny's book will convince any reader that Charny's mind is steeped in a piety that shapes its thought and expression.

This apparently straightforward, even simplistic piety requires much closer analysis, however. For Charny's piety can easily mask the fundamental layer of lay independence that undergirds it, emerging in places like some geological stratum exposed by weathering. We will not understand Charny if we fail to take into consideration each aspect of his religiosity—his deep piety and a marked spirit of lay independence—or if we fail to recognize the strength of each. Charny's lay piety, an amalgam fused from seemingly contradictory elements, can tell us much about the way he made sense of the world round him. It is personal to its maker. Yet it speaks to much more general issues of chivalry and religion, to the efforts at self-understanding essayed by knights who felt a need to fit their violent vocation into the framework of Christian teaching and who perhaps wanted to

---

104. Stella Mary Newton, *Fashion in the Age of the Black Prince: A Study of the Years 1340–1365* (Bury St. Edmunds, 1980), 15.

understand, as well as buttress, their place of dominance within the hierarchy of Christian society.[105]

Charny's piety is one of the features that most swiftly and forcefully strike any reader of his book. His tone is insistently religious, at times even puritanical. His providential view is almost a mental reflex. He insists again and again that whatever happens in the world is the will of God, that one must therefore take reverses patiently and accept honors humbly. The lasting rewards in life are not randomly handed out; fortune may seem for a time a rogue force, but it has no permanent power. God will distribute the real rewards to His warriors for their good deeds.

An important feature in all such discussions is Charny's appropriation of religious ideas and language. The process is better described as a laicization rather than a secularization of ecclesiastical language, for the animating power of the words is drawn almost intact from the sphere of religion into that of the everyday life of men-at-arms. For example, Charny borrows something of the coloration of traditional medieval Christian denigration of the body in contrast to the immortal soul. He speaks of "this puny body that lives only the space of an hour." This phrase might sound strange in the mouth of a knight much given to the praise of prowess, the ultimate display of bodily strength. But Charny uses descriptions of this sort to castigate the inadequate bodies of the slothful and the timid, those who do not make the most of their bodies, fearing to risk them in the all-important quest for honor. In his mind denigration of the body in words does not connect at all with deeds of *prouesce*, for it is by such feats that a knight gains honor which (like the soul), is immortal.

In fact the religious contrast of body and soul is paralleled more than once in Charny's book by the knightly contrast of worldly possessions or worldly comforts and all-important honor. That is, mere possessions or comforts rank on the chivalric scale of the good alongside the mere body on the ecclesiastical scale, but chivalric honor stands alongside the ecclesiastical ranking of the soul.

Significantly, in discussing Judas Maccabeus as the ideal knight Charny emphasizes the two great gifts God granted him: earthly honor and eternal salvation. In Charny's mind these gifts clearly inhabit the same mental and ethical universe. However Christian their form in his book, such ideas reveal the perduring belief of warriors that daring and hardship are rewarded

---

105. For general discussions of chivalry, piety, and the limitations of ecclesiastical dominance, see Keen, *Chivalry*, 18–63; Richard W. Kaeuper, *War, Justice and Public Order: England and France in the Later Middle Ages* (Oxford, 1988), 186–87.

by bliss; Geoffroi expected his heavenly reward with the Lord of Hosts as ardently as any Viking anticipated Valhalla.

Just as striking is Charny's appropriation of the concept of suffering righteously, or even martyrdom, which resonated so powerfully in medieval Christianity.[106] Accustomed to thinking of knights in shining armor as lords of their world, we may be surprised by discussions of the warriors' suffering; we might expect the palm of martyrdom to appear more often in the hands of those occupying the lesser layers of society, that is, among those who paid for the knightly display and so often felt the effects of sword and torch in the hands of the knights.

It is important to Charny to say how hard it is to be a knight, how hard to give up the ease he condemns, to work the body constantly and risk it in battle. Striving to explain, he emphasizes the suffering a good knight willingly undergoes; he states in the *Livre Charny* that knights carry heavier loads than beasts of burden.[107] In his mind—and he was scarcely alone in this line of thought—suffering and the risk of violent death in a good cause connect with religious ideas, perhaps even (distantly if not explicitly) with the sacrifice and violent death of Christ.[108]

It seems significant, then, that in his *Book of Chivalry* he asserts (and here he keeps company with Llull)[109] that knights suffer more than the clergy: "the good order of knighthood . . . should be considered the most rigorous order of all, especially for those who uphold it well and conduct themselves in a way in keeping with the purpose for which the order was established." Considering the "hardships, pains, discomforts, fears, perils, broken bones, and wounds which the good knights . . . have to suffer frequently, there is no religious order in which as much is suffered"

---

106. For citations giving many examples of the idea that crusaders who died on campaign might be popularly regarded as martyrs, see James A. Brundage, *Medieval Canon Law and the Crusader* (Madison, WI, 1969), 30, n. 1. The word martyr, as we would expect, comes to be used widely and in a more laicized form: the knights who died on the battlefield at Poitiers, for example, are martyrs according to the *Chronique des quatre premiers Valois*, ed. Luce, 54; Honoré Bonet uses the term for the laborers troubled by war; see the quotation in Hewitt, *Organization of War Under Edward III*, 138.

107. Quoted and discussed in "Le Livre Messire Geoffroi de Charny," ed. Piaget, 410–11.

108. The romances give many examples of the link of suffering with religious virtue. See, for example, *Quest*, trans. Matarasso, 204; *The Vulgate Version of the Arthurian Romances*, ed. H. Oskar Sommer (Washington, DC, 1909–13), VI, 138; *The High Book of the Grail: A Translation of the Thirteenth-Century Romance of Perlesvaus*, trans. Nigel Bryant (Cambridge, 1978), 170, 237, 238; *Le Haut Livre du Graal: Perlesvaus*, ed. William A. Nitze and T. Jenkins (Chicago, 1932–37), 265, 367, 369–70. Malory gives Gawain a revealing speech in his account of the "Quest of the Holy Grail." *Works*, ed. Eugene Vinaver, 2nd ed. (Oxford, 1971), 535: "I may do no penaunce, for we knyghtes adventures many tymes suffir grete woo and payne."

109. *The Book of the Ordre of Chyvalry*, ed. Byles, 95: "For no men put theyr bodyes in so many peryls as done the knyztes."

(40.10–13). In his verse treatise on chivalry, Charny speaks with considerable realism and frankness about the knight's suffering in battle: arrows and lances rain down on him; he sees his friends' bodies sprawled on the ground all around him; he is well-mounted and could escape, but to flee would be a loss of honor. "Is he not a great martyr," Charny asks, "who puts himself to such work?"[110]

The powerful language of martyrdom allows Charny to accomplish several important goals at once. He vents feelings about the weariness of constant campaigning that would otherwise sound like mere complaining. He expresses what must have been a genuine, if usually unspoken, fear on the part of men who regularly faced other men armed with edged weapons. He casts a mantle of righteousness over the knightly vocation, reinforcing the notion that its practitioners and others should see it, for all its violence, as pleasing in the eyes of God. He uses the suffering of knights inversely to elevate their status, a point to which we will return below.

The piety that led Charny to appropriate religious language for his discussion of chivalry left fascinating traces beyond the pages of his book.[111] As early as 1343, when he was planning to found a church on his estate at Lirey, Charny obtained permission from Philippe VI to amortize (to take out of feudal circulation) land worth 140 livres.[112] Five clerics would serve the chapel, praying and saying masses continuously for Charny and his family and for the king and the royal family (the latter being Philippe's condition for giving Charny license for amortization). Over the remaining years of his life, Charny sent to the papal court a number of requests for himself and his church. He obtained the right to have a portable altar, to receive from his confessor a plenary indulgence "in articulo mortis" (i.e., just before death), to hear a first mass of the day before sunrise, to have a family cemetery next to his church at Lirey, and to have his body divided into parts for burial in separate locations (as was the aristocratic religious fashion).[113]

---

110. *Livre Charny*, ll. 363–593, in "Critical Edition," ed. Taylor, quotation at 457–58. For other references to martyrdom, see ll. 130 ff, 863.

111. For what follows see P. Savio, "Ricerche sopra la Santa Sindone," *Pontificium Athenaeum Salesianum* I (1955), 120–55, which prints the documents.

112. Perrett, "Essai sur l'histoire du Saint Suaire," 61, argues that Anselme, the source for the amortissement of 1343, must have misread the date, which should be corrected to a decade later. Savio prints Anselme's statement and the papal document (with the 1343 date) in "Ricerche sopra la Santa Sindone," 122.

113. The relevant requests and papal responses are printed by Savio, "Richerche sopra la Santa Sindone." See also the useful studies by Ulysse Chevalier, "Etude critique sur l'origine du Saint Suaire de Lirey-Chambery-Turin" and "Autour des origines du Suaire de Lirey," parts 2 and 4 respectively of *Bibliothèque Liturgique* 5 (1900), especially 9–21, 129–50.

To modern eyes, however, perhaps the most intriguing indication of Charny's piety inheres in his ownership of the piece of linen cloth known today as the Shroud of Turin.[114] This remarkable cloth, long regarded by some as the actual burial wrapping of Christ, seems to bear an imprint from the front and back of his crucified body.

Charny has long been recognized as the first historical owner of the Shroud; the recent scientific dating of the Shroud allows us to speculate that Charny may well have been its original owner. Controlled tests conducted at several laboratories date the Shroud to 1260–1390 ("with at least 95% confidence")—the likelihood of manufacture being, of course, most pronounced in the middle of this range of years.[115] These tests indicate that the Shroud was made in Charny's lifetime.

Although virtually no aspect of the history of the Shroud has escaped controversy, Charny's involvement is slightly less entangled than others. For our purposes the Shroud simply but effectively complements the picture of pronounced religiosity displayed in Charny's writing. Nonetheless his ownership raises interesting questions that cannot be brushed aside altogether.

Exactly how and when the Shroud came into Charny's possession remains tantalizingly unknown. Charny's church at Lirey eventually housed the Shroud, but in the repeated papal grants Charny secured for this chapel he makes no mention of the Shroud whatsoever.[116] In fact, only a few thin, if strong, strands of evidence convincingly link Charny to the Shroud.

Shortly after Charny's death, a papal letter referred to the Shroud which had been "generously given to him" (*liberaliter sibi oblatam*). Geoffroi's son (the second Geoffroi de Charny) inherited the Shroud and caused considerable scandal by his profitable public showings to crowds of pil-

---

114. A recent survey of the issues, concentrating on the work of Ulysse Chevalier, is given in Victor Saxer, "Le Suaire de Turin aux prises avec l'histoire," *Revue d'Histoire de l'Eglise de France* 76 (1990), 21–55.

115. For the results of controlled testing carried out by mass spectrometry (first developed at the University of Rochester) in laboratories in Arizona, Oxford, and Zurich, see P. E. Damon et al., "Radiocarbon Dating of the Shroud of Turin," *Nature* 337 (1989), 611–15, and two articles by H. E. Gove: "Progress in Radiocarbon Dating the Shroud of Turin," *Radiocarbon* 31 (1989), 965–69, and "Dating the Turin Shroud—An Assessment," *Radiocarbon* 32 (1990), 87–92. I am grateful to Gove for copies of these papers and for much advice and helpful conversation. The results of these tests make any speculation about a relationship between Geoffroi de Charny and a Templar by a similar name (burned at the stake in 1314) rather pointless; there is, in any case, no evidence linking the two men beyond the coincidence in name.

116. Savio, "Ricerche sopra la Santa Sindone," discusses all these papal privileges. Chevalier, "Etude critique," 131 and "Autour des origines," 9 notes the absence of any mention of the Shroud.

grims. In a memorandum sent to the papal court, probably in early 1390,[117] the bishop of Troyes, Pierre d'Arcis, referred to exhibitions of the Shroud made thirty-four years earlier "or thereabouts" and investigated at that time by his episcopal predecessor in Troyes, Henri de Poitiers.[118] We might wish that Pierre d'Arcis had been more precise, but his rough date does suggest that showings of the Shroud took place about the time Charny died in 1356 on the battlefield of Poitiers. The bishop stoutly opposed a renewed series of such displays and denounced the motives of those who had made them. But for the purposes of our inquiry the question is whether the earlier showings were made by Charny or by others after his death. Had the pious knight engaged in practices that later brought episcopal investigation of fraud?

A fascinating piece of evidence appeared with the proper identification only in 1960 of a lead pilgrim's badge, now in a Paris museum. This badge bears an unmistakable representation of the Shroud, the arms of Charny, and those of Geoffroi's second wife, Jeanne de Vergy.[119] It seems at first glance that steps had been taken to encourage a flow of pilgrims to see the Shroud in Charny's lifetime and that this traffic justified the manufacture — and sale — of badges for the faithful to wear in display of their active piety. One of these found its way back to Paris. Yet Victor Saxer makes the plausible suggestion that the arms on the badge could represent not Geoffroi I and his wife but his infant son Geoffroi and his widow. If so, the profitable displays of the Shroud were the work of Jeanne de Vergy and the clerics of the church at Lirey.[120]

Fortunately, we need not get enmeshed in the webs of controversy that have accumulated over the years from scholarly and popular interest in the Shroud. We can note in passing, however, how many of the problems associated with the Shroud would be resolved by the suppositions that the

---

117. Perrett, "Essai sur l'histoire du Saint Suaire," 63 n. 70, suggests that Anselme's dating of 1389 is incorrect since D'Arcis shows an awareness of the letters of the Avignon Pope Clement VII, written 6 January 1390.

118. Ulysse Chevalier printed this document as appendix G of his "Etude critique." Henry Thurston discussed the document and provided an English translation in "The Holy Shroud and the Verdict of History," *The Month* 1 (1903), 17–29. See also Guillaume Mollat, "Clément VII et le Suaire de Lirey," *Le Correspondant* 210 (1903), 254–59.

119. Arthur Forgeais, *Collection de plombs historiés trouvés dans la Seine* (Paris, 1865), 105–8 described and published a drawing of this badge, but he incorrectly identified it as the Shroud of Besançon. The correction appears in Perret, "Essai sur l'histoire du Saint Suaire," 62. A photograph of the badge appears among the illustrations between pages 226 and 227 in Ian Wilson, *The Shroud of Turin* (New York, 1978). The badge is at present in the Musée de Cluny, Paris (Ref. 75 CN 5261).

120. Saxer, "Le Suaire de Turin aux prises avec l'histoire," 30.

cloth was of Eastern manufacture, that Charny obtained it while on crusade in 1345–46, and that he considered it a splendid icon, an aid to pious devotion, rather than an actual relic from the life of Christ.[121] He would not then have felt any need to mention it among the relics of his church at Lirey in his correspondence with the papacy; his possession of the Shroud as icon need not have aroused any controversy at all. Only later, when his widow and the clerics at Lirey blurred the crucial line between icon and relic, did an episcopal investigation lead to charge and countercharge.

Of course these bits of solid evidence and a bit of informed guesswork fail to answer the scores of questions they provoke, but they do suggest that Charny's piety led him to obtain the marvelous cloth he owned. Chevalier points out that a holy cloth would be a most attractive object of popular devotion at just this time. The cloth known as the Veronica (bearing an imprint of Christ's face), shown in Rome during the papal jubilee of 1350, had drawn pilgrims in vast numbers.[122] We can only note that in his final years two pieces of sacred cloth, the oriflamme and the Shroud, fittingly represented the major facets of chivalry and religion as they blended in Charny's life.

Piety of one sort or another was, of course, the common thread woven into both emblems. Nonetheless, Charny, like most knights of his age, read a significant degree of lay independence into his religious life and belief. Charny's piety was no less real for taking directions quite different from the narrow paths prescribed for knighthood on idealized ecclesiastical charts; at times he seems to step around clerical authority with an easy knightly confidence that his beliefs and actions win direct divine approval.[123] The phenomenon is no less significant for being the predictable mentality of a seigneur. Men possessed of sheer physical power in any age have usually valorized the form of their lives and the shape of their social and political control by reference to religious ideas. Some of them have also demon-

---

121. Since I wrote these thoughts, the interesting article of W. S. A. Dale, "The Shroud of Turin: Relic or Icon?" *Nuclear Instruments and Methods in Physics Research* B29 (1987), 187–92, has come to my attention through the kindness of Professor Harry Gove. Dale notes that an icon known as the *epitaphios sindon*, which bears resemblances to the Shroud of Turin, was featured as the focal point for devotion in the lenten services of the Orthodox Church. He also notes the tradition that a somewhat similar icon, the Shroud of Besançon (destroyed in 1794), was given to another crusader, Otho de la Roche, for his valor at the siege of Constantinople in 1205.

122. Chevalier, "Autour des origines du Suaire de Lirey," 17–20,

123. At the end of section 26 below, for example, Charny suggests that his standards for good lay governance could be applied to the entire clerical hierarchy from the pope to the priests, but checks himself and adds, "but it does not befit lay people to speak more of this, rather they should hold their peace as best they can."

strated a piety that could spring from deep spirituality. If the balance of motive in Charny's mind, let alone the content of his soul, lie beyond scholarly reach, we can nonetheless note with profit when and how our theoretician of chivalry parted company with the high claim of the clerics, as arbiters of Christian society, to direct and judge the truth of religious ideas and practices.

By the time Charny wrote, the idea of a tripartite division within Christian society occupied an established and venerable place in medieval thought.[124] The social world functioned because of the respective functions of those who fought, those who prayed, and those who worked. But the first two orders, knighthood and priesthood, received the most elaborate theoretical attention. It comes as no surprise to find that clerical writers emphasized the preeminence of their own order. The analogy of the soul's superiority to the body was often invoked. Guibert of Nogent caught the sense of innate clerical superiority well when he suggested that for a cleric to take up knighthood would be "a shameful act of apostasy," so superior was the clerical role.[125] The influence of such views appears in the vernacular manuals on chivalry, which repeat the traditional and careful formula that knights enjoyed a status above all others save only the priests; the anonymous author of the *Ordene de chevalerie* took this stance early in the thirteenth century, as did Ramon Llull nearer the end of the century.[126] Yet this view scarcely won unanimity of opinion. The romances that knights read could flatly insist that chivalry was the highest order God had created.[127]

Charny conservatively repeats the formulation of the earlier vernacular manuals, and is second to none in his reverence for the clergy, especially for the secular clergy (more than the monks) since they perform the mass. But he modulates this hymn of praise so insistently that he ends in a quite different key. In his *Livre Charny* he advises parents how to know which son is to become a knight and which a priest. The son who likes to run, jump, and hit is on the road to knighthood; the son who never wants to sing or

---

124. Georges Duby, *The Three Orders: Feudal Society Imagined*, trans. Arthur Goldhammer (Chicago, 1978).
125. Quoted in Duby, *The Three Orders*, 219. For Guibert, the source of the taint lowering knightly status was not violence but sex.
126. *Ordene*, ll. 425–80, in *Roman des eles*, ed. Busby, 117–18; *The Book of the Ordre of Chyvalry*, ed. Byles, 23–24, 76, 115.
127. Chrétién de Troyes, *Le roman de Perceval ou le conte du graal*, ed. William Roach (Geneva, 1956), ll. 1632–35: "Le plus haute ordene... Que Diex ait faite et comandee: C'est l'ordre de chevalerie."

laugh should become a priest.[128] In a more serious vein, the emphasis on suffering and martyrdom, noted before, wins the knight greater praise in Charny's eyes than any cleric could merit. After cataloguing the pains and tribulations endured on campaign, Charny asks pointedly, "And where are the orders which could suffer as much?" He insists that a good knight can wear his armor as purely and devoutly as any priest wears his vestments for divine service. Moreover, a knight must keep his conduct as thoroughly honest as any priest's, "ou plus" (or more). The necessity to be a good Christian is even more imperative for the knight because he lives in constant peril and must be ready to die at any moment. This point bears weight with Charny, who repeats it more than once: the knight has the greatest need of all to be a good Christian.

There can be no thought that a life of fighting counts against a man-at-arms. Though some say a man cannot save his soul through fighting, Charny assures his audience that they can save or lose their souls in any profession. But Charny is, of course, interested in knights not bakers, and one suspects that he thinks God is inclined in the same martial direction. The knight's arms, Charny insists, are those of God when he uses them to secure reason and right, when he calls for divine help. Those who fight well but die in the fray need not fear; they will be taken into God's select company to enjoy paradise forever. His terms are never so explicit, but perhaps in his musings he pictured an otherworldly Company of Heaven replacing and perfecting the Company of the Star.[129]

In all such lines of thought, Charny shows a very important general trend in the way in which knights came to think of their hard lives and good service. The careful, specific, and highly discriminating clerical praise of knights from earlier centuries was intended to guide and control knightly behavior rather than to praise the general company of knights indiscriminately; but knightly minds tended to apply such praise to all knights (or at least to all but a very small set of admittedly bad fellows, as we will see below). In short, knights generalized and laicized a clerical message which in its original form always balanced praise for good behavior among

---

128. *Livre Charny*, ll. 1390–1440, in "Critical Edition," ed. Taylor.

129. The idea appears in romances of the preceding century. In the *Queste*, for example, one of the omnipresent hermits tells Lancelot that the true knight (Galahad) "entrera la celestiel chevalerie," *La Queste del Saint Graal*, ed. Pauphilet, 116. (Matarasso nicely renders this as "join the company of the knights of heaven," *Queste* 134.) Perceval in this same romance prays that he may never sin in such a way that he "perde la compaignie des chevaliers celestielx." *Queste*, 92.

an elite few with sulfurous denunciation of the vile behavior of knights in general.

The point is clearly illustrated by noting the fate of the ideas announced two centuries earlier by the great twelfth-century monastic and uncrowned pope, St. Bernard of Clairvaux.[130] St. Bernard wrote words of glowing praise and comfort specifically for the order of the Knights Templar in contrast to the great mass of knights who were obviously rushing to perdition. These few sanctified monk/knights won the great abbot's praise as ideal warriors who fought only the pagan enemy and avoided the pitfalls of mere earthly chivalry. The great body of knights, who blindly followed earthly chivalry, made prowess and tourneying laudable ends in themselves; they remained strangers to the great virtue of chastity. Only the "new knighthood" of the Temple, as he wrote in a treatise sent to the master of the new order, "ceaselessly wages a twofold war both against flesh and blood and against a spiritual army of evil in the heavens. . . . What a glory to return in victory from such a battle! How blessed to die there as a martyr!" The great mass of knights, by contrast, are still mired in "worldly knighthood, or rather knavery, as I should call it." Thinking of the generality of knighthood Bernard thunders blandishments in his best style:

What then, O knights, is this monstrous error and what this unbearable urge which bids you fight with such pomp and labor, and all to no purpose except death and sin? You cover your horses with silk, and plume your armor with I know not what sort of rags; you paint your shield and your saddles; you adorn your bits and spurs with gold and silver and precious stones, and then in all this glory you rush to your ruin with fearful wrath and fearless folly.[131]

---

130. Bernard is the classic source for such ideas. Jean LeClercq notes how much the knightly life is for Bernard, a matter of asceticism and discipline. "Saint Bernard's Attitude Toward War," *Studies in Medieval Cistercian History*, II, ed. John R. Sommerfeldt (Kalamazoo, MI, 1976). Bernard should not be thought, however, the only source for the idea of limiting knightly virtue to Templars. John of Salisbury, for example, says the Templars are virtually the only men he knows who are engaged in legitimate warfare. *Polycraticus*, ed. C. C. J. Webb, CVII, ch. 21 (Oxford, 1909), II, 198.

131. *On Grace and Free Choice: Praise of the New Knighthood*, in *The Works of Bernard of Clairvaux*, vol. 7, *Treatises III*, trans. Daniel O'Donovan and Conrad Greenia (Kalamazoo, MI, 1977), 127–67. For the Latin see *Sancti Bernardi Opera*, 8 vols., vol. 3, *Tractatus et Opuscula* (1963). These strictures are unmistakably imprinted in the actual Rule of the Templars, with its slighting reference to the generality of knights as "you who until now have led the lives of secular knights, in which Jesus Christ was not the cause, but which you embraced for human favor only. . . . This [earthly] knighthood despised the love of justice that constitutes its duties and did not do what it should, that is, defend the poor, widows, orphans, and churches, but strove to plunder, despoil and kill." *The Rule of the Templars: The French Text of the Rule of the Knights Templar*, trans. J. M. Upton-Ward (Woodbridge, 1992), 19.

An echo of this message of warning still clearly resonates in Charny's prose, but just as clearly it takes on transformed meaning there. The proportions of the elect and the reprobate have been reversed; most knights now merit the praise St. Bernard lavished on the select few; only a few fourteenth-century knights, Charny professes to believe, merit the vitriolic criticisms the great Cistercian had poured on knighthood in general. The constant factors that link St. Bernard and Charny are the ideals of hard service and even martyrdom in a good cause (winning the approval of God who sacrificed himself for his people), and the foolishness of vain display, rather than true and disciplined devotion.

Of course even St. Bernard found it necessary to extend his blessing to all crusaders. Other clerics had already moved in this direction, broadening the field of knights to be praised. From the launching of the first crusade some clerical authors had urged knights to fight in the right causes and had promised the joys of heaven in reward. "God in our time has introduced the holy war," Guibert of Nogent wrote, in a classic statement of the theme, "so that the knighthood and the unstable people, who shed each other's blood in the way of pagans, might have a new way to win salvation. They need not choose the life of a monk and abandon the world in accordance with the vows of a monk, but can obtain God's grace through their own profession, in their accustomed freedom and secular dress."[132] Ecclesiastical pronouncements meant to popularize the crusade were echoed by less official statements with the same view; Roland being carried off to bliss by flights of angels was undoubtedly a stock image by Charny's day.[133] Charny follows the ecclesiastical lead in predictable ways when praising the fight in defense of Holy Church and against the enemies of the faith; he calls it warfare "righteous, holy, certain, and sure" (35.217).

Yet clerics, who had long urged such warfare as a knightly duty, had over the same long period condemned much of knightly life in general and had always assumed the authority to determine the causes for which knights might fight with a clear conscience. They had for centuries insisted specifically that the mock warfare of the tournament did not qualify as such a case of clean conscience; they had even denied burial in sanctified

---

132. *Recueil des historiens des croisades*, 16 vols. (Paris, Académie des Inscriptions et Belles Lettres, 1841–1906), IV, 124, quoted in Carl Erdmann, *The Origins of the Idea of Crusade*, trans. Marshal W. Baldwin and Walter Goffart (Princeton, NJ, 1977), 336–37.

133. See laisse 175 and laisse 176. Justifications of violence in a sacred cause appear throughout the poem.

ground to knights killed in the rough sport.[134] Such clerical condemnation had never made much headway against the compelling popularity of the tournament in all its particular forms. The checkered pattern of royal prohibitions, royal regulation, and royal sponsorship of the tournament had likewise fallen short of really effective control. By the fourteenth century even ecclesiastics seem to have given up with a sigh and a grumble. Kings came to terms with the tournament by becoming its grand sponsor, insofar as they could, especially through the medium of the royal chivalric orders so prominent in Charny's lifetime.[135] Across the Channel in England the duke of Lancaster wrote an acceptance of tournament into his pious treatise.[136] Even Llull, the former knight become quasi-friar, had earlier assumed that tournaments occupied honorable space in the life of his model knight.[137] Likewise, Charny's praise for jousting and fighting in the *mêlée* as the first two honorable levels of prowess does not ruffle the smooth surface of his piety in the slightest. Had he been present generations earlier at the deathbed of the great William Marshal, Charny would surely have nodded in sage agreement with Marshal's classic opinion in response to sharp questioning about his lifetime participation in tournament:

. . . listen to me for a while. The clerks are too hard on us. They shave us too closely. I have captured five hundred knights and have appropriated their arms, horses, and their entire equipment. If for this reason the kingdom of God is closed to me, I can do nothing about it, for I cannot return my booty. I can do no more for God than to give myself to him, repenting all my sins. Unless the clergy desire my damnation, they must ask no more. But their teaching is false — else no one could be saved.[138]

The lay independence so prominent in this declaration stands out in Charny's work not only in his acceptance of these "deeds of arms of peace," but even more in his discussion of the "deeds of arms of war." War, after all, was the supreme theater for the knightly manifestations of prowess that meant so much to him. He thus must walk, however swiftly, through the tangled and prickly field of just war theory in order to reach safe ground on which all the men-at-arms of his audience can use their weapons with clear consciences. He is familiar enough with scholastic doctrine on just war to

---

134. Barber and Barker, *Tournaments*, 139–51.
135. Kaeuper, *War, Justice, and Public Order*, 199–211; Boulton, *Knights of the Crown*, passim.
136. *Le livre de seyntz medicines*, ed. Arnould, 78; Arnould, "Henry of Lancaster and His 'Livre des Seintes Medicines,'" 360–61.
137. *Book of the Ordre of Chyvalry*, ed. Byles, 31, 75.
138. Quoted in translation by Sidney Painter, *William Marshal, Knight-Errant, Baron, and Regent of England* (Baltimore, 1933), 285–86. For the statement in the original French see *L'Histoire de Guillaume le Marechal*, ed. Paul Meyer, 3 vols. (Paris, 1891–1901), vol. 2, 304–5.

use the term "necessity" in valorizing knightly warfare. Such theoretical bounds, however, have very little effect in limiting the field of licit warfare in his view. Charny insists on the legitimacy of the fighting in which knights were so constantly engaged in the France of his own day: "for when lords have wars their subjects can and must fight for them." He assures knights that they can enter these battles with moral confidence as well as chivalric gusto. The due and proper service to the lord from whom they hold their lands is best demonstrated by feats of arms, taking the risk of losing it all: life, honor, possessions. Moreover they can enter battle with clear conscience to avoid their own disherison or dishonor, or to protect defenseless young women, widows, or orphans. Few conflicts in contemporary Europe could not fit under one of these elastic rubrics. In all such causes, Charny argues, the fighting is beneficial to both body and soul. If they do well with their bodies, the fighting men will win great honor; if they die, their souls are saved, unless of course their great sins prevent it. The laicized echo of St. Bernard's earlier voice from the cloister appears again in Charny's opinion.

Through Charny's treatise, then, we can peer into the religious mentality of a respected fourteenth-century French knight. The view is instructive. His piety appears at first to be as conventional as it is omnipresent. Charny seems almost driven to garnish his text with constant references to Our Lord and the Blessed Virgin.[139] He is at pains to emphasize the need to reverence priests and their sacred services. His prolix piety forms the very framework of his thought even as he analyses his own profession of knighthood.

This point is worth emphasizing for piety and chivalry do not occupy separate spaces in his consciousness; rather they fuse into one inseparable whole. For Charny piety and chivalry were virtually interchangeable qualities in men of war. Through the hard martyrdom of their profession knights acted in accordance with God's will. So clear was this certainty in Charny's mind that clerical cavils about this particular point or that could be shrugged off as nonessential. The order of chivalry was the keystone that kept the great arch of Charny's world standing firm. What other order could compare with it? The essential role of the clergy in a sacramental religion was obvious. Yet Charny believed that in broad domains of their lives the great host of his warriors served God without a need to acknowledge the stringencies of ecclesiastical control. Right order in the world (in-

---

139. This could be a combination of personal piety and the desire to invoke the names of the holy patrons to whom the Company of the Star was dedicated.

cluding, of course, true religion) was secured finally through the power and self-sacrificing service of the Order of Knighthood. This was the essence of knightly lay piety, not its qualification or denial. Spiritual rectitude and physical force fused in the knightly mission. As Maurice Keen has acutely observed, Charny ends his book appositely with a combination prayer and war cry: "Pray to God for him who is the author of this book. Explicit Charni, Charny."[140]

Charny and Chivalric Reform

The smooth and proper running of the world thus depended on the state of chivalry, the properly dominant force within the world. What a serious problem confronted the kingdom of France, then, if French chivalry failed to live up to its high vocation. Charny wrote as this disturbing problem cast its deepening shadow over chivalry's birthplace. Both Charny's book and his age come into sharper focus when we consider this atmosphere of crisis and the urgent need for reform.

To the extent that it represented an ideal code, chivalry always appeared to its thoughtful practitioners—and certainly to their clerical contemporaries—to stand in need of reform. William Marshal's biographer announced that chivalry was dead in the early thirteenth century; he took the common line of some contemporary poets that the problem stemmed from the imprisonment of largesse and voiced a hope that the young English king Henry III would liberate generosity and "set all the world joyful."[141] Raoul de Hodenc in *Le Roman des eles* had similarly argued that chivalry was threatened by a failure of largesse, lost in the contemporary emphasis on prowess.[142]

The fear in Charny's day and in Charny's text is much more serious; the need for reform, in fact, drives Charny's text. Far from purveying a conventional topos of the past glories of an imagined golden age, Charny feels an urgent need to respond to a clear and present danger. Perhaps the

---

140. Keen, "Chivalry, Nobility and the Man-at-Arms."
141. *Histoire*, ed. Meyer, ll. 2686–2712, 4297–4319. If the author expects royal leadership, he also worries about the rising and restrictive power of kingship that turns knights errant and tourneyers into courtroom pleaders.
142. *Roman des eles*, ed. Busby, ll. 116–43.

atmosphere had darkened in Charny's early youth as the King of France brought down the venerable Order of the Temple, charging these model monk-knights with shocking immorality and heresy and arresting nearly 2,000 brothers.[143]

Charny, however, points to a specific problem as the focus of his fears for chivalry. He is not worried about largesse and he never mentions the Templars. He does talk tirelessly about that most essential chivalric trait, prowess. The crisis at its most basic level stemmed from the serious and repeated defeats of French knighthood; they failed to show the needed prowess. On the sea at Sluys in 1340, and in the long awaited set-piece land battle at Crécy in 1346, French men-at-arms had been beaten badly. Their English foes held Calais, a base for future operations and irritating raids. Clearly the glittering ranks of knights led by the kings of France were unable to provide the defense on which so much of their claim to honor and their enjoyment of dominance and wealth finally rested. The English and their allies underscored the point repeatedly with their campaigns through French territory, leaving behind them a swath of charred and looted villages.[144]

Unable to provide for defense, French chivalry likewise proved unable to maintain unity within the ranks of the powerful. As they failed to demonstrate the great virtue of prowess, their loyalty began to disintegrate as well. Here was a second major chivalric virtue in decline, their reliable adherence not only to their king, but to the working ideals of their *ordo*, the ideals which gave steadfastness and cohesion to their social group. An entire set of problems that might be individually labeled political or military or social therefore converged. The Valois kings who had succeeded the senior line of the Capetian dynasty in 1328 feared, with good reason, that their hold on the crown was somewhat shaky. Although a certain level of quarreling between the king and some great lords was to be expected, the issue took on new dimensions with the defection to the English of two great lords, Robert d'Artois and Geoffroi de Harcourt, with the summary execution of the constable, Raoul, Count of Eu on royal orders, and with the flickering ambitions of Charles of Evreux and Navarre always threatening to burst into open flame. Any reasonably acute observer would have feared

---

143. An overview of the order is provided by Malcolm Barber, *The New Knighthood: A History of the Order of the Temple* (Cambridge, 1994). For the trial, see Georges Lizerand, *Le Dossier de l'affaire des Templiers*, 2nd ed. (Paris, 1964).

144. See the descriptions in Hewitt, *The Organization of War* and *The Black Prince's Expedition*.

the factionalism that would, in time, make the Hundred Years War a veritable civil war in France.[145] Many observers began to raise doubts about the balance between virtuous performance and high privilege among the chivalric strata of society.

Many critics worried over the deficiencies of French chivalry even before the crowning disaster of the battle of Poitiers. Two particular charges worked moralists into a lathered fury: first, as the defense of the kingdom crumbled, the nobles and their followers collected ever larger sums of money which they spent frivolously; second, and just as bad in the eyes of moralists, they risked the wrath of God by a shameful and costly display of vanity in the outrageous clothing they now sported.[146] The well-traveled Provincial of the Carmelite Order, Jean de Venette, who seems to have been closely in touch with popular opinion, poured out these strictures more than once in his chronicle. Under the year 1340, for example he wrote:

Men were now beginning to wear disfiguring costumes. This was especially true of noblemen: knights, squires, and their followers, but it was true in some measure of burgesses and of almost all servants. Garments were short to the point of indecency, which was surprising in a people who had up to this time conducted themselves becomingly. . . . Men thus tricked out were more likely to flee in the face of the enemy, as the events afterwards many times proved.[147]

In his entry for 1346 he added the financial theme:

Officials were being enriched, the king impoverished. Money was contributed to many nobles and knights that they might aid and defend their land and kingdom, but it was all spent for the useless practices of pleasure, such as dice and other unseemly games.[148]

In an entry for the year 1356, preceding his account of the battle of Poitiers, he rails at a bad situation gone worse: "the luxury and dissoluteness of many of the nobles and the knights became still more deeply rooted." Reminding his readers of knightly dress already immoral by becoming scanty and form-fitting, he now denounced the fashion to "adorn themselves from

---

145. Cazelles, *Société politique*, 1–195; Perroy, *Hundred Years War*, 69–124; Jean Favier, *La Guerre de Cent ans*, 75–156.
146. A dramatic change in clothing style did actually occur, beginning around 1340. See Newton, *Fashion in the Age of the Black Prince*. I owe this reference to Montgomery Bohna.
147. *The Chronicle of Jean de Venette*, trans. Jean Birdsall, ed. Richard A. Newhall (New York, 1953), 34.
148. *Chronicle of Jean de Venette*, 45.

head to foot with gems and precious stones." The knights were buying up jewels with such enthusiasm that prices shot up dramatically in Paris. Jean pours scorn on them:

> By night they devoted themselves immoderately to the pleasures of the flesh or to games of dice; by day, to ball or tennis. Wherefore the common people had reason to lament, and did lament greatly, that the taxes levied on them for the war were uselessly spent on such sports and converted to such uses.[149]

Jean de Venette's quotable report of widespread and trenchant criticisms was joined by many others. The *Grandes Chroniques de France*, in sections written between 1344 and 1350, expressed the view that God was punishing the nobility of France for their pride, greed, and indecency of dress. The flower of French chivalry had been cut down on the battlefield at Crécy in punishment for these very sins.[150] The continuator of the Chronicle of Guilliaume de Nangis denounced the nobles for their long beards and tunics so short they displayed their backsides, "which caused in the general populace a considerable derision." The author at once connects such morals with a tendency to flee in the face of the enemy.[151]

Clearly a tide of criticism was already gathering the force that would carry it to flood stage after Poitiers.[152] In the wake of this battle, rhetorical treatises such as the one written by the Benedictine brother Francis Beaumont would declare French chivalry a subject for satire, its soft cowardice standing in painful contrast to its pride; the knights who had run like rabbits, leaving their brave king to be captured, had elevated pleasure and luxury above discipline and military art, in the process bringing the ruin of the French state.[153]

This low estimate of the current state of French chivalry was not contradicted by the king. Jean II, far from being the blindly chivalrous fool pictured by some, actually shared many of the criticisms that scorched the

---

149. *Chronicle of Jean de Venette*, 62–63.
150. *Grandes Chroniques de France*, ed. Jules Viard, Société de l'Histoire de France IX (Paris, 1937), 285. See the discussion in Newton, *Fashion in the Age of the Black Prince*, 9–10.
151. Quoted in Charles de Beaurepaire, "Complainte sur la bataille de Poitiers," *Bibliothèque de l'Ecole des Chartes* 12, ser. III, 2 (1850), 259.
152. The anonymous author of the brief "Complainte sur la bataille de Poitiers" rapidly warms to his task of castigating the failures of French chivalry. In line 3 he writes of "leur traison"; by line 15 he speaks of "leur grant traison"; by line 49 it has become "La tres grant traison." See the text printed by Charles de Beaurepaire, "Complainte," 260–63.
153. Discussed and printed by André Vernet, "Le tragicum argumentum de miserabili statu regni Francie de François de Monte Belluna (1357)," *Annuaire-Bulletin de la Société de l'Histoire de France* (1962–63).

pages of the chroniclers.[154] His view may well have taken shape several years before his accession, after he had witnessed defeat and shameful retreat on the battlefield at Crécy. His doubts were fully confirmed at the dénouement of the battle of Poitiers as he saw his army routed, himself captured.

But however much he distrusted the results the current state of French knighthood might produce on the battlefield or in the council chamber, he obviously believed in the crucial importance of a reformed chivalry for the success of his reign and the good governance of his realm. It is difficult to imagine what alternatives could have presented themselves in his mind; chivalry, as we have seen, constituted a given, the self-definition of noble life, the framework within which religion, violence, and love took on acceptable meaning.

Thus a reform of chivalry claimed a prominent place among the other schemes for reform that marked the early years of his kingship.[155] Within a year or so of his accession Jean reorganized his council, reissued the great administrative reform ordinance of 1303 (with suitable modifications), promulgated a *reglement pour les gens de guerre* (setting the size of military companies, specifying duties and wages), and announced the formation of his Company of the Star.

The place of a renewal of chivalry within the constellation of other reform measures could easily be missed; the modern view is less inclined than the medieval one to see chivalry as an essential component of rational governance. But if we can imagine that Jean thought of his problems as much in terms of human morality as of institutional change, then the Company of the Star takes on its proper luster.[156]

The importance of Charny's book as a reform document within the contemporary military and political context becomes obvious. Working out his reform goals involved Charny in a delicate balancing act of the sort any reformer faces in discussing an institution or set of ideas currently under criticism. The reformer must walk the tightrope stretched between the high poles of two needs. First, he must praise the current system as essential

---

154. Cazelles, *Société politique*, 35–47.
155. For what follows, see Cazelles, *Société politique*, 60–157; Boulton, *Knights of the Crown*, 167–210.
156. Of course the need to reform knightly morality and to improvise better institutional arrangements for taking advice from nobles may well have fused in Jean II's mind. As Boulton observes, "as the Company seems to have included many and perhaps most of the leading members of the nobility of the kingdom, and as there was no other regular assembly in which the king could consult with representatives of the second Estate, it is very likely that Jean meant to ask the knights for 'loyal counsel' on matters of concern to the nobility as a whole." *Knights of the Crown*, 194.

and, second, he must recognize the serious problems that must be solved if the system is to function ideally. A writer can fall off on either side and compound problems by overemphasizing either the ideal or its difficulties. Charny carries out this balancing act with a fair amount of skill.

His book established links with the specifically political dimension of the royal reform movement most directly in the section that imitates the well-known "mirror of princes" genre. Two long lists of rhetorical questions, filling half a dozen folio pages of the text (24.81ff), debate the reasons for the institution of kings and princes. The first list suggests the possibility of a thoroughly disreputable conception of kingship, one that sees authority simply as license for ease, private enrichment at common expense, and cowardice and neglect of defense. Charny answers each of these questions with a resounding negative: kingship cannot have such origins. The second set of questions asks whether true kingship is based on good governance in war and peace. Charny gives an enthusiastically positive answer to each question. His views here are conventional[157] but powerfully expressed. In his effort to make the point clear he makes it repeatedly: kings have been chosen because they have the strength to suffer the pains needed to work for good government. The basis of authority is a sense of duty, not entitlement to ease and empty mastery. By first stating his case in two long catalogues of rhetorical questions, turning each negative statement into a positive injunction for good governance, Charny doubles the impact of his message. He likewise balances his mini-sermon on current problems with a defense of the proper functioning of kingship.[158]

---

157. As noted below, the elaboration of a raison d'être for kingship runs parallel to that for knighthood. Charny may well have known earlier treatments of this theme of good kingship and good lordship in knighthood. A clear example appears in the *Lancelot do Lac* (ed. Kennedy, 142–47) when the Lady of the Lake presents a high conception of chivalry to Lancelot. She tells him a creation myth about chivalry. When the original human equality failed to secure orderly life, as greed and strife appeared, knighthood arose to provide order and defense for all. The knight must thus be courteous without baseness, gracious without cruelty, compassionate to the needy, generous, ready to confound robbers and murderers, and a fair judge who acts without favor or spite. The sense of duty, even of heavy obligation thus accompanies privilege at every step. As we have seen, Llull takes much the same position in his book. Kennedy suggests that he may in fact be following the *Lancelot do Lac*, "Social and Political Ideas in the French Prose *Lancelot*," *Medium Aevum* 36 (1957), 103.

158. That a layman would use such rhetorical patterning in a treatise on chivalry provides interesting evidence on lay culture. Charny's elaboration of a major topic through two lists of questions with contrasting answers at least resembles some figures found in rhetorical manuals. Geoffrey of Vinsauf's *Poetria Nova*, for example, explains *disjunctio* as the figure that "distinguishes alternatives, accompanying each with a reason and bringing both to a conclusion." *Poetria Nova of Geoffrey of Vinsauf*, trans. Margaret F. Nims (Toronto, 1967), 61. Though we need not imagine formal rhetorical training on his part, Charny could frequently have been

Moreover, he specifically states that this consideration of good governance applies not only to kings but to all those in positions of privilege and power, that is to the entire hierarchy of lords. These words were meant to resound in the hall of the Noble Maison when the Company of the Star gathered there formally; they were meant to remain within the minds of the leading knights and men-at-arms of the realm when they went back to their own estates. The message is intended to inform and reform the practice of governance by knights at all levels.

Charny had long been associated with ideas of governmental reform and the need to consider the common good. He was a member of the political circle of the future King Jean II (then Duke of Normandy) when, in 1347, one member of this circle wrote for Jean a prose treatise, framed by short poems, entitled *L'Estat et le gouvernement comme les princes et seigneurs se doivent gouvener* (translated into English in the next century as *The III Considerations right necesserye to the good governaunce of a prince*). Jean-Philippe Genet, who edited this text, considered the possibility that Charny might have been its author, though he finally concluded that Jean de Marigny (who became archbishop of Rouen in 1347) was a more likely candidate. For our purposes it is important that Charny breathed this atmosphere of ideas about political reform and may well have heard this earlier treatise read and discussed in the court of the future Jean II.[159]

If broad notions of political reform were circulating in mid-fourteenth-century France, chivalry was the specific set of essential ideals and practices temporarily under a cloud and in need of *reformatio*. By writing on behalf of the new chivalric order founded by the king of France, Charny skillfully carried out the reformer's balancing act; he of course gave free rein to his inclination to praise chivalry to the skies, but he also, without calling too much attention to the tarnish and corrosion (seen all too clearly by other critics, outside the charmed circle), identified problems and urged reforms that might realize the potential of chivalry and blunt the criticisms voiced against it. High praise of chivalry and strict catechizing of its adher-

---

exposed to rhetorical prose. He shows here a sensitivy to rhetorical patterns and their effects. I am grateful to Marjorie Woods, University of Texas, Austin, for helpful advice on these points.

159. Jean-Philippe Genet, *Four English Political Tracts of the Later Middle Ages*, Camden Fourth Series 18 (London, 1977), 174–219 prints the mid-fifteenth-century English translation of this text and discusses the original. He notes that Charny's *Livre de chevalerie* "includes several passages focused upon political problems," but concludes that "Charny made no allusion to another work which he had written, and the style of his *Livre* bears no resemblance to that of *L'Estat*" (178).

ents formed (to borrow the sword imagery so dear to writers of the vernacular treatises) opposite edges of the same blade.

We have already noted the scale of his praise for chivalry, and his view that knights, and indeed all men-at-arms, followed the most demanding and most honorable vocation of all. He never tires of praising the worth and honor of all forms of knightly endeavor, even while establishing his dynamic scales of increasing chivalric virtue, from the lesser feats of arms in peacetime to the more comprehensive and demanding feats of arms in war. In fact, we have seen that in Charny's eyes the good knight swings his sword on behalf of God Himself, that he is a loyal son of the true Father of Chivalry who dispenses the divine gift of honor on earth and eventually welcomes His true warriors into paradise.

However, Charny knows that matters do not go so smoothly in the world and that chivalry has fallen short in the lives of its contemporary French practitioners. Perhaps as much of his book speaks to the problems of chivalry as to its praise. Yet behind all his criticisms stands an unfaltering belief that reform is possible and that the key to reform is a return to individual prowess.

This general belief informs Charny's most strikingly precise criticism of contemporary French knighthood. On the emotional issue of style he agrees wholeheartedly with the moralists who object to clothing so shameful that the wearer should be embarrassed to appear in it. Men who wear clothing molded to reveal the body and who with disgusting vanity cover their clothing with rich ornament can only have forgotten shame, and those who have forgotten shame have forgotten honor as well. It is only appropriate for women to adorn their bodies with jewels, because they lack the opportunity to win honor through prowess; for men the matter stands otherwise.[160]

This all-pervasive concern for the high demands of prowess clearly distances Charny from the *Roman des eles*, which worried that the element of prowess in knighthood might overwhelm largesse, and also from Llull's book, which worried about the classic knightly sin of pride. Charny's scale of knightly virtue, as we have noted more than once, rests on increasing displays of prowess.

Any modern reader, and certainly any modern military historian, may

---

160. Georges Duby provides perceptive comments on how significant dress could be in the eyes of medieval people, how shocking sudden changes appeared to them. *The Three Orders*, 54–55.

wonder at this emphasis on personal prowess and the failure to advance reform through a discussion of battlefield tactics, let alone through some broader concept of strategy as the means for revitalizing French knighthood. Why are such lines of thought so conspicuously absent? The reflexive modern answer would likely be that medieval knights thought little and charged often, that there truly was no medieval science of warfare. In fact, as John Gillingham[161] has demonstrated from sound evidence, great twelfth-century knights such as Richard I and William Marshal practiced a policy emphasizing military objectives over displays of individual prowess. Their wars were based on administrative effectiveness and involved strategies of ravaging enemy territory; their leadership was scarcely confined to a simple-minded search for dramatic and risky battlefield confrontations. Moreover they were open about this preference. When Marshal advised Henry II to fool the French by pretending to disband his forces and then secretly assembling them for a swift campaign of ravaging, the English king praised William's advice as "most courteous" (*molt corteis*).[162] In the generations between Marshal and Charny, no one could doubt that administrative efficiency supporting warfare continued to grow or that commanders had enthusiastically maintained their preference for ravaging over fighting set-piece battles.[163] The success of the English along just these lines can be traced by their scorched progress through the kingdom of France; their evident success must have burned itself into Charny's consciousness as well. Why, then, in so practical a treatise as the *Livre de chevalerie*, does he not suggest specific tactical and strategic responses?

If we could interview Charny we might find him somewhat puzzled at the stark alternatives implied in our questions.[164] Of course warfare is a matter of manoeuver, he might say; of course you ravage your enemies' territory whenever possible (and here he might elaborate his graphic plans for an invasion of the England he actually saw only as a prisoner). He could

---

161. John Gillingham, "Richard I and the Science of War in the Middle Ages," *War and Government in the Middle Ages: Essays in Honour of J. O. Prestwich*, ed. John Gillingham and J. C. Holt (Bury St. Edmunds, 1984), 78–92; Gillingham, "War and Chivalry in the History of William the Marshal," *Proceedings of the Newcastle Upon Tyne Conference, 1987*, ed. P. R. Coss and S. D. Lloyd, Thirteenth-Century England 2 (Bury St. Edmunds, 1988), 1–15.

162. Gillingham, "War and Chivalry," 6. The future Richard I, who was present, agreed that this was ideal advice.

163. For abundant evidence, with many citations, see Hewitt, *The Organization of War* and Kaeuper, *War, Justice, and Public Order*.

164. William Marshal might be equally puzzled. The pragmatic warrior who urged King Henry to avoid battle and conduct a *chevauchée* showed a delight in prowess all his life. As Gillingham points out, however, he took part in only one or two real battles, along with many skirmishes and sieges. "War and Chivalry," 12.

point to a portion of his text enjoining young knights to learn all they can about the best techniques of campaigning (17). But these are lessons to be learned only in the field, not from a book.

The granite foundation on which all such campaigning rests is that complex of military virtues he would sum up as prowess. This is the fit subject for his book. In formal writing for the royal chivalric order, why belabor details of military practice on which all seasoned warriors broadly agreed? The clear need is for French knighthood to hear again the clarion call of chivalry, to give up the soft life and be willing to undertake the pains and privations of knighthood. Perhaps that would mean besieging some stronghold through endless rainy days on bad rations. It might bring that glorious apotheosis of prowess, a full-blown battle. In either case it is a set of personal qualities that Charny wants his knights to have and that he thinks absolutely necessary, a kind of military morality with prowess as its center. As he writes, "anyone who wants to attain this high honor, if he retains his physical health and lives for long enough, cannot and should not be excused from achieving it" (19.136–38); "but no one should or can excuse himself from being a man of worth and loyal, if he has the will" (24.15–16).

Such a personal emphasis need not surprise us. After all, Charny's stress on individual will, so evident in his book, fits the tenor of thought in the mid-fourteenth century. Popular religious enthusiasm in Charny's age also emphasized issues of personal morality. We cannot forget that chivalry functioned as a form of aristocratic lay piety; we cannot forget that Charny's book is intensely pious.

Recognizing how much Charny stresses individual prowess as a key to chivalry, we must also take account of his reforming interest in motive and maturity. Time and again he assures his audience that the motives of men-at-arms can always be read as honorable. But those who fight primarily for gain must be careful lest they endanger the victory while they search for spoils or quarrel among themselves as they find them. Even the poor man-at-arms can be rich in honor. Better to spend goods in the search for honor than the reverse. Shame is the great fear of the true warrior; compared to loss of honor, death itself is a trifle.

Being a hardy fighter is not enough, though it is praiseworthy in itself. The great goal is not simply to win each contest, but to become a *preudomme*, a man of worth. Such a man will have moved through three stages in each of three essential component categories of worthiness. First, he will have progressed beyond simple-minded goodness and the formalities of

charity and church attendance to genuine love and service of God. Second, his intelligence will not be of the merely malicious or merely subtle sort, but will have attained what is good and reasonable. Third, he will show valor beyond the disorderly type found in seekers of individual good only; he will demonstrate a more mature prowess in military action abroad as well as at home, following good leaders. Finally, he will become such a seasoned commander himself, wise in his military experience. The man who combines in his own actions the final stage of each category Charny says will be the ideal layman, "supreme among all lay people," the model for emulation.

Can such a combination of qualities be found in a single man? Speaking to this point Charny shows his characteristic combination of the practical and the pious in his reform program. He praises emulation of the great without demanding perfection. He recognizes that the full fusion of characteristics would be rare, especially in his own troubled age. Historical examples—a fascinating list including Samson, Absalom, St. Peter, Julius Caesar—show flaws in even the famous from biblical and classical ages. There are, however, other great examples to remind men who aspire to such perfection what is possible. He cites that "saint chevalier" Judas Maccabeus in the Old Testament. This hero of Ancient Israel, Charny assures his audience, was indeed the ideal knight, motivated by piety and prowess, guided and rewarded by God (35.151–80).

Above all, Charny's contemporaries who strive to emulate such great models must remember that perfection can never be attributed to human effort alone, but rather to God's wonderful grace. Like the Calvinists of later centuries, Charny powerfully combines the most urgent calls for strenuous human effort with the most thorough sense of absolute divine election.

Thinking along these lines does not eliminate all the tensions between individual prowess and the larger requirements of sound military planning and action. Some of this tension is surely inherent in chivalry, not merely in Charny's conception of it. But such analysis does help to make better sense of the text at hand.

Charny's sense of urgency about the necessity of prowess (whatever cautions are necessary) and the crippling failure of will among his contemporaries emerges most clearly when he turns to knights who do not live up to the code. The subject leaves a bitter taste in his mouth and he touches on it only briefly, expressly stating his great relief when he can return to talk of the good knights. But the political and military realities in France by the middle of the fourteenth century left him little choice. He is desperately

worried that prowess has atrophied. Even when he dispenses seemingly casual advice, especially to young aspirants for knighthood, Charny is likely to warn against some enemy of prowess—living to eat, sleeping late in soft beds, and so forth. Timidity, even more than sloth or indolence, is the insidious enemy of prowess.

Charny comes as close to humor as his dignity and a high sense of mission will allow when he writes of the cowardly warrior. His humor is dark and biting. How else could he deal with men of war who have failed to understand the great lesson that it is better to die with honor intact than to live shamefully? In these passages he writes a more withering sarcasm than any chronicler; always the reformer, though, he carefully defines the focus of his target. Not all French knights are to blame, and certainly true chivalry—if only the will to exercise it can be restored—will produce prowess that matches the enemy blow for blow, come what may. The true knight will not retreat from a battle, but will stand his ground and do all the harm he can to his enemies.

Charny's text strongly reinforces Jean II's ideas for the Company of the Star. According to Jean le Bel, the members of the royal company of knights swore an oath that they would never flee a battle.[165] The letter notifying members of the Company of their election provides confirmation: one clause specifies that any member who shamefully fled from a battle would be expelled from the order until he had cleared his name.[166]

If Charny worried about prowess, then, he also worried about that second great chivalric virtue, loyalty. Only loyalty can assure the necessary hierarchy and fighting that is justifiable and enobling. Even before the battle of Poitiers the factionalism of the French noblesse and the relative breakdown of order generated a good deal of fighting that defied the classification of legitimacy even by Charny's generous standards. Some men, he admits, wear armor but are not really good men-at-arms. These dishonest, disorderly men make war without reason and seize, rob and wound people without the proper defiance. Others may avoid such direct misdeeds, but act in this fashion through their subordinates and receive them after the fact. Such men, he sternly warns, are unworthy to live or to enjoy the company of truly good men-at-arms. The pains and hardships these men incur in fighting are not signs of their virtue, but a foretaste of the greater pains that await them in hell.

In the meantime, had the Company of the Star developed along the

---

165. Quoted and discussed in Boulton, *Knights of the Crown*, 182.
166. Boulton, *Knights of the Crown*, 196.

lines its founder intended, the members of the Company with a penchant for the dishonorable would have faced the threat of a different foretaste of hell: a public recounting of all their adventures, honorable or otherwise, in a plenary meeting of the knightly order, with the deeds immortalized in the book kept by three clerks.[167] The Company of the Star, guided by Charny's treatise, could provide both the carrot and the stick to urge knights toward honor in this life and its reward in the next.

Just how closely Charny's book fits the reform program of Jean II will appear if we set the ideas we have found in the *Livre de chevalerie* alongside the royal statement of intent contained in the letters of October, 1352, endowing the college of canons, chaplains, and clerks to serve the Company of the Star. The preamble to these letters is given at length below as the best statement of Jean's hopes for the reform of French chivalry through his grand company.[168]

Jean by the Grace of God King of France. . . . Among the other preoccupations of our mind, we have many times asked ourself with all the energy of reflection, by what means the knighthood of our realm has, from ancient times, sent forth into the whole world such a burst of probity, and has been crowned with so lively an aureole of valiance and honour; so well that our ancestors the Kings of France, thanks to the powerful intervention of heaven and to the faithful devotion of this knighthood, which has bestowed upon them the sincere and unanimous concourse of its arms, have always triumphed over all the rebels whom they have wished to reduce; that they have been able, with the aid of divine favour, to restore to the pure paths of the Catholic Faith the numberless victims that the perfidious Enemy of the human race, through ruse and artifice, had made to err against the true faith; and finally that they had established in the realm a peace and security so profound that, after many long centuries, some of the members of this order, unaccustomed to arms and deprived of exercises, or for some other cause unknown to us, have immoderately plunged themselves into the idleness and vanity of the age, to the contempt of honour, alas, and of their good renown, to diminish their gaiety of heart in exchange for the comfort of their persons. For this reason we, mindful of former times, of the honourable and constant prowess of the aforesaid liegemen, who brought forth so many victorious, virtuous, and fortunate works, have taken it to heart to recall these same liegemen, present and future, to a perfect union, to the end that in this intimate unity they will breathe nothing but honour and glory, renouncing the frivolities of inaction, and will, through respect for the prestige of the nobility and knighthood, restore to our epoch the lustre of their ancient renown and of their illustrious company, and that after they have brought about the reflow-

167. See note 72, which provides sources for a parallel with the practice of Arthur's court in the *Lancelot do Lac*.
168. Quoted in Boulton, *Knights of the Crown*, 184–85, from AN Mem. de la Chambre des Comptes, C, f. 121; and Register JJ 81, f. 288r.

ering of the honour of knighthood through the protection of divine goodness, a tranquil peace will be reborn for our reign and our subjects, and the praises of their virtue will be published everywhere. Therefore, in expectation of these benefits and of many others, we . . . have founded [the Company of the Star and its college of clerics]. And we have firm confidence that with the intercession of the said most glorious Virgin Mary for us and our faithful subjects, the Lord Jesus Christ will mercifully pour out his grace upon the knights of the aforesaid company or association, with the result that the same knights, eager for honour and glory in the exercise of arms, shall bear themselves with such concord and valiance, that the flower of chivalry, which for a time and for the reasons mentioned had faded into the shadows, shall blossom in our realm, and shine resplendent in a perfect harmony to the honour and glory of the kingdom and of our faithful subjects.

All the familiar themes are here. Chivalry has been the grand force for good, the strong arm of true faith, favored by God, the agency of defense, the guarantor of good and peaceful governance, the procurer of glorious victories. But the flower of chivalry has faded, lost under dark shadows cast by current difficulties and weakness. Only vigorous reform can restore a knighthood that will throw off sloth and immorality and be "eager for honour and glory in the exercise of arms." The anxious king and the honored knight who carried his banner and wrote as theoretician of chivalry saw the same issues and spoke to them in the same language.

Yet we must not make the error of generalizing this agreement into a belief that kingship and chivalry were always compatible. Charny's book and Jean le Bon's letters contain much that is important and informative about chivalry and governance in the broadest sense; they show significant areas of congruence. Both men wrote in a time of crisis that demanded unity if the accustomed social and political order of the kingdom were to survive. The problems that nearly overwhelmed France shortly after each wrote painfully confirmed their wisdom. Earlier kings acting in different circumstances, and other knights less committed to the necessity of reform measures, could have spoken to their relationship in different terms.

The ambiguity stemmed from the common sense of duty and entitlement, the common stock from which kings and knights drew their ideas about their proper roles and rights. That many knights clearly thought themselves to be kinglets is evident from the political history of medieval Europe. Kings and knights together shared responsibility for the legitimate use of force, in theory always practiced in the interests of defense and justice. Many French lords had long claimed this use of force as their legitimate right. But the proper division of labor and profit involved in such high duties was complicated by the growing reality of royal sovereignty. In the

Coutumes de Beauvaisis for example, the great lawbook Philippe de Beaumanoir finished in 1283, one chapter is devoted to the practice of private war and another to truces. As Beaumanoir says,

> Although custom allows these wars in the Beauvais region, between gentlemen,[169] for a *casus belli*, the count (or the king if the count will not) can require the parties to make peace with each other or to make a truce.[170]

In Charny's own lifetime the crown was busy regulating private war, that is, war between knights within the realm. A royal act of 1338–39 confirmed for Aquitaine the right of lords in that duchy to war against each other so long as they respected certain conditions: the two sides must respectively give and accept formal notification of the war and they must likewise cease their war at the commencement of the king's own war. An act of 1352 renewed the prohibition of private wars during royal war, and another edict in 1354 affirmed the concept of the *Quarantaine le Roy* (attributed to Saint Louis), which imposed a forty-day truce during which relatives of the principals involved could declare their intentions regarding the war.[171]

If Charny is a royalist, he is also, as we have seen repeatedly, much in favor of the chivalric war which French kings were trying to bring within the sphere of their control. In one of his most concise statements Charny tells all his men of war that they must strive for the highest honors "by force of arms and through good deeds (*par force darmes et de bonnes euvres*)." For several generations the late Capetian kings of France, like their Plantagenet cousins across the Channel, had been rapidly and forcefully expanding their jurisdiction, even against the independence of lords and knights. They claimed precisely that *not* all feats of arms done within their realms were, in fact, good works, and insisted on their sovereign right to secure public order even against the impulse—claimed as legal right—among the chivalric classes to demonstrate prowess in quarrels and private wars. Vigorous monarchs had brought into their courts whole classes of actions in which one side had acted "by force and arms, against the king's peace," or "by illegal and prohibited arms,"[172] phrases that contrast sharply with Charny's state-

---

169. He notes a few lines later that "According to our custom war cannot begin between commoners or between townsmen."

170. *The* Coutumes de Beauvaisis *of Philippe de Beaumanoir*, trans. F. R. P. Akehurst (Philadelphia, 1992), 611.

171. *Ordonnances des rois de France*, ed. E.-J Laurière et al., 22 vols. (Paris, 1723–1849), vol. 2, 61–63, 552–53. See Raymond Cazelles, "La Réglementation royale de la guerre privée de Saint Louis à Charles V et la précarité des ordonnances," *Revue Historique de Droit Française* 4th ser. 38 (1960), 530–48.

172. Kaeuper, *War, Justice, and Public Order*, 244, 264.

ment of approval for honor achieved "by force of arms and through good deeds." As Philippe Contamine has observed of Charny, "In his eyes, the war of the king of France is in no way privileged; it appears as only one of the guises which the profession of arms could wear."[173]

Charny's discussion of lawless knights was suitably brief for a reform treatise with a delicate mission. But the phenomenon was writ much larger in life, as any perusal of the legal records of the French or English monarchies would quickly demonstrate.[174] Problems existed not simply because of the faults of individual men who regrettably could not live up to the high standards of chivalry, but because the roles of kings and knights overlapped in areas significant enough to cause conflicts.

To recognize this fact is not in any sense to devalue Charny's treatise, with its emphasis on cooperation. Rather, it shows how much pressure the problems experienced in fourteenth-century French political society placed on both chivalry and kingship in that kingdom. "Among the other preoccupations of our mind," King Jean wearily began, when he wrote of his new chivalric order. As English armies ravaged his realm, as he worried over factionalism and disloyalty, Jean II was not thinking about sovereignty vis à vis knighthood with the touchiness and vigor of a Philippe le Bel, his royal predecessor of a generation earlier.[175] In an age of crisis Geoffroi de Charny, for his part, was willing to try to recall French knights to displays of prowess in following the king's banner which he personally bore with such honor.

But was the text he wrote really important in the history of chivalry? Was it widely read and influential? It seems highly unlikely that Charny's text had anything like the audience that Llull's book on the same subject commanded. As Maurice Keen notes, outside Germany at least, Llull's book became the standard treatise on chivalry.[176]

The reason for the lesser influence of Charny's book is not hard to find. His ideas seem to have been so closely associated with the Company of the Star that his book declined with that order. The *Livre de chevalerie* probably did not reach the elite primary audience, and certainly did not reach the wider secondary audience of its intentions; thus, like Jean le Bon's reform of chivalry, it failed.

It is true that in some measure the ideas in the book may be echoed in

---

173. Philippe Contamine, *Guerre, état, et société à la fin du Moyen Age* (Paris, 1972), 187. He returns to this theme in "Geoffroy de Charny," 115.
174. Kaeuper, *War, Justice, and Public Order*, chap. 3.
175. Joseph R. Strayer, *The Reign of Philip the Fair* (Princeton, NJ, 1980).
176. Keen, *Chivalry*, 11.

the treatise of Jean de Beuil, *Le Jouvencel*, written more than a century later around 1466.[177] The author appears to have read Charny; Malcolm Vale even calls him Charny's heir. *Le Jouvencel* was truly popular, as its printing in five editions between 1493 and 1529 attests.[178] Yet *Le Jouvencel* belongs to a new direction taking shape in the conception of knighthood by the late fifteenth century, while Charny's work, in its essential characteristics, looks back to an earlier tradition. The new humanist view, whether appearing in Jean de Beuil's book, in Christine de Pisan's *Epitre d'Othéa à Hector*, or in the anonymous *Knyghthode and Bataile* (c. 1457),[179] concentrates even more than Charny on the working details of a knightly career in the field, in local administration, or as a courtier in royal service. Above all, as Beverly Kennedy has argued, such works move away from a religious view that considers knighthood a great temporal order of Christendom and "assume that both the motives and the rewards for [the knight's] moral behaviour will be as much, if not more, of this world as of the next. They assume that the knight is a careerist."[180] Thus Charny's book was neither a contemporary success nor an early contributor to the wave of the future.

But the importance of Geoffroi de Charny's *Livre de chevalerie* rests finally with us rather than with a diminishing audience of knightly readers in fourteenth- or fifteenth-century Europe. As students of his age we can profitably listen to his ideas with greater attentiveness than did his contemporaries. He has much to teach us, about chivalry as a form of lay piety among aristocratic males, about the self-definition and valorization embedded in a demanding code of behavior, about the ambivalent relationship of chivalry and public order, and about a vocation as religious in its high aspirations as it was violent in its essential activity.

177. *Le Jovencel*, ed. Camille Favre and Léon Lecestre, 2 vols. (Paris, 1887–89).
178. Malcolm Vale, *War and Chivalry*, 31: "Jean de Beuil's stress on the rigours of a military training, the privations of a soldierly existence and the skills demanded of the man-at-arms make him the fifteenth-century successor to Charny, whose writings he may well have read. It is instructive to note that this element in the chivalric tradition was part of that handed on to Renaissance nobles and soldiers."
179. *Knyghthood and Bataile*, ed. Roman Dyboski and Zygford M. Arend (London, 1935).
180. Beverly Kennedy, *Knighthood in the Morte Darthur* (Bury St. Edmunds, 1985), 16.

THE
BOOK OF CHIVALRY

Editorial Introduction

Literary Background to the *Livre de chevalerie*

ALTHOUGH GEOFFROI DE CHARNY'S DEBT to the two treatises on chivalry, *l'Ordene de chevalerie* and *Le libre del orde de cavallería* of Ramon Llull (details of which will be given in the notes to the text and translation) has long been acknowledged by scholars, not as much attention has been paid to the influence of the medieval courtly lyric and Arthurian romance on the work of Charny. The themes of the twelfth-century verse romances of Chrétien de Troyes have already been explored in relation to the development of concepts of chivalry by scholars working on both literature and history, but not so much has been done on the great prose romances of the thirteenth century. That these manuscripts were widely read is suggested by the large number of them that have survived and by the allusions to these romances and borrowing from them in the works of knights such as Philippe de Novare and Philippe de Beaumanoir as well as Ramon Llull.[1] The Prose *Lancelot*, of which the first version (the non-cyclic version, edited by me and referred to in the notes) appeared very early in the thirteenth century and may well predate *l'Ordene de chevalerie*, contains both the oath the knights had to swear that they would tell the truth about their adventures on their return to Arthur's court and the references to the recording of the accounts of their adventures by Arthur's clerks in a big book.

The words of the oath which, according to Jean le Bel, the knights of the Compagnie de l'Etoile had to swear when they set out to perform deeds of arms recall those which, according to the early thirteenth-century Prose *Lancelot*, all Arthur's knights had to swear when they left court on a quest, as do those passages describing the recording of these adventures by the

---

1. For a discussion of the wide reading of prose romance by knights see Elspeth Kennedy, "The Knight as Reader of Arthurian Romance," *Culture and the King: The Social Implications of the Arthurian Legend, Essays in Honor of Valerie M. Lagorio*, ed. Martin B. Schichtman and James P. Carley (New York, 1995), 70–90.

King's learned clerks which appear to be modelled on similar passages in the Prose *Lancelot*:

Aprés, par lo comandement lo roi s'agenoille Hectors devant les sainz, si jure ce que li rois li devise, si con a cel tans estoit costume: que il querroit lo chevalier a son pooir tant comme queste devoit durer — c'estoit un an — et que il ne vanroit sanz lui o sanz veraies enseignes por coi an savroit de voir que il l'avroit trové: *et que de chose qui li avenist an sa queste ne mantiroit a son pooir, ne por sa honte covrir, ne por s'anor avancier*. Itel sairement juroient tuit cil qui an la queste aloient au tens que les mervoillouses avantures avenoient el reiaume et es fiez de Logres, si com vos avez oï autrefoiz an cest conte. (*LK*, 406)[2]

Hector knelt before the holy relics and swore what the King told him to swear, for at that time such was the custom: that he would seek the knight to the best of his ability as long as the quest should last — that was a year — and that he would not come back without him or without true evidence that he had found him; *and that he would not lie about anything that happened in his quest, whether to hide his shame or to increase his honor*. All those who went on a quest swore such an oath at the time when the marvelous adventures happened in the kingdom of Logres, as you have heard.

Et furent mandé li clerc qui metoient an escrit les proeces as conpaignons de la maison lo roi. (*LK*, 571)

And the clerks were sent for who set down in writing all the deeds of prowess of the companions of the King's household.

Jean le Bel writes:

Et y (at the Maison de l'Etoile) debvoit le roy, chascun an, tenir court plainiere de tous les compaignons au mains, et y debvoit chascun raconter toutes ses aventures, aussy bien les honteuses que les glorieuses qui avenues luy seroient des le temps qu'il n'avroit esté a la noble court, et le roy debvroit ordonner .ii. ou .iii. clercs qui escouteroient toutes ces aventures, et en ung livre mettroient affin qu'elles fussent chascun an raportees en place par devant les compaignons, par quoy on poeut sçavoir les plus proeux et honnourer ceulx qui mielx le deserviroient. (*Chroniques* II, 204–6)

and the king should each year hold a full court of all the companions, and each one should recount all his adventures, the shameful as well as the glorious, which hap-

---

2. *Lancelot do Lac: The Non-Cyclic Old French Prose Romance*, ed. Elspeth Kennedy, 2 vols. (Oxford, 1980) (abbreviated *LK*), vol. 1, 406. Similar passages are to be found in later branches of the cycle. See, for example, *Lancelot: roman en prose du XIIIe siècle*, ed. Alexandre Micha, 9 vols. (Paris-Geneva, 1978–83) (abbreviated *LM*), LXXXIV, 68, CI, 1–11. Except where otherwise stated, all translations from French are by Elspeth Kennedy.

pened to him during the time he spent away from the noble court, and the king should order two or three clerks to listen to all these adventures and put them in a book so that they would be reported each year in front of the companions, so that the most valiant should be known and those honored who most deserve it.

In this account of Lancelot's early adventures, which later in the thirteenth century came to form the first branch of the Lancelot-Grail cycle[3] the Lady of the Lake gives a discourse on chivalry in which she explains to the young Lancelot the origin of chivalry after the Fall of Man, the function of the knight as member of one of the three orders, as defender of justice, of the weak (widows and orphans) against the wicked and powerful, and of the Holy Church against its enemies.[4] She also explains the significance of the knight's armor. Philippe de Beaumanoir and Ramon Llull give accounts of the origin of kings and/or knights which, to judge from certain verbal similarities, they both draw from the Prose *Lancelot*. Charny too gives an explanation of the origin of kings and of the duties of princes and knights in which he appears to take material both from Llull, but also from the Prose *Lancelot*.[5] Charny, unlike Llull but like the Prose *Lancelot*, does not mention the division of the men into thousands from which one is chosen.

The link between the *Livre de chevalerie* and Arthurian romance is made explicit when Charny refers to Guinevere in his explanation of the importance of secrecy in love and speaks disapprovingly of those who want to boast of conquests of ladies, whether true or fictitious:

3. The earliest manuscript of the Prose *Lancelot* brings the story to an end with the death of Lancelot's friend Galehot, and does not contain a Grail Quest or a *Mort Artu*; this version has been published as *Lancelot do Lac: The Non-Cyclic Old French Prose Romance* (see n. 2 above). In the cyclic version of the romance, written a few years later, the account of Lancelot's adventures up to his installation as a knight of the Round Table was taken over unchanged, but the last two episodes in the earlier version were rewritten to prepare the way for a Grail Quest with Lancelot's son as the new Grail hero.
4. Georges Duby in Chapter 22 of *Les trois ordres: ou l'imaginaire du féodalisme* (Paris, 1978) analyzes the Lady of the Lake's account of the origin of chivalry and suggests that it gives greater importance to the knight than to the clergy and thus represents a desacralization of knighthood. However, if all men have to obey the knight (*LK*, 144.15–16) and the Church must sustain him spiritually (*LK*, 144.36–37), it is also stressed that he must serve the Church; when he receives the order of knighthood, he has to make a solemn promise to God that he will perform faithfully the duties of a knight (*LK*, 145.25–37), and if he fails to do so, he will have sinned in the sight of God. When the cyclic romance develops, knights are given a very important role in the allegory of the Quest for the Holy Grail. It is Galahad, a type of Christ, who achieves the adventure of the Holy Grail, and at the solemn part of the mass ("el segré de la messe") is invited to look inside the holy vessel and contemplate the spiritual mysteries. *La Queste del Saint Graal*, ed. Albert Pauphilet (Paris, 1923), pp. 277–78.
5. For particular verbal echoes from Llull and the prose romance see Notes to the Text and Translation.

et ce n'est mie le plus grant deduit que l'en puisse avoir que de dire: "J'ayme celle la", ne de vouloir en faire telx semblans que chascun doie dire: "Celi aime trop bien par amours celle dame la." Et moult en y a qui dient qu'ilz ne vouldroient pas amer la royne Genyevre, s'il ne le disoient ou s'il n'estoit sceu. Y celles gens aimeroient miex que chascun dist et cuidast qu'il amaissent trop bien par amours et ja n'en fust rien, que ce qu'il amassent et bien leur en deust venir et fust tenu bien secret. (19.193–200)

The greatest pleasure to be derived from love is not to be found in saying "I love so and so" nor in behaving in such a way that everyone will say: "That man is the lover of that lady." And there are many who say that they would not want to love Queen Guinevere if they did not declare it openly or if it were not known. Such men would prefer it to be said by everyone that they were the accepted lovers of ladies, even if this were not true, than that they did love and had met a favorable response, were this to be kept secret.

This allusion recalls both the need for secrecy in love (a recurring theme in both lyric and romance: Lancelot in the Prose *Lancelot* always refuses to name the object of his love, even if it means remaining in prison (*LK*, 303), and the central role of love as the inspiration for the young knight Lancelot's achievements. In both the prose romance and the *Livre de chevalerie*, unlike *L'Ordene de chevalerie* or Ramon Llull's treatise, or indeed, the Lady of the Lake's discourse on chivalry, the importance of *amer par amors* as an incentive for bold endeavor is given considerable stress.[6] *Amer par amors* or *amer finement*, or *amer leialment* are the terms used to designate the idealized love celebrated in lyric and romance. This is a love which ennobles a young man through his desire to prove himself worthy of the love of his lady, whether by the quality of his song or by his prowess at arms. In the Prose *Lancelot*, it is said that Claudas has *amé par amors* in his youth, but had given it up because he wanted to have a long life. He explains why he has said this:

---

6. It is interesting that two thirteenth-century knights, Philippe de Novare and Philippe de Beaumanoir, both readers of the Prose *Lancelot*, do not make use of any of the passages in the romance that emphasize the importance of love in the development of the career of a young knight. Philippe de Novare paraphrases passages from the Prose *Lancelot* in *Les quatre âges de l'homme, traité moral de Philippe de Navarre, publié pour la première fois d'après les manuscripts de Paris, de Londres et de Metz*, ed. Marcel de Fréville, SATF (Paris, 1888), 23–24, to stress the need for a young knight to listen to the advice of his elders, drawing from an episode in the romance where relations between lord and vassal are explored. Philippe de Beaumanoir follows closely the Lady of the Lake's account of the origin of chivalry in his explanation of the origin of *gentilhommes* chosen to help the king maintain justice, *Les Coutumes de Beauvaisis*, ed. A. Salmon, SATF, 2 vols. (Paris, 1884–85), §1453. Both men wrote books on customary law.

"Por ce, fait il, que cuers de chevalier qui finement aimme ne doit baer qu'a une chose: c'est a tot lo monde passer; ne nus cors d'ome, tant fust preuz, ne porroit soffrir ce que li cuers oseroit emprandre, que ançois ne lo convenist fenir. Mais se la force del cors fust si granz que ele poïst aconplir les hardemenz del cuer, ge amasse par amors tote ma vie et passasse toz les prodomes de totes iceles proesces qui puent estre en cors de boen chevalier, car il ne puet estre tres preuz d'armes, se il n'aimme tres leialment, et ge conois tant mon cuer que ge amasse leiaument sor toz leiaus." (*LK*, 30–31)

"Because," he said, "the heart of a knight who truly loves [finement aimme] should have only one aim: that is to surpass the whole world; nor can the body of any man, no matter how worthy, suffer what the heart would dare to undertake without perishing. But if the strength of the body were so great that it could achieve the bold undertakings of the heart, I would love truly [amasse par amors] all my life and would surpass all men of worth and valor in the qualities of prowess to be found in the physical person of a good knight, for no one can be of great valor at arms if he does not love loyally, and I know my own heart well enough to be certain that I would love more loyally than all those who are loyal."

The prose romance then confirms that he spoke the truth:

Car il avoit en s'amor estoit de merveilleuse proesce, et avoit eü los et pris de sa chevalerie en maintes terres. (*LK*, 31)

For he had, while in love, been of marvellous prowess and had won praise and honor for his chivalry in many lands.

To be compared with Charny's remarks on the benefit for good men-at-arms of *amer par amors*:

Si doivent icelles gens vivre loiaument et liement, entre les autres choses amer par amour honorablement, que c'est le droit estat de ceulx qui celi honour veulent acquerir. (19.183–85)

And these people should live loyally and joyfully, and, amongst other things, love a lady truly and honorably, for it is the right position to be in for those who desire to achieve honor.

The Lady of the Lake, who had not mentioned the importance of *amer par amors*, in her discourse on chivalry, later sends a damsel to tell Lancelot something she had forgotten to say to him before he left for Arthur's court:

"Ce fu, fait ele, que vos ne metoiz ja vostre cuer en amor qui vos face aparecir mais amander, car cuers qui por amor devient pareceus ne puet a haute chose ataindre, car il n'osse. Mais cil qui tozjorz bee a amender puet ataindre a hautes choses, autresin com il les ose anprandre." (*LK*, 205–6)

"It was," she said, "that you set your heart on a love which will improve you, not make you grow indolent, for a heart which for love becomes indolent cannot achieve great deeds, for it does not dare to do so. But a man who always aims to improve can achieve great deeds, as he dares to undertake them."[7]

Lancelot himself ascribes all his great deeds to the inspiration of his love for Guinevere, when he tells her (*LK*, 345–46) that it was her words of farewell, when as a young knight he left Camelot on his first adventure, which had inspired all his great deeds. She had said to him "A Deu, biax douz amis" (*LK*, 165), and he had given these words a deeper meaning than she had originally intended. In a later branch of the cyclic romance, when Guinevere has expressed her fears lest Lancelot's love for her may have endangered his chances of achieving the adventure of the Holy Grail, Lancelot declares firmly that he owes everything to that very love.[8]

"Sachiez que je ja ne fusse venu a si grant hautesce com je sui, se vos ne fussiez, car je n'eusse mie cuer par moi au conmancement de ma chevalerie d'amprandre les choses que li autre laissoient par defaute de pooir. Mais ce que je baoie a vos et a vostre grant biauté mist mon cuer en l'orgueil ou j'estoie si que je ne poïsse trouver aventure que je ne menasse a chief; car je savoie bien, se je ne pooie les aventures passer par prouesce, que a vos ne vandroie je ja, et il m'i couvenoit avenir ou morir. Dont je vos di vraiement que ce fu la chose qui plus acroissoit mes vertuz." (*LM*, LXXXV, 3)

"I tell you that I would never have attained the heights which I have reached, were it not for you, for I would never at the beginning of my career as a knight have had the courage on my own to undertake the adventures which other knights had left alone through lack of the power to achieve them. But the fact that I was aspiring to you and your great beauty gave my heart such proud confidence that there was no adventure I could find which I did not achieve, for I knew well that if I could not succeed in the adventures by my prowess, I would not attain you, and I had to reach

---

7. See also *LK*, 296.21, where the Lady of Malehaut assumes from the evidence of Lancelot's great deeds that Lancelot must love *par amors* some one in a high position.
8. Lancelot accepts in the *Queste del Saint Graal*, 66, that his love for Guinevere was a sin which had impaired his quality as a knight and caused his failure at the Grail Quest. Yet in the next branch, *La mort le Roi Artu*, ed. Jean Frappier, 3rd ed. (Paris, 1964), § 129, lines 132–36), he reminds Arthur of his debt to him as savior of the kingdom, and this refers to exploits he performed *after* he had fallen in love with Guinevere.

you or die. Thus I tell you truly that it was the thing which most increased my powers."

This idea of the importance of love as a source of inspiration for a young knight as it is presented in the Prose *Lancelot* is recalled both by Charny's allusion to Guinevere and by his use of the phrase *amer par amors*. However the expression is given a special meaning, well adapted to his practical approach, when he associates it with the men-at-arms who at the beginning of their career are so naïve (*nice*) that they are unaware of the great honour that they could win by deeds of arms; yet nevertheless they succeed so well because they put their hearts into winning the love of a lady (12.1–4). The young Lancelot may be called *pas senez tres bien* (not very sensible) by Guinevere when he falls into a lover's trance on his first sight of her and cannot reply to her questions (*LK*, 158), but we have already been given indications of his great destiny and heroic quality, and he is fully aware, when he leaves for Arthur's court, of the honor he can win through deeds of arms.

This move from the idealized world of romance onto a more practical level is also to be found in Charny's treatment of a theme to be found in the Prose *Lancelot*, namely that the lady's honor will be increased if she inspires a knight to great deeds, as the Lady of the Lake tells Guinevere (*LK*, 557). Charny's lucky and simple young man may have a lady of such quality that she will not let him waste his time but sends him off to win honor where good men-at-arms should seek it and makes him put more effort into it than he might otherwise have had the will to do, without demanding, like some ladies in Arthurian romance, that he should undertake artificial and unnecessary tasks to prove his love.[9] These ladies who give such good practical advice and thus "make" good men-at-arms deserve to be honored according to Charny (12). In Charny the honor gained by the lady with the valiant lover in comparison with the lady whose lover has achieved nothing is brought to life in concrete terms: the pride of the lady whose lover has demonstrated his prowess, and is acclaimed when he enters the hall, and the embarassment of the lady whose lover has not dared to

---

9. An example of such artificial tests or tasks imposed by ladies on knights as proof of the quality of their love can be found in Chrétien de Troyes' *Erec et Enide*, where in the Joie de la Cour episode Mabonagrain's lady insists that he should remain within the enchanted enclosure and defend it against all other knights. Another example is to be found in the Prose *Lancelot*: Gauvain defeats a knight whose lady has commanded him to challenge to a duel with lances every knight who passes through the Lande des Set Voies; she has promised to grant him her love if he does this for a month without being defeated (*LK*, 422–24).

take up arms and has achieved nothing (20). The love of a lady can be useful in other ways. For Charny, if a man-at-arms is not increasing his skill in the use of lance or sword, he will be better employed conversing with ladies than spending his time in bad company, gambling with dice or playing real tennis (1971–93). Thus the familiar phrases concerning the importance of true love for a lady to be found in both the Prose *Lancelot* and *Le livre de chevalerie* are given a more explicitly practical slant by Charny.

It would seem very probable that Charny also knew the *Roman de Perceforest*,[10] a fourteenth-century romance that provides a pre-history to the *Lancelot-Grail* cycle, as he gives a very similar account of the death of Julius Caesar as that given in that romance. One of the editors of this text, Gilles de Roussineau, argues that the romance must have been completed by 1344, as he believes that Edward III based his unfulfilled plan for a palace to house the Knights of the Garter on a building described in the romance, the Franc Palais, which held a table designed to seat three hundred knights.

The Manuscripts

There are two manuscripts of *Le livre de chevalerie*:

Manuscript *B* (Brussels, Bibliothèque Royale de Belgique: 1124–26).[11] This late fourteenth-century manuscript is described as French. It consists of 136 folios of parchment and contains: ff. 1–40, *Le livre Charny* (in verse); ff. 41–82, *Les demandes pour la joute, les tournois et la guerre*; ff. 83–136, *Le livre de chevalerie*. It begins:

"L'autre jour mon chemin aloie"

It ends on f. 136r:

"Priez a Dieu pour celui qui ce livre fait a.
EXPLICIT CHARNI: CHARNY:"

---

10. See *Perceforest: Le Roman de Perceforest, quatrième partie*, ed. Gilles Roussineau, 2 vols., Textes Littéraires Français (Geneva, 1987), abbreviated *Perceforest* 4, vol. 1, pp. xii–xiv. See also note to Text, 35.108–20. Trans., 35.111–123.

11. For a full description of the manuscript see Camille Gaspar and Frédéric Lyna, *Les principaux manuscrits à peintures de la Bibliothèque Royale de Belgique* (Paris, 1937; reprinted Brussels, 1984), 410–12, and *La Librairie de Philippe le Bon: Exposition organisée à l'occasion du 500ᵉ anniversaire de la mort du duc, Catalogue rédigé par Georges Dogaier et Marguerite Debae* (Brussels, 1967).

The whole page measures 237 × 171 mm., the writing 157 × 98 mm., and there are 24 to 25 lines per page. There is a change of hand at f. 102 r. The gatherings are usually of 8 leaves with catchwords, many of which have disappeared. The nineteenth-century binding is of calf. At the beginning of each work and of each section of the *Demandes* there is a large decorated initial in red and blue, on a gold ground, with vine leaves in the margin and a dragon and smaller decorated initials elsewhere. The arms of Jean Sans Peur are painted on the four margins of ff. 1, 41, 46, 51, 83; these are not always placed symmetrically and seem to have been added later. According to Camille Gaspar and Frédéric Lyna, Jean Sans Peur probably bought the volume and had his arms added as a mark of ownership. This seems to have been the manuscript "de la Bibliothèque de Bourgogne" used by Kervyn de Lettenhove for his edition of the text, although from time to time he gives readings which are quite different from those of this manuscript.

Manuscript *P* Paris, Bibliothèque Nationale, nouvelles acquisitions françaises, 4736. This fifteenth-century manuscript contains the *Demandes* ff. 1–35, and the *Livre de chevalerie*, ff. 36–87. It begins: "Demandes pour la jouste que je Geffroy de charni fais a hault et puissant princes des cheualiers nostre dame de la noble maison," and ends on f. 87: "vous deuez desirer souuerainnement de tous vos coeurs de y venir de voz encommencemens jusque a vos definemens." The page measures 230 × 155 mm. and there are 30 lines per page.

Manuscript *B* has been chosen as our base manuscript in preference to *P*, in which there are a number of omissions and which breaks off before the end of the text.

The Hands of Manuscript B

Both before and after f. 102r, where a change of scribe has been detected, the hand is reasonably legible. The letters *m, n* are usually clearly distinguishable from combinations of *u, i*, although after f. 102r there are a few cases where the distinction may not be quite so evident; the same is true of *c* and *t*. For example, at **24.79** Lettenhove reads *delices* where, in the opinion of the present editor, it looks more like *delites*; at **41.39** Lettenhove read *tresmuscier*, where the reading looks more like tresnuitier. The groups *ct* and *tt, sf* and *ff* tend to look very similar. Lettenhove seems to have had some difficulty in distinguishing final *s* and final *z*.

The Language of Manuscript B

The following remarks are not meant to provide an exhaustive account of the scribes' language, but are designed to shed light on the interpretation and editorial treatment of the text. Except where otherwise indicated, the "standard" form is used by the scribe as well as the "deviant" one. As will be seen, the language of neither scribe is strongly dialectal; the second scribe displays rather more features that were originally characteristic of the North or East, although a number of these had spread into other regions by the fourteenth century. For some features we have taken as an interesting point of comparison the edition of another text, *Perceforest*.[12] This was written at the same period, the middle of the fourteenth century, but with a later base manuscript, copied in the second half of the fifteenth century.

SPELLING

Vowels

1. *a* for *ai*: *comparasons* 40.8. The spelling *a* for *ai* (from [*a* + *yod*]), of which there are the occasional examples in *B*, was a common feature of the North and East.[13]

2. *a* for *e* and *e* for *a*. Alternation between *e* and *a* before *r* is common in Middle French and is to be found in *B*, for example, *marveilleusement* 24.64 (Pope, 187). This alternation also occurs before other consonants: *astache* (for *estache*) 43.37, *alongier* 24.97, alongside *eslongier* 25.39; cf. *Perceforest* 4, xliv.

3. *ey* for *e* (from Latin tonic free [*a*]), common in the North and North East (Pope, 107, 491); *grey* 21.22, 35.41.

4. Reduction of *iee* to *ie*, common in the thirteenth century in the North and East, but was also found in a wider area in Middle French (Pope, 193,

---

12. *Perceforest, troisième partie*, ed. Gilles Roussineau, 2 vols., Textes Littéraires Français (Geneva, 1988), abbreviated *Perceforest* 3.
13. Mildred K. Pope, *From Latin to Modern French with Especial Consideration of Anglo-Norman: Phonology and Morphology*, 2d ed. (Manchester, 1952), 488, abbreviated to Pope.

488, 494): *ville gaaignie* 15.7. See also *l'onneur qu'il ont pourchacie* 17.71, but there is some hesitation over the gender of *onneur*. See below, *Morphology*, 1.

5. *i* for *ie*, characteristic of North and North East (Pope, 193, 488): *fivres* 42.76.

6. *ie* for *i* before intervocalic *r*; *messieres* 35.84.[14]

7. *chie, che, chei, chai* as alternative spellings: *chietiz* 25.54, *chietives* 22.33, 26.10; *chetifs* 19.115; *cheitives* 26.11; *chaitives* 19.120.[15]

8. *i* for *ei* or *oi*: *damiselles* 43.1, 6, 10, 24. To be found in the North and East (Pope, 165, 489, 494). See also *guerrier* 15.25, 17.2, 35.188 (for the more usual *guerroier*) and *guerrient* 7.24, *guerria* 35.102; *festier* 20.4.

9. Also to be noted: *villanz* or *villans* for *vaillanz* or *vaillans*: *villanz* 35.4, 23; *villans* 35.4, 6, 25. P also reads *vill-* for *vaill-*.

10. *eil* for *ueil*: *veil je* 19.36; *veille* 35.68, 42.169, 44.23; *veillent* 39.11; but *vueillent* 19.72. Reduction of *ue* to *e*, especially for palatalized *l*, found in certain regions, West, South Center and South East in the thirteenth century, but becomes more widespread in Middle French (Pope, 203).

11. *ou* and *o* as alternative spellings (Pope, 210–11): *coulonme* 35.74; *prouffit* 35.99; *voulentiers* 24.103; *vous* for *vos* (possessive) 23.11, 12, 27. See also *Morphology*, 6.

12. Also to be noted: *preuesce* for *prouesce* 35.20.

13. *oi* for *ui*: *poissance* 35.36, 59, 42.149; *poissances* 35.38; *poissans* 35.54, 42.123; *poissant* 35.58. This is the usual form in the text, but *puissance* does occur, 43.49. This absence of breaking before a palatal is to be found in the North East and East (Pope, 163, 491).

14. *en* and *an* alternate: *dengier* 23.57; *senz* for *sanz*, meaning "without," 35.209; *dempnacion* 35.60; *consciance* 42.20; *liemant* 37.14.

---

14. Pope, 498, describes *ie* for *i* as characteristic of South Center and West, but Roussineau, *Perceforest* 3, xxi, identifies such forms as inverse spellings well attested in the North.
15. This alternation after palatal consonants is also noted by Roussineau, *Perceforest* 4, xliv.

15. *ain, ein,* and *en* alternating: *amaindri* **35**.49; *maine* **35**.60; *peine* **16**.26; *paine* **35**.60; *consaintement* **25**.48. Such alternation in spelling was common in Later Old and Middle French (Pope, 179).

16. *aum* for *am*: *aumes* ("souls") **40**.33; *souffisaument* **25**.84; *espeuciaument* **40**.3. According to Pope, 489, velarizing and rounding of [*a*] before [*m*] was beginning to be current in the second half of the fourteenth century in the Northern region. Note also one example of *eu* followed by *m*: *obeïsseument* **42**.29. The letter *u* is clearly differentiated from *n* in these examples.

17. *jennes* **19**.37; *jones* **34**.5; *joennes* **19**.70. According to Pope, 182, *uen* was sometimes reduced to *en*.

18. After the change of hand (f. 102r, **21**.10), there is in general some hesitation over final feminine *e*, which is sometimes omitted and sometimes added, especially before a word beginning with a vowel, where the words would run together in pronunciation, or at the end of a phrase (a sense group), where there would be a pause. For an example of omission before a vowel, see *plair[e] a* **43**.9; for one of addition at the end of a phrase, see: *ainsi comme desus est dite* (emended to *dit*). In some cases, where the last letter of the preceding or following word is repeated, a mechanical error on the part of the scribe may be an important contributory factor. This is possibly the case in the following examples. Omission: *boir[e] et mengier et dormir* **39**.22; *pour fair[e] raison* **25**.23. Addition: *mettre toute* (emended to *tout*) *orgueil* **36**.27; *ainsi comme il est dessus dite* (emended to *dit*), *ne* **40**.14; *les premieres* (emended to *premiers*) *esleuz* **24**.78; *lequele* (emended to *lequel*) *de* **42**.17. There is one example which does not fit into any of the above categories: *celle fol[e] creance* **35**.55.

Consonants

1. There is uncertainty over final *s* which often disappears (see below under *Morphology*). Final *s* alternates with final *z*: *nulz* **39**.3, *nuls* **25**.36; *perdrez* **21**.11, *dormirés* **21**.10.

2. Final *l* occasionally disappears after *i* before a word beginning with a consonant: *selon ce qu'il fait et qu'i vaut* **19**.140; *qu'i leur* **42**.46. This is a widespread feature in thirteenth- and fourteenth-century French.

3. Double consonants for single are quite often found: *pensser* **23**.91; *neccessité* **17**.59, 67.

4. Alternation between the spellings *s* and *c* to represent the sound [s]: *se* (for *ce*) **42**.97; *avansement* **17**.56; *ces* (for *ses*) **19**.6.

5. *p* added after nasal once: *dempnacion* **35**.60.[16]

6. *ng* for *gn*: *eslongier* **25**.39, 50.

7. Disappearance of nasal consonant before *s*: *asseignent* (for *enseignent*) **23**.26.

8. *rm* for *m*, *nm* in *arme, armes* for *ame, ames* (soul): **35**.177, 211, 237, **44**.58.

Morphology

1. There is sometimes hesitation over the gender of nouns beginning with a vowel or a silent *h*: *honnour* is usually feminine **19**.127, but is treated as masculine **19**.129, 130, **20**.40; *ordre* is usually feminine, but *li ordre de chevalerie* **35**.223; *en cest ordre* **39**.2. See also *bon ordenance* **24**.23; *bonne ordenance* **24**.31.

2. The distinction in form betwen masculine nominative and oblique in relation to a noun preceded by an article is still often preserved. The indication of case is in general maintained with greater consistency in the form of the definite article than in that of the noun. *li* is the form almost always used for the nominative in the singular and *le* for the oblique, with only the very occasional deviation (for example: *li peuple* as oblique **25**.11). In the plural there are rather more deviations, for example: *que ne font les povres compaignons* **18**.4; *les huis furent fermés* **35**.112. There is somewhat more hesitation in the use of flexional *s* in relation to nouns and adjectives and the indefinite article. The regular pattern, often observed, can be illustrated by the following examples: *li debaz de deux bons est* **17**.37–38; *pour le fait* **10**.11; *li autre compaignon, qui voient les bons* **18**.8–9. But deviations from this are not infrequent, for example: *et pour ce vous enseignent li bons* **21**.34;

---

16. Cf. *Perceforest* 4, xlix.

li un des fais d'armes vaille miex que li autre 3.16; *laquelles des deus dames* 20.1; *traire les dens toute l'une aprés l'autre* 19.62. This hesitation is particularly marked after the verb *estre*, for example: *sont il regardés* 19.14; *qui sont si seur et si honorables* 44.15.

3. The pattern is much more confused in relation to the demonstratives: *cilz* (*icilz, ycilz*) is used in both singular and plural for the nominative: 1.6, 24.18; *celi* is used as both nominative masculine singular, 19.195, and oblique masculine singular, 4.10; *cil* 16.4, *cilz* 22.17, *ycilz* 24.18 *ycelz* 25.7, *ceulz* 26.2 are used as nominative plural forms; *ceulx* is also, of course, the normal form for oblique plural 5.4. *Cest* is used as nominative singular 39.27 *cesti* 4.5, *cestui* 19.130 as oblique singular.

4. Feminine forms of adjectives that derive from the third declension in Latin are to be found: *grant* 35.13 is used more frequently than analogical forms such as *grandes* 35.153 *tel* is often used as a feminine form, for example, *tel grace* 10.17, but *tele* is also often used, 15.21 in the plural, *telx* 6.3, *telz* 9.10 *tiex* 19.8, are all feminine forms as well as *teles* 9.8.

5. Personal pronouns: *il* and *ilz* are both used as masculine nominative plural; *eulx, eulz* is the tonic form of the oblique plural, but is also sometimes used as a nominative plural 19.219, 21.21; *li* is sometimes used as the tonic form of the masculine third person singular before an infinitive and after a preposition 5.13, 18.15, 35.159.

6. Possessives: the form *vous* rather than *vos* is on one folio used for the possessive adjective 23.11, 12, 27.

7. Relative pronouns: *que* is sometimes used for *qui* as the subject of a clause: *ne que jamais y soient* 35.28; *qui* is sometimes used as direct object: *qui souverainement l'en doit plus tenir a preux* 34.1–2; see also 40.2. *Cui* is, of course, used as a dative 35.178.

8. The present indicative: the strong stem is preserved in some verbs, for example: *menjue* 20.4, *menjuent* 21.30, *parolent* 23.8, *scevent* 3.6.

9. The ending *-és* alternates with *-ez* in the second person plural and the past participle.

10. In the present subjunctive, there is one example of the Burgundian form of the third person singular: *doubtoit* **42**.190; see Pope, 497. Also in the present subjunctive, for the first person plural, the ending *-iens* is found once: *parliens* **16**.2. This form, characteristic of the North and East, gained ground in the central region in the later thirteenth and fourteenth centuries, see Pope, 343.

11. In the imperfect subjunctive of verbs with an infinitive in *-er*, the third person plural ending *-aissent* is occasionally used: *amaissent* **19**.198. This form is characteristic of the East, see Pope, 383, 494.[17]

12. In the future and conditional, *vr* is reduced to *r*: *n'aroit* **19**.22 This was a Northern feature which became more widespread in the Middle French period, see Pope, 368. Forms such as *vouroit* **19**.86, *vourroit* **24**.57, where there is no interconsonantal glide between *l* and *r*, were also originally characteristic of the North, see Pope, 489.

13. There is one example of a "surcomposé" tense: *que ce qu'il y fussent onques euz montez* **24**.54–55. Such forms are found occasionally in thirteenth- and fourteenth-century texts, see *Perceforest* 4, lxvii.

14. *Se* is sometimes used instead of the coordinating conjunction *si*: **30**.1, **31**.1, **35**.109.

Syntax

Some of the features listed below, particularly those which concern the structure of the sentence, probably stem from the author rather than the scribes.

1. Some of the curious combinations of singular and plural to be found in the text may arise from uncertainty over final *s*, as for example: *laquelles des deux dames doit avoir* **20**.1.

2. There are, however, a number of instances of a third person plural verb with a singular subject, as for example: *lesquelz un chascun doivent tenir a*

---

17. Cf. *Perceforest* 4, lxi, where the forms are described as characteristic of the North and North East as well as the East.

saiges 31.1–2; *pour ce que de touz iceulz ramentevoir seront trop lonc* 35.147. On the other hand, a singular verb may be found after two subjects: *li bien et honnour lui demeure* 19.168–69.

3. On several occasions there are sudden switches between singular and plural. For example: *Si devez savoir que en nulle maniere nul qui soit en cestui monde, ne qui onques y furent, ne que jamais y soient, ne peuent avoir eues, ne n'ont, ne jamais n'avront* 35.27–29.

4. A sudden switch between *tu* and *vous* is to be found within one passage: 19.52–57.

5. The negative *ne* is not expressed after the coordinating conjunction *ne* on a number of occasions, for example: *et nulle melencolie ne vous en devez donner se vos besoignes ne sont si bien faictes, ne se portent si bien* 19.158–59. See also 20.15–16, 20.25, 21.22.

6. An example of an unusual construction only to be found in *B* (*P* has *est* instead) is the use of *et* in the following phrases: *la meilleur condicion des trois manieres et de preudommie* 35.17–18; *la meilleur des trois manieres et de preuesce* 35.20.[18] See also 42.123, where *P* has the same reading as *B*.

7. Very long sentences with a complicated succession of subordinate clauses, sometimes with a break in construction, are characteristic of the text (in both *B* and P). See, for example: 24.65–78, 35.13–24, 35.39–49, 35.92–105, 35.138–146, 42.46–57, 42.119–131. This type of sentence is not so typical of those passages which are closely based on earlier sources, such as the description of the knighting ceremony modeled on the account given in *L'Ordene de Chevalerie* (see 36.3–57 and Notes to Text and Translation).

Editorial Treatment

Base manuscript *B* has been followed as closely as possible. "Grammatical" corrections concerning, for example, the flexional system have not been made unless the text would be very obscure without them, for such "deviations" would seem to be characteristic of the language of the scribe and of

---

[18]. In both cases *P* reads *manierest de*, which appears to be an unsuccessful attempt at correction, and *L* removes the *et*.

the period. However, in the case of hesitation over final feminine *e*, where mechanical error seems in most cases to have played a significant role (see above, Vowels, 18), corrections have been made. Other small mechanical errors such as the omission or repetition of a word have been corrected where it is possible to be reasonably sure of what has been left out or repeated. However, *P*'s text is very close to that of *B* except that it has more omissions arising from jumps from like to like; it therefore sheds little light on the passages where B's text is corrupt as it either presents the same reading or an equally incomprehensible one: see, for example, 1964.

Abbreviations have been expanded in the usual way, according to the form in which they are most often written out in full in the manuscript. I have distinguished between *i* and *j*, *u* and *v*, and have followed the normal editorial conventions for the use of the acute accent and cedilla. The diaeresis has been employed sparingly, mainly to distinguish between forms such as *pais/pays* (peace) and *païs/paÿs* (country), and between verbal forms such as *oy/oi* (present indicative) and *oÿ/oï* (past participle) of the verb *oïr*. Some modern punctuation has also been added to facilitate the interpretation of the text.

In the translation, we have endeavored to produce an accurate version of the text which is readable yet preserves as much as possible of the flavor of the original. This is not always easy, as the sentences of Geoffroi de Charny are often long and rambling. It has sometimes been necessary to divide them, but in general we have tried to follow the natural development of the author's processes of thought as reflected in the structure of his sentences. His strong personal involvement in all the complexities of chivalric ideals and practice is mirrored in his often somewhat convoluted style and in the frequent changes of grammatical structure in mid-sentence as he strives to convey his meaning. Such characteristics are to be found in other writings of the fourteenth century, but are particularly pronounced in the prose of Geoffroi de Charny, who, for all his knowledge of both treatises on knighthood and chivalric romance, was a knight and warrior rather than a professional writer.

Le Livre de chevalerie

1   Pour ce qu'il m'est venu en memoire de parler de plusieurs estas de gens d'armes qui ont esté pieça et encores sont, en voeil je un petit retraire et faire aucune mencion briefment. Et bien en peut on parler, car toutes telz choses sont assez honorables, combien que les unes le soient assez, et les autres plus, et adés en plus, jusques au meilleur. Et tousjours la meilleur voie seurmonte les autres; et cilz qui plus y a le cuer va tousjours avant pour venir et attaindre au plus haut honneur, et pour ce convient il que nous viegnons a parler de ceste matiere au commencement.

2   Premierement du mains au plus, et bien me semble que nulz ne s'en doit ne peut tenir a mal paiez, car nulz ne pourra dire qu'il y ait fors que bien et verité, ou autrement seroit mal du retraire. Et pour ce vueil je parler de pluseurs estaz de genz d'armes en la meilleur maniere que je pourray, car c'est drois que chascuns en recorde le bien la ou il n'y a point de mal a tous hommes d'armes qui se arment volentiers pour quelconque mestier d'armes qui soit. La ou il n'y a (f.83v) reproche, il n'y peut avoir nul mal fors que bien. Et pour ce prie je a Dieu qu'il me doint maniere et matiere de en parler tousjours en bien.

3   Si dirons premier d'une maniere de gens d'armes qui bien font a loer selon le fait d'armes dont leur volenté est d'entremettre. Ce sont li aucun qui ont bon corps sain et appert, et qui se tienent nettement et joliement, ainsi come il affiert bien a joenne gent douz et courtois et de bonne maniere entre la gent, et de nulles males oevres ne se veulent entremettre, mais pour le fait d'armes de joustes sont il si appert come il veulent, et pou scevent

Translation

Introduction

1 Because I am minded to examine the various conditions of men-at-arms, both of the past and of the present, I want to give some brief account of them. And it is right to do so for all such matters are honorable, although some are honorable enough, others more honorable on an ascending scale up to the most honorable of all. And always the noblest way rises above all others, and those who have the greatest heart for it go constantly forward to reach and achieve the highest honor, and for this reason we must start by speaking of these matters from the beginning.

2 First, let us turn to the lesser before moving to the greater; and it seems to me that no one should be dissatisfied by this method of proceeding, for no one will be able to say that in what is written there is anything other than the good and the true; otherwise it would not be right to tell of it. I therefore want to speak of divers conditions of men-at-arms in the best way that I can, for it is right that each of us should record what is good, where there is nothing bad, in relation to all men-at-arms who willingly take up arms for whatsoever form of the practice of them. Where there is no reproach, there can be no evil but only good. For this reason I pray that God may grant me that I do justice to my subject as far as both manner and matter are concerned.

The Scale of Prowess and Types of Men-at-Arms

3 We shall first speak of a class of men-at-arms who are worthy of praise in terms of the kind of pursuit of arms they are willing to undertake. These are the ones who are physically strong and skillful (agile) and who conduct themselves properly and pleasantly, as is appropriate for young men, gentle, courteous and well mannered toward others, who have no desire to engage in any evil undertaking, but are so eager to perform deeds of arms at jousts

feste ou emprise de jouster, que a leur pouoir n'y soient; et se bien leur en chiet, que le plus souvent les forjoustent, ou sont en debat d'avoir le pris. Et pour ce que Dieu leur a donné tele grace de eulx si bien gouverner en celui fait d'armes, le prennent il si a gré que ilz en delaissent et entreoublient les autres mestiers d'armes, mais toutevoies est li mestier bon et bien avenant a faire et bel a regarder. Et pour ce di je qu'il est bien de le faire pour celi qui le fait, quant Dieu lui en donne tele grace du bienfaire; car tuit fait d'armes font bien a loer a tous ceulx qui bien y font ce qu'il y appartient de faire. Car je ne tieng qu'il soit nul petit fait d'armes fors que tous bons et grans, combien que li un des fais (f.84r) d'armes vaille miex que li autre. Et pour ce di je que: qui plus fait, miex vault.

4 Dont de l'autre nous estuet parler, auquel tout plain de gens d'armes entendent a faire leurs corps: ce sont les faiz d'armes des tournoiemens. Et veraiement il font bien a loer et priser; car il convient grans mises, grans estofes et grans despens, travail de corps, froisseures et bleceures, et peril de mort aucune foiz. Et pour cesti fait d'armes en y a aucuns que bon corps qu'ilz ont fort et appert et delivre le font si tres bien qu'ilz ont en ce mestier grant renommee pour leur bienfait, et dont pour ce qu'il le font souvent, et bien leur en croist leur renommee et leur cognoissance et en leurs marches et entour leurs voisins; et ainsi veulent continuer de poursuivre en celi fait d'armes pour les graces que Dieu leur en a faictes. Et de cesti mestier d'armes se tiennent pour contens pour les grans los qu'il en ont et entendent a avoir. Et vraiement il font bien a loer, combien que: qui plus fait, miex vault.

5 Dont me convient aprés ces fais d'armes de pays dessus nommez parler d'autres estas de gens d'armes pour la guerre, que pluseurs en pluseurs manieres en attendent a faire leurs corps en celi mestier. Et pour ce parlerai je premierement de ceulx qui suient et hantent les guerres en leurs paÿs sanz aler en loyntaines marches, (f.84v) et qui moult font a loer pour leurs grans faiz et emprises qu'ilz ont faiz et font de leurs senz et de leurs corps et de leur main, comme ceulx qui ont guerre en leur chief pour deffendre leur honneur et leur heritage,° come de ceulx qui veulent faire guerre pour aidier a deffendre l'onneur et heritage de leurs amis charneulx, come de ceulx qui

that if they hear of any festivities or other occasions for jousting, they will be there if they can; if all goes well for them they will usually win their contest or be in the running for the prize. And because God has bestowed on them such grace as to conduct themselves well in this particular pursuit of arms, they enjoy it so much that they neglect and abandon the other pursuits of arms; that is not to deny that it is a good pursuit, attractive for the participants and fair to see. I therefore say that it is good to do for him who does it, when, by the grace of God he does it well; for all deeds of arms merit praise for all those who perform well in them. For I maintain that there are no small feats of arms, but only good and great ones, although some feats of arms are of greater worth than others. Therefore, I say that he who does more is of greater worth.

Deeds of Arms at Tournaments

4   We should then talk of another pursuit at which many men-at-arms aim to make their reputation: that is at deeds of arms at tournaments. And indeed, they earn men praise and esteem for they require a great deal of wealth, equipment and expenditure, physical hardship, crushing and wounding, and sometimes danger of death. For this kind of practice of arms, there are some whose physical strength, skill, and agility enable them to perform so well that they achieve in this activity such great renown for their fine exploits; and because they often engage in it, their renown and their fame increases in their own territory and that of their neighbors; thus they want to continue this kind of pursuit of arms because of the success God has granted them in it. They content themselves with this particular practice of arms because of the acclaim they have already won and still expect to win from it. Indeed they are worthy of praise; nevertheless he who does more is of greater worth.

Deeds of Arms in Local Wars

5   After speaking of the above-mentioned peacetime activities in the practice of arms, I should now turn to another category of men-at-arms, those involved in war, for many aim to make their reputations in this calling in a number of different ways. I shall therefore speak first of those who seek out and participate in the wars in their own locality without going into distant regions and who deserve praise for their great exploits and undertakings which they have achieved and are achieving by their good sense, their physical strength and dexterity as those who have to wage war on their own behalf in order to defend their honor and inheritance,° or those who want

demeurent et servent leur droit seigneur en ses guerres pour deffendre et garder l'onneur et heritage de leur dit seigneur soubz qui ilz tiennent leur chevance, car la foy et loyauté qu'ilz doivent a leur seigneur ne peut estre miex monstree que de li servir et aidier loyaument a tel besoing come de fait des guerres qui est si pesant come de mettre corps, honneur et chevance tout en aventure.

6   Et autres en y a encores qui veulent servir leurs amis, quant ilz ont a faire aucun fait de guerre; et aucuns en y a qui n'ont de quoy yssir de leurs paÿs. Et quant Dieu donne grace a telx gens dessus nommez de bien faire et de bien guerrier et d'emporter grace en pluseurs bonnes journees que il peuent avoir, itele gent doit l'en prisier et honorer qui si bien se sont portez et gouvernez en leurs marches, et bien semble que autre part le deussent il bien faire. Et si ose je bien dire que toutes gens d'armes qui bien l'ont fait en ce mestier (f.85r) et a qui il en est bien pris et souvent et fust fait en leur paÿs tant seulement, que en leur paÿs et entre toutes gens l'en les doit honorer ainsi come l'en doit honorer bonnes gens d'armes et ainsi come il appartient a eulx de si tres noble oevre come de fait d'armes de guerre qui passe tous autres, excepté Dieu servir.

7   Si avons parlé de ceulx; et des gens d'armes qui en leur paÿs font les faiz d'armes chascun selon ce qu'il lui semble le miex a faire, certes nul ne peut parler ne ne doit fors qu'en bien et en toute honneur, especiaument de fait d'armes de guerre en quelque paÿs qu'il soit fait sanz reproche. Et toutesfoiz me semble il que en ce fait d'armes de guerre peut l'en faire en un jour tous les trois mestiers d'armes come de jouster, de tournoier et de guerroier; car en guerre convient il jouster de fer de glaive et ferir d'espee come a tournoiement et encontrer d'estoc et d'autres glaives° come pour la guerre. Et pour ce doit l'en prisier plus et honorer gens d'armes pour la guerre que nulles autres gens d'armes qui soient; car pour le fait d'armes de joustes, li aucun se tiennent a paiez de ce qu'ilz en font sanz autres faiz d'armes faire. Et aussi pour les tournois, li aucun s'en tiennent pour content sanz pou faire autre mestier d'armes. Et ces deus mestiers d'armes sont tous compriz ou fait d'armes de guerre. Et pour ce (f.85v) est ce grant chose et honorable que tous ces mestiers d'armes dont li aucun se tiennent a paiez d'un chascun pour soy, que les gens d'armes pour la guerre les font tous

to wage war to assist in the defense of the honor and inheritance of their kinsmen, or like those who stay to serve in the wars to defend the honor and inheritance of their rightful lord who maintains them, for the faith and loyalty which they owe to their lord cannot be better demonstrated than by serving him and assisting him loyally in such urgent need as that of war which is so grave as to put person, land and resources all at risk.

Deeds of Arms in Local Wars
6   There are others still who want to serve their friends or kinsmen, when they are at war, and there are some who have not the means to leave their own locality. And when God by his grace grants that such people as are mentioned above perform great exploits, fight well and distinguish themselves in several successful days of combat which they may have, such people should be valued and honored who have conducted themselves so well within their own region. It seems indeed that they would also have done well elsewhere. And I am prepared to say that all men-at-arms who have done well in this art of war and who have often been successful, even if it were only in their own district, should be honored among all men in their own locality as one should honor good men-at-arms and as is appropriate in relation to such a very noble activity as the practice of arms in war, which surpasses all other except the service of God.

Deeds of Arms in War Are the Most Honorable
7   We have spoken of those men, and of the men-at-arms who in their own region, perform deeds of arms in the way which seems best to them; indeed no one should speak except in favorable and honorable terms, especially in relation to armed exploits in war, in whatever region, provided that they are performed without reproach. But it seems to me that in the practice of arms in war it is possible to perform in one day all the three different kinds of military art, that is jousting, tourneying, and waging war, for war requires jousting with the point of the lance and striking with the edge of the sword as in a tournament, and attacking with the swordthrust and other weapons,° as war demands. Therefore one should value and honor men-at-arms engaged in war more highly than any other men-at-arms; for in the practice or arms in jousts some are pleased enough with what they do without undertaking any other deeds of arms. The same is true in relation to tournaments, for some are satisfied with taking part just in them and not in any other use of arms. And these two uses of arms are both to be found in armed combat in war. It is therefore a great and honorable thing that these

ensemble tous les jours qu'ilz ont a faire sur les champs. Et pour ce devez amer, prisier, loer et honorer touz ceux a qui Dieu donne grace d'eulx trouver en pluseurs bonnes journees d'armes pour la guerre, quant ilz emportent grant grace et grant renommee de leur bienfait; car des bonnes journees viennent et croissent les grans honneurs, que par les bonnes journees sont esprouvez les bons corps, liquel en demeurent preus et en leur paÿs mesmes sanz aler dehors. Si avons parlé d'icelles bonnes gens d'armes qui ainsi bien guerrient en leur paÿs mesmes et ont trouvees les bonnes journees.

8   Si dirons d'une autre maniere de gens d'armes qui entendent faire leurs corps en alant hors de leur paÿs et en pluseurs manieres qui toutes sont bonnes et honorables, combien que les unes vaillent miex des autres.

9   Si dirons de ceulx qui entendent leurs corps a faire par grant emprise d'entreprendre a aler en lointains voiages et pelerinages et en pluseurs paÿs estranges et lointains, et moult (f. 86r) d'estranges choses et diverses peuent veoir, dont autres gens qui point n'avroient hors esté s'esmerveilleroient pour les merveilles estranges et diverses choses que racontent et dient ceulx qui les ont veues, et envis le peuent croire, et s'en moquent li aucun et dient que c'est tout bourde. Et il doit sembler a toutes gens de bien que cilz qui ont veu teles choses en peuent et doivent miex parler et dire la verité que ceulx qui n'y veulent ou osent aler; ne nulz ne doit ne peut dire par raison qu'ilz bourdent s'il n'ont esté la. Et pour ce devons nous telz gens qui ainsi ont esté en lointains et estranges voiages volentiers oïr, veoir et honorer; car vraiement nulz ne peut aler en telx lointains voiages que le corps ne soit en peril maintes foiz. Et pour ce devons nous telz gens d'armes honorer qui a grant mise et a grant travail et en grant peril se mettent en aler et en veoir les lointains païs et estranges choses, combien que, a la verité dire, toutes gens qui mettent leur entente a faire lointains voiages, entre ceulx qui sont acoustumez, et qui tousjours veulent aler pour veoir nouvelles et estranges choses et pou arrestent et ne peuent mie trouver ne estre es fais d'armes si communement comme sont autres qui si tres lointains voiages ne quierent mie et qui plus s'arrestent et attendent les faiz d'armes (f.86v) de guerre. Et bien puet estre que en faisant les lointains voiages leur en peut avenir aucune bonne aventure, mais non mie si souvent, quar en tout plain de pais

uses of arms, of which some feel they have achieved enough by performing just one, should all be carried out together by men-at-arms engaged in war each day they have to fight on the battlefield. For this reason you should love, value, praise, and honor all those whom God by his grace has granted several good days on the battlefield, when they win great credit and renown for their exploits; for it is from good battles that great honors arise and are increased, for good fighting men prove themselves in good battles, where they show their worth in their own locality without traveling outside it. We have now dealt with those good men-at-arms who have fought well in their own region and have found good battles to take part in.

8   We shall next consider another category of men-at-arms, those who intend to make their reputation, traveling outside their own territory, in several different ways, which are all good and honorable, although some are of greater value than others.

Men-at-Arms Who Undertake Distant Journeys and Pilgrimages
9   We shall first consider those who aim to make their reputation by a great enterprise, undertaking distant journeys and pilgrimages in several far-away and foreign countries; they may thereby see many strange and unusual things at which other men who have not traveled abroad would wonder because of the strange marvels and extraordinary things described by those men who have seen them; and those who listen can scarcely believe what they hear, and some say mockingly that it is all lies. And it should seem to all men of worth that those who have seen such things can and should give a better and truer account of them than those who will not or dare not go there, nor should nor can any one reasonably say, without having been there, that such people lie. We should therefore be glad to listen to, behold, and honor those who have been on distant journeys to foreign parts, for indeed no one can travel so far without being many times in physical danger. We should for this reason honor such men-at-arms who at great expense, hardship, and grave peril undertake to travel to and see distant countries and strange things, although, to tell the truth, among all those who are intent on distant journeys, there are some who make a habit of it and who always want to go and see new and strange things and do not stay anywhere long and cannot find and take part in armed exploits as often as others who do not seek out such very distant journeys and who stay longer in one place and wait for the opportunity to perform great deeds of arms in war. It may well happen that in making these distant journeys they

peut l'en aler ou l'en n'oseroit porter nulz harnois de guerre ne aler en estat d'omme d'armes mais comme pelerin ou en estat de marcheanz. Et pour ce est il semblant a aucuns que l'en ne voie pas si souvent les faiz d'armes come l'en les pourroit veoir et trouver en autre maniere. Toutevoies doit l'en bien prisier et honorer telz gens qui ainsi mettent leurs corps en peril et travail pour les estranges choses veoir et lointains voiages faire. Et de ce faire leur soufist pour les grans choses estranges qu'ilz y ont veues et encores ont volenté de veoir. Et vraiement c'est grant bien; mais toutesfoiz di je: qui plus fait, miex vault.

10   Dont nous convient parler encore d'un autre estat de gens d'armes qui moult font a loer. Et ce sont ceulx qui, par pluseurs neccessitez qui ne font a ramentevoir, se partent de leur païs, ou pour profit qu'il y pensent a avoir plus grant qu'il n'avroient ou pourroient avoir en leur païs mesmes. Et par ceste maniere se partent de leur païs avant qu'il soit nul compte d'eulx par nul fait d'armes, et plus volentiers demorassent en leur païs se il peussent bonnement. Mais toutesfoiz s'en partent et vont en Lombardie ou en (f.87r) Touscane, en Puille ou es autres païs, la ou l'en donne soulz et gaiges, et la se demeurent et se mettent en estat de chevaux et d'armeures parmi les solz et les gaiges qu'ilz reçoivent. Et par ce peuent il veoir, aprendre et savoir moult de biens pour le fait de la guerre, car ilz peuent estre en telx païs ou marches la ou il peuent veoir et faire en fait d'armes moult de biens. Et pluseurs foiz a Nostre Sires donné grace a pluseurs qui sont alez en la maniere que j'ay dessus dite, tant de la renommee des grans biens qu'ilz y ont faiz de leurs corps et de leur main es bons faiz d'armes ou il se sont trouvez, come de proffiter avecques l'onneur. Et quant Dieu leur a donné tel grace d'onnour pour leurs bons faiz en ce mestier, icelles gens font a loer et honnorer partout, mais que il ne delaissent mie pour leur proffit trop tost du continuer; car qui trop tost le delaisse, de legier s'abaisse de renommee, et nulz ne se doit delaissier de bien faire, que quant le corps ne peut plus, si doit avoir le cuer et la bonne volenté. Et a moult de gens est il miex cheu et avenu a la fin que ilz n'avoient esperance a leur encommencement selon la maniere de leur emprise. Et pour ce di je que: qui miex fait, miex vault.

may from time to time encounter some fine adventure, but not very often, for when, in the midst of a time of peace, it is possible to go where one would not dare to go equipped for war nor as a man-at-arms, but only as a pilgrim or a merchant. It seems therefore to some that one does not come across opportunities to practice the military art so often in this way of life as might be encountered in another way of life. Nevertheless one should honor and respect such men who subject themselves in this way to physical danger and hardship in order to see these strange things and make distant journeys. And they find satisfaction in doing this because of the wondrously strange things which they have seen and still want to see. And indeed it is a fine thing, but nevertheless I say: he who does more is of greater worth.

Deeds Performed Outside One's Locality for Pay or Other Rewards

10 Now we must consider yet another category of men-at-arms who deserve much praise. That is those who, for various compelling reasons which need not be mentioned here, leave their locality, perhaps for the profit they might expect to get from this, which might be greater than anything they could obtain in their own locality. And in this way they leave their locality before they have gained any reputation there, and they would have preferred to remain in their own region if they could well do so. But nevertheless they leave and go to Lombardy or Tuscany or Pulia or other lands where pay or other rewards can be earned, and there they stay and are provided with horses, and armor is included in the pay and rewards they receive. Through this they can see, learn and gain knowledge of much that is good through participating in war, for they may be in such lands or territories where they can witness and themselves achieve great deeds of arms. And many times Our Lord has favored a number of those who have departed in the way I described above both with renown for their great achievements through their physical strength and skill in the good armed combats in which they were engaged so that they drew profit as well as honor from them. And when God has by His grace granted them honor for their great exploits in this military activity, such men deserve to be praised and honored everywhere, provided that they do not, because of the profits they have made, give up the exercise of arms too soon, for he who too quickly gives it up may easily diminish his reputation. And no one should give up performing great exploits, for when the body can do no more, the heart and determination should take over; and there are many people who have been more fortunate in the end than they had hoped for

11 Une autre maniere de gens y a qui ne se veulent partir de leur lieu ne entremettre d'armes pour autrui se l'on ne leur fait grant profit avant qu'ilz se veullent partir, et rien du leur n'i (f.87v) voudroient mettre, combien qu'il aient bien de quoy, et pou fait en l'armeure; mais toutevoies quant il chiet bien a teles gens de bien faire en iceli mestier d'armes et en pluseurs bonnes journees en la compaignie de ceulx de qui ilz prennent les proffiz, ycelles gens d'armes font bien a loer pour les biens qu'ilz ont faiz es bons faiz d'armes la ou ilz se sont trouvez en deservant les proufiz qu'ilz en ont eu. Mais di je encores: qui miex fait, miex vault.

12 Une autre maniere de gens d'armes y a qui sont en leur encommencement si nice que il ne cognoissent mie la grant honneur qu'il pourroient acquerir pour les faiz d'armes; mais toutevoies leur avient si bien, quar ilz mettent leur cuer en amer par amours,° et si bien leur en chiet que leur dames mesmes, de leur tres grant honnour et des tres grans biens qui en elles sont, ne les veulent mie laisser sejourner ne perdre leur temps d'avoir tel honneur come d'onneur d'armes; si les en avisent et puis leur commandent que eulx aillent travailler et acquerir les biens et grans honnours la ou les bons les quierent; si les y font aler oultre ce que par avant n'en avoient eu nulle volenté. Mais toutevoies leur avient il de telles et de si bonnes aventures qu'il est grant compte de leur bienfait et de la bonté que ilz acquierent en pluseurs bonnes places (f. 88r) et journees la ou ilz se sont trouvez. Et bien les doit l'en loer et honorer et les tres bonnes dames aussi qui ainsi les ont faiz et par qui ilz se sont faiz. Et bien doit l'en honorer, servir et tres bien amer icelles tres bonnes dames et autres que je tien toutes a dames, qui ainsi font* les bons, et par elles sont faiz chevaliers et les bonnes genz d'armes.° Et pour ce toutes bonnes gens d'armes sont tenuz de droit de garder et deffendre l'onnour de toutes dames contre tous ceulx qui voudroient dire ne mesdire ne faire le contraire. Mais revenir me convient es gens d'armes es faiz et en la maniere que j'ay dit devant. Et encore di je que: qui miex fait, miex vault.

Deeds Undertaken for Rewards

11   There is another category of men who do not want to leave their own area nor to bear arms for another if they do not reap great rewards before they are willing to depart, and do not want to put any of their own resources into the undertaking, even if they have the wherewithal to do so, and contribute little toward the armor. Yet, all the same, when such men are fortunate enough to perform well in this practice of arms in several good battles in the company of those from whom they take their material rewards, these men-at-arms deserve praise for what they have achieved in the good armed combats in which they have participated, thus deserving the material rewards which they have had from this. But I say yet again: he who does best is most worthy.

Deeds Undertaken for Love of a Lady

12   There is another category of men-at-arms who when they begin are so naïve that they are unaware of the great honor that they could win through deeds of arms; nevertheless they succeed so well because they put their hearts into winning the love of a lady.° And they are so fortunate that their ladies themselves, from the great honor and superb qualities that reside in them, do not want to let them tarry nor delay in any way the winning of that honor to be achieved by deeds of arms, and advise them on this and then command them to set out and put all their efforts into winning renown and great honor where it is to be sought by valiant men; these ladies urge them on to reach beyond any of their earlier aspirations. Such naïve men-at-arms may nevertheless be so fortunate as to encounter such good adventures that their deeds of prowess and achievements in a number of places and fields of battle are held to be of great account. And they should be praised and honored, and so also should the noble ladies who have inspired them and through whom they have made their name. And one should indeed honor, serve, and truly love these noble ladies and others whom I hold to be ladies who inspire men to great achievement, and it is thanks to such ladies that men become good knights and men-at-arms.° Hence all good men-at-arms are rightly bound to protect and defend the honor of all ladies against all those who would threaten it by word or deed. But I must now return to the kind of men-at-arms who act in the way described above. And again I say: he who does best is most worthy.

13   Si me convient dire d'un autre estat de gens d'armes qui bien font a loer pour la grant et bonne volenté qu'ilz ont de mettre le leur en poursuivre les faiz d'armes, dont avient il moult de foiz en leurs paÿs et dehors, et y mettent si grandement du leur pour aler plus honorablement que ilz leur semble que ilz en doivent plus tost venir a leur entente du tré haut honnour a quoy ilz ont volenté de venir. Et quant Dieu leur donne grace de trouver les faiz d'armes, il les font si tres bien come bonnes gens d'armes ont acoustumé du faire. Mais quant il (f.88v) vient en meilleur point et saison d'attendre et de trouver les faiz d'armes, dont avient il moult de foiz que il convient qu'il s'en partent pour le grant estat dont ilz se chargent et les grans missions qu'il veulent faire, dont il ne peuent demorer ne attendre le temps ne la saison que ilz tant desirent, si s'en vont a grant mesaise de cuer. Et li aucun veulent tant mettre en un an qu'il les en convient sejourner dix. Dont est ce grant dommage quant il convient que bon corps sejourne pour outrageuse mise; car miex vaut raconter et dire que l'en ait esté aux journees d'armes tous seulx avecques les autres et raconter son bienfait, quant Dieu li en a donné grace, que dire que l'en maine si grant estat et que l'en ait itrop despendu et que l'en n'ait peu attendre jusques au temps. Mais toutevoies pour la grant et bonne volenté qu'il ont de bien faire et ont fait la ou ilz se sont trouvez, les doit l'en priser et honorer, que c'est raison. Mais pour ce est il bon a toutes gens qui veulent faire leur corps qu'il mainent tel estat qu'il puissent durer a poursuivre les biens par qui les bons sont faiz. Et pour ce est il que: qui plus fait, miex vault.

14   Or me convient encore parler d'une autre maniere de gens d'armes qui bien font a loer. Ce sont li (f. 89r) aucun qui moult mettent du leur et travaillent leurs corps pour querir, attaindre et trouver les faiz d'armes et en pluseurs pays; et bien peut avenir de en trouver assez, et en moult de bonnes places se sont trouvez sanz nul reproche. Mais tant y a qu'il est pou de nouvelle de leur bienfait fors tant qu'il y ont esté, qui est moult bele chose; car quant plus voit l'en du bien, et plus en doit l'en savoir et parler et conseiller es places la ou l'en se trueve et en autres besoignes. Et pour ce font il

Men Who Spend Recklessly to Perform Deeds of Arms

13   I must now speak of another category of men-at-arms who deserve praise for their great determination to put their own resources into the pursuit of opportunities for performing deeds of arms, opportunities often to be found both in their own territory and outside it; they put a great deal into traveling in a more honorable style, for it seems to them that this should enable them to achieve more quickly that goal of great honor for which they strive. When through the grace of God they find opportunities for deeds of arms, they fight as well as good men-at-arms are wont to do. But when it comes to waiting for the best time and season to find occasions for deeds of arms, then it often happens that they have to depart, because of the great state and outward show with which they burden them and the great expenditure to which they choose to commit themselves; hence they cannot stay and wait for the due time and season which they desire so much, and they go away, sad at heart. And there are some who want to put as much in one year as would require a longer stay. It is then a great shame when a good career is held back by excessive spending, for it is better to give an account of how one has been on one's own without a retinue, to take part in armed combats along with other people, and to tell of one's exploits, when God has by his grace granted them, than to say that one lives in such great state and that one has spent too much and has not been able to stay until the right moment. Yet for the great determination that such men have to perform great deeds, which, indeed, they do perform where they have found the opportunity, these men should be esteemed and honored, for that is only right. But because of this, all those who want to establish their reputation should maintain themselves at such a level that they can continue to strive for those achievements which establish them as good men-at-arms. And for this reason it is true that: he who does best is most worthy.

Sacrifices Made by Men-at Arms Whose Deeds Remain Unknown

14   I must now consider yet another category of men-at-arms who deserve praise: that is those who devote a good part of their own financial resources and suffer physical hardship in the search for opportunities for deeds of arms in a number of countries; and they may well find many such opportunities and incur no reproach on many good fields of combat. But it so happens that few learn of their exploits but are only aware of the fact that they have been there, which is in itself a fine thing; for the more one sees great deeds, the more one should learn what is involved and should

bien a loer et honorer; combien qu'il soit petit compte de leur bienfait, n'y ont il fait nul mal; car grant chose est en tel besoigne du bien arrester et regarder. Mais: qui plus fait, miex vault.

15 Si m'estuet encore parler d'un autre estat de gens d'armes qui bien font a loer, qui ont bon corps et appert, hardiz et bien travaillans, dont li aucun de ceulx sont volentiers tousjours des premiers en alant par maniere de coureurs come pour gaigner proye et prisons et autres biens sur les ennemis de ceulx avecques qui ilz sont. Et moult bien, moult appertement et sagement le scevent faire; et pour ce qu'il mettent leur entente sur le gaing, moult de foiz leur avient que a l'entrer en une ville gaaignie par force, ceulx qui (f.89v) si grant desir ont de gaignier si se boutent ça et la et se departent de leurs compaignons, qui n'entendent de rien a cela fors que a parfaire leur emprise et leur fait. Et moult de foiz avient que telx manieres de genz qui courent et tirent ainsi aux grans gaings sont tuez en cela faisant, et ne scet l'en moult de foiz comment, une foiz par leurs ennemis, l'autre pour la rimour qui muet des uns aux autres pour gaigner. Si avient moult de foiz, par le deffault de ceulx qui courent au gaing avant que l'en soit au dessus de son fait, que l'en puet reperdre ce que l'en cuide avoir gaigné et les corps avec. Si peut avenir encores de telx gens qui grant volenté ont de gaigner, que quant ce avient que l'en a afaire sur les champs, pluseurs sont qui regardent a prendre prisons et autre gaing; et quant il les ont pris et autres biens, il ont plus grant volenté et desir de sauver leurs prisons ou leur gaaing que de secourir et aidier de mettre la journee a bonne fin. Et bien puet avenir que par tele maniere peut l'en perdre la journee. Et l'en doit bien doubter le gaing qui fait perdre honneur, corps et avoir. Et pour ce doit l'en mettre en ce mestier plus son cuer et s'entente a l'onnour, qui tous temps dure, que a proffit et gaing que l'en peut perdre en une (f.90r) seule heure. Et toutes foiz doit l'en bien loer et prisier telx gens d'armes qui scevent guerrier et grever et gaaigner sur leurs anemis, car ilz ne le peuent faire sanz grans travaulx et hardement. Mais encore dirai je que: qui plus fait, miex vault.

16 Or est il donques raisons que, aprés tous ces estas et manieres d'armes dont nous avons parlé, nous parliens du droit entier estat qui est et peut

talk and take advice at the places where feats of arms are performed or where one is engaged in other activities. And because of this they deserve to be praised and honored: although their deeds have been of little account, they have done no ill; for it is very important in such activity to pause and look. Hence so it is that he who does best is most worthy.

Those Who are Brave But Too Eager for Plunder
15 I now need to consider yet another category of men-at-arms, who deserve praise, who are strong and skillful, bold and sparing no effort, some of whom always want to be at the forefront, riding as foragers to win booty or prisoners or other profit from the enemies of those on whose side they fight. And they know well how to do it skillfully and cleverly; and because they are so intent on plunder, it often happens that on the entry into a town won by force, those who are so greedy for plunder dash hither and thither and find themselves separated from those of their companions who have no thought for gain but only for completing their military undertaking. And it often happens that such men, those who ride after and hunt for great booty, are killed in the process — frequently it is not known how, sometimes by their enemies, sometimes through quarrels in which greed for plunder sets one man against another. It often occurs that through lack of those who chase after plunder before the battle is over, that which is thought to be already won can be lost again and lives or reputations as well. It can also happen in relation to such people who are very eager for booty that when there is action on the battlefield, there are a number of men who pay more attention to taking prisoners and other profit, and when they have seized them and other winnings, they are more anxious to safeguard their captives and their booty than to help to bring the battle to a good conclusion. And it may well be that a battle can be lost in this way. And one ought instead to be wary of the booty which results in the loss of honor, life, and possessions. In this vocation one should therefore set one's heart and mind on winning honor, which endures for ever, rather than on winning profit and booty, which one can lose within one single hour. And yet one should praise and value those men-at-arms who are able make war on, inflict damage on, and win profit from their enemies, for they cannot do it without strenuous effort and great courage. But again I shall repeat: he who does best is most worthy.

How the Highest Standard in Deeds of Arms Is Achieved
16 Having considered all these different forms of the practice of arms, it is now time to speak of the truest and most perfect form which exists

estre en pluseurs gens d'armes, ainsi come vous pourrés oïr ci aprés ensuiant. Ce sont cil qui, de leur propre nature et de leur propre mouvement, des lors que cognoissance se commence a mettre en eulx en leur joennesce, et de leur cognoissance ilz oent et escoutent volentiers parler les bons et raconter des faiz d'armes, voient volentiers gens d'armes armez et leurs harnois, et si voient volentiers beaux chevaux et beaux coursiers; et ainsi come ilz viennent en aage, si leur croist leur cuer ou ventre et la tres grant volenté qu'ilz ont de monter a cheval et d'eulx armer. Et quant ilz sont en aage et en estat qu'ilz le peuent faire, ilz n'en demandent conseil, ne n'en croient nullui qui les en vueille conseillier qu'il ne s'arment ou premier fait d'armes qu'il treuvent, et d'ileuc en avant tousjours de plus en plus; et ainsi come ilz croissent d'aage, ainsi croissent il de bonté et en fait (f.90v) d'armes de paiz et en fait d'armes de guerre. Et d'eulx mesmes pour la grant et bonne volenté qu'il y ont, aprennent il l'usage et la maniere du faire, et tant qu'il ont la cognoissance de tousjours faire et tirer au plus honorable, tant de tous faiz d'armes come en autres manieres, de tous bons gouvernemens qui a leurs estaz appartiennent. Et lors s'appensent et avisent et demandent de tout ce qui est bon a faire pour le plus honorable. Si le font briefment et liement et n'attendent pas que l'en les amonneste, ne que l'en les en avise. Et ainsi semble il* que telx gens sont faiz et se font d'eulx mesmes, dont se doit doubler le bien qui ainsi en teles gens se met, quant de leur propre mouvement et bonne volenté que Dieu leur a donnee, il cognoissent le bien; et rien n'espargnent, ne corps ni avoir, qu'il ne mettent peine de le faire. Et bien nous peut apparoir en leur maniere de venir avant; car le premier mestier d'armes qu'il puissent cognoistre en leur commencement, c'est le fait d'armes de joustes, dont le font il volentiers et liement. Et quant Dieu leur donne grace de bien jouster souvent, si leur plaist le mestier et leur croist leur volenté qu'ilz ont d'eulx armer. Dont leur vient il a cognoistre, aprés cesti mestier d'armes de jouster, les faiz d'armes des tournoiemens. Si leur semble* et voient et cognoissent que les tournoiemens sont plus honorables, (f.91r) qui bien y font, que les joustes. Dont se mettent eulx a armer pour les tournois le plus briefment qu'ilz peuent. Et quant Dieu leur donne grace de le bien faire baudement et liement et ouvertement, dont leur semble il bien que le tournoier leur acroist leur renommee et leur bien plus que les joustes ne faisoient. Si delaissent plus les joustes qu'ilz n'avoient acoustumé pour aler aux tournois; et de plus en plus leur acroist leur cognoissance tant qu'il voient et cognoissent que les bonnes gens d'armes pour les guerres sont plus prisiez et honorez que nul des autres gens d'armes qui soient. Dont leur semble de leur propre cognois-

and is to be found in a number of men-at-arms, as you can learn in what follows. It is embodied in those who, from their own nature and instinct, as soon as they begin to reach the age of understanding, and with their understanding they like to hear and listen to men of prowess talk of military deeds, and to see men-at-arms with their weapons and armor and enjoy looking at fine mounts and chargers; and as they increase in years, so they increase in prowess and in skill in the art of arms in peace and in war; and as they reach adulthood, the desire in their hearts grows ever greater to ride horses and to bear arms. And when they are old enough and have reached the stage when they can do so, they do not seek advice nor do they believe anyone who wants to counsel them against bearing arms at the first opportunity, and from that time forward, on more and more occasions; and as they increase in years, so they increase in prowess and in skill in the art of arms for peace and for war. And they themselves, through their great zeal and determination, learn the true way to practice the military arts until they, on every occasion, know how to strive toward the most honorable course of action, whether in relation to deeds of arms or in relation to other forms of behavior appropriate to their rank. Then they reflect on, inform themselves, and inquire how to conduct themselves most honorably in all circumstances. They do this quickly and gladly, without waiting for admonitions or exhortations. Thus it seems that such men have made a good reputation for themselves through their own efforts; in this way they double the good to be found in them, when from their own instinct and the will for good which God has given them, they know what is right and spare neither themselves nor what they own in their effort to achieve it. This can be clearly apparent to us in the way that they come forward; for, at the outset, the first exercise in the use of arms which they can encounter is jousting, and they are eager to do it. And when God by his grace grants them frequent success in jousting, they enjoy it, and their desire to bear arms increases. Then after jousting, they learn about the practice of arms in tournaments, and it becomes apparent to them and they recognize that tournaments bring greater honor than jousting for those who perform well there. Then they set out to bear arms in tournaments as often as they can. And when, by God's grace, they perform well there, joyfully, gladly, and openly, then it seems to them that tournaments contribute more to their renown and their status than jousting had done; so they no longer take part in jousts as often as they were wont to do, and go to tournaments instead. Their knowledge increases until they see and recognize that the men-at-arms who are good in war are more highly prized and honored than any

sance que en ce mestier d'armes de guerre se doivent mettre souverainement pour avoir la haute honnour de proesce; car par autre mestier d'armes ne le pueent il avoir. Et si tost come ilz en ont la cognoissance, si delaissent a faire si souvent les faiz d'armes de pays et se mettent es faiz d'armes de guerre. Si regardent et enquierent et demandent ou il fait le plus honorable selon le temps en quoy ilz sont. Dont vont il celle part et puis veulent savoir de leur bonne nature tous les estas de fait de guerre et ne se pueent tenir a paiez d'eulx mesmes se ilz ne voient tout le desir qu'ilz ont du savoir et de y estre.

17 (f.91v) Si veulent savoir et veoir comment l'en met sus une chevauchee pour guerrier et courre sus a ses ennemis, et veoir l'ordenance des coureurs,° les ordenances qui se font de gens d'armes et des gens a pié, et la maniere de beau chevauchier en alant avant, et du beau retraire seurement et honorablement quant il en est temps. Et quant ilz ont veu cela, il ne leur soufist pas qu'ilz ne veullent estre et savoir comment villes et chasteaux se peuent deffendre, tenir, garder et furnir contre leur ennemis tant d'assaut come de siege et de tous aprochemens que l'en leur puet faire, ce que l'en doit faire a l'encontre par dedanz; et encore ne s'en veulent ilz mie deporter atant, combien que en ce fait d'armes se soient trouvez a leur tres grant honnour. Si veulent il savoir encore tousjours plus pour ce qu'ilz oient parler comment l'en puet mettre siege devant villes et chasteaulx. Dont vont querant a leur pouoir comment ilz puissent estre en telles places. Et quant ilz y sont, si prennent grant delit a veoir comment le siege se met pour enclorre la ville ou chastel, comment li batiffol° se font oster leurs yssues et les tenir plus court, comment la mine se fait en autres artifices come d'engins, de truyes, de buyres, de chas et de baffrois,° et en autres manieres, come d'assaillir au mur, de monter par eschielles et de percier les murs et d'entrer enz (f.92r) et* prendre par force. Dont sont il a aise quant Dieu leur a donné grace d'i estre et avoir veu et avoir bien fait en ce fait d'armes. Et quant plus voient celes gens et font de bien, dont leur semble il de leur bonne nature que ilz n'aient rien fait et leur semble qu'ilz soient tousjours a l'encommencier. Et pour ce encore ne leur soufist pas que pour ce qu'ilz ont oÿ parler comment l'en se puet et doit combatre sur les champs, gens d'armes contre autres, et ilz oyent recorder a ceulx qui y ont esté les grans biens que les bons y ont faiz, dont leur semble il bien que ilz n'ont rien veu ne rien fait se ilz ne se

other men-at-arms. It therefore seems to them from their own observation that they should immediately take up the practice of arms in war in order to achieve the highest honor in prowess, for they cannot attain this by any other form of armed combat. And as soon as they realize this, they give up participating so frequently in exercising their skill at arms in local events and take up armed combat in war. They look around, inquire, and find out where the greatest honor is to be found at that particular time. Then they go to that place and, in keeping with their natural good qualities, are keen to discover all the conditions of armed combat in war, and cannot be satisfied with themselves if they do not realize to the full their wish to find themselves there and to learn.

How to Study the Art of War
17   They want to observe and to find out how to set up an expedition to attack and fight one's enemies, and to observe the deployment of light horsemen,° the deployment of men-at-arms and foot soldiers, and the best way to advance in a fine attack and to make a safe and honorable withdrawal, when it is the time to do so. And when they have observed that, they then will not be content until they have been present at and learned about the defense of castles and walled towns: how they can be held, guarded, and provisioned against both enemy attack and siege, and against all advances against them which can be made; what should be done in relation to an encounter from within. And they still do not want to give up at this point, even though they have achieved great honor in this form of the practice of arms; they always want to learn more because they hear people talk about how one can lay siege to walled towns and castles. Then they do their best to seek out the places where such sieges are going on. And when they come there, they take great pleasure in seeing how a siege is set up to surround the town or castle, how the *battifol*° are made to block the way out for the besieged, and to exert more pressure on them, how mining is carried out under the cover of devices such as sows, *buyres*, cats, and belfries,° and other matters, such as how to mount an attack on the walls, to climb up on ladders, and to pierce the walls and to enter and take by force. They are then glad when God by his grace has granted that they should have been there, observed, and performed well during this military operation. And the more these men see and themselves perform brave deeds, the more it seems to them, because of the high standards their natural nobility demands of them, that they have done nothing and that they are still only at the beginning. And as a result of this, they are still not

treuvent en ce noble fait d'armes come de bataille. Dont mettent peine de aler en pluseurs lieux et de travailler leurs corps par tous païz en mer et en terre. Et quant Dieu leur donne grace de trouver et veoir si tres hautes be-
30 soignes come de batailles, avecques ce qu'ilz aient grant gré et grant grace de leur bienfait, dont doivent bien telles gens mercier Nostre Seigneur et servir du bien qu'il leur a fait et monstré pour continuer en ces mestiers d'armes. Et quant il cognoissent quel bien et quelle honnour c'est, dont leur croist leur volenté de travailler pour querir telx faiz d'armes. Et quant bien
35 leur en chiet du trouver, c'est tres grant bien; et a qui il en chiet le miex de y estre souvent et de y bien faire son devoir en son paÿs et en autres, tant (f.92v) vault il miex des autres qui mains avroient fait. Et li debaz de deux bons est es honorables,° que li uns vaille miex que l'autre, et chascun bon de cest mestier d'armes doit on priser et honorer, et regarder les meilleurs
40 et aprendre d'eulx oïr et escouter, et demander de ce que l'en ne scet, car par raison ilz en doivent miex parler, aprendre et conseiller que li autre, quar ilz ont veu et sceu, fait, esté et essaié en toutes manieres d'armes ou li bon ont apris le bien et aprennent. Et ainsi par raison doivent bien savoir parler de tout ce que a tout fait d'armes et pluseurs autres estaz doit appartenir. Et
45 quant a ainsi parler pourroient aucuns debatre et faire question duquel ou desquelx l'en doit tenir plus grant bien, ou des povres compaignons qui font et ont fait leurs corps en la maniere que dessus est dite, ou des grans seigneurs qui leurs corps veulent faire et ont fait es mesmes manieres, et egalment de toute bonté en sens et maniere et de l'ouvrage de fait d'armes et de
50 la main. Mais il semble que a ce peut l'en trop bien respondre, car raisonnablement li povre compaignon font bien a priser et loer qui de leur povreté se mettent a tel travail et a tel labour, dont il vienent a si haute bonté et a si grant cognoissance que la renomee de leurs biens faiz s'espant et estent ainsi come partout dont avant n'estoit nul compte, ne ne fust, se avant ne se
55 fussent enhardiz et mis a faire les bons fais d'armes ainsi (f.93r) come dit est. Et pour celle honnour leur vient cognoissance, avansement d'estat, profit, richesce et acroissement de tout bien. Dont leur est il plus necessaire faire et avoir fait ces biens dessus diz que a grans seigneurs; car aux grans seigneurs n'est il nulle neccessité d'aler nulle part pour estre cogneuz, que
60 leur estat les font assez cognoistre, ne d'aler nulle part pour estre serviz et honorez, car ilz le sont assez de leurs estaz mesmes, ne necessité ne les puet esmouvoir d'aler hors pour proufit avoir, car ilz sont assez riches. Aprés n'est il pas grant besoing qu'ilz voisent hors pour avoir aaise ne deduiz, car en leur terre et en leur paÿs en peuent eulx avoir assez. Dont doit en sou-
65 verainement plus grant compte faire des emprises du travail et du peril de

satisfied, for they have heard talk as to how one should fight on the battlefield, men-at-arms against others, and they hear those who were there recall the great exploits that good warriors achieved there; then it seems to them that they have seen and done nothing if they do not take part in such a noble form of military activity as a battle. They therefore take pains to travel to different places and to endure great physical hardship in their journeys through many countries across land and sea. And when, through the grace of God, they find out and witness such supremely noble affairs as battles, were they also to be granted the grace and favor of performing great deeds, then such men should indeed thank Our Lord and serve him for the kindness he has shown them and the assistance he has given in their continuance of these military pursuits. And when they recognize what a great benefit and honor it is, this increases their determination to strive to seek out opportunities for such deeds of arms. And when they are fortunate enough to find them, this is very good; and he who is the most fortunate in often taking part in them and in doing his duty well in his own region and in others is of that much greater worth than those who have done less. The question which is the better of two revolves around the honors,° of which one is more worthy than the other. Every man who does well in this military vocation should be prized and honored, and one should observe those who are best and learn by listening to them and by asking about what one does not know, for they ought rightly to know better how to explain, teach, and advise than the others, for they have seen and known, taken part in, experienced, and proved themselves in all forms of armed combat in which good men have learned and learn how to excel. It therefore follows that they should know how to speak about everything that concerns armed combat and many other matters. And in relation to such talk, some might argue over and question which might be the kind of person from whom one might derive the greatest benefit. Would it be the impoverished companions who make and have made a name for themselves in the manner explained above, or would it be the great lords who want to make their reputation and have done so in the same way, and are of equal worth in wisdom and in conduct, and in skill and performance in combat? It seems to me that one can give a good answer to this question, for the impoverished fighting companions rightly deserve esteem and praise, those who with their limited resources set out to make such strenuous efforts and exertions, through which they achieve such noble prowess and such great understanding that the renown of their exploits spreads everywhere, which, up until then, had been held to be of little account, nor would they ever

corps ou li grant seigneur se veulent mettre et se mettent de leur bonne volenté sanz aucune neccessité mais sanz plus pour avoir honnour de corps sanz autre loyer attendre pour leur grant mise et travail qu'il font et sueffrent en faisant les biens et faiz d'armes dessus diz, que l'en ne doit de ceulx qui en attendent aucuns proffiz ou avancemens et essaucemens de leurs estas pour les desertes et guerdon de l'onneur qu'il ont pourchacie ou pourchacent.

18 Et s'il est ainsi que l'en tiegne plus grant compte des uns, li autre ne valent de rien mains, car tout est bien pour ceulx qui bien font. (f.93v) Mais toutevoies peuent li grant seigneur trop plus porter grant loange de leur bonté en pluseurs bonnes manieres que ne font les povres compaignons qui valent aucune foiz autant ou miex que li aucun grant seigneur. Maiz la raison si est tele que quant uns grans sires et qui est sires de paÿs est bons en telle maniere come dessus est dit, il en aime miex et prise plus les bons pour la cognoissance qu'il a des biens qu'il a veuz qu'il ont faiz. Et li autre compaignon, qui voient les bons estre honorez par les grans seigneurs pour leur bonté, ont plus grant volenté de venir a ce bien quant ilz voient qu'il est si bien cogneuz. Et ainsi pouez vous veoir que plus tost se font et sont fait cent hommes bons ou fait d'armes par un bon grant seigneur que ne seroient dis par deus bons povres hommes, car li grans sires les maine et si les aime et les honnore et prise et leur fait proffit, et le doubtent, aiment, honorent et prisent pour le bien qu'ilz voient et cognoissent qui est en li avecques les amours, honours et proufiz qu'il leur fait. Lors se travaillent de faire bien de plus en plus. Et pour ce est il que uns bons sires et bon chevetaine de paÿs refait tout un païs, et un chetif sires anientist une grant partie

have won this reputation if they had not first had the courage to set about achieving the good deeds of arms spoken of above. And from this honor they gained recognition, rise in status, profit, riches and increase in all benefits. It is, therefore, more necessary for them, in their own interest, to perform and have performed these above-mentioned noble deeds than it is for great lords who have no need to go anywhere to become known, as their rank ensures that they are well known; nor do they need to travel about in order to be served and honored, as their rank entitles them to this; nor can necessity move them to go forth in search of financial gain, for they already have considerable riches. Nor do they have any great need after this to travel abroad in search of pleasure or entertainment, for they can have as much as they want in their own land and territory. One should therefore take far greater account of undertakings involving physical hardship and danger which the great lords are prepared to and do embark on of their own free will without any need to do so other than to achieve personal honor, with no further expectation of any reward for the money and effort which they devote to performing these great deeds of arms; these enterprises should be valued more than those of men who expect some profit or advancement or rise in status as a reward for the honor which they have won or are winning.

The Great Influence of a Valiant Lord

18 If it is thus true that greater account is taken of some, the others are not to be valued less because of this, for there is good in all those who perform great deeds. Nevertheless the great lords may be given higher praise for their valor in a number of worthwhile activities than are the impoverished fighting companions who are sometimes worth as much or more than some great lords. But the reason is that when a great nobleman, lord of extensive lands, is of great worth in the way explained above, as a result he loves and values men of worth all the more for the knowledge he has of the great deeds he has seen them perform. And the other companions, who see that good warriors are honored by the great lords for their prowess, become more determined to attain this level of prowess. Thus you can see that one hundred men skilled in deeds of arms make themselves a name all the sooner through one great and worthy lord than would ten by two poor men of great worth, for the great lord has them in his company and loves, honors, and values them and rewards them, and they respect him, love, honor, and esteem him for the great valor they see in him in addition to the love, honor, and reward that he has bestowed on them. Then they strive to attain greater heights of prowess. And for this reason a

du bien de son paÿs. Et li povre bon compaignon ne puet mener aucun a sa
20 mise, ne faire (f.94r) profit. Et si ne tient on pas si grant compte d'estre
honorez d'un bon povre come d'un bon grant seigneur. Ne li bon povre ne
sont tant doubté ne obeÿ a un besoing come sont li grant seigneur, mais
pour ce n'est ce pas que li bien tout entier ne soit et demeure a ceulx qui le
font, soient povres ou riches: et qui plus en fait, plus li en demeure et miex
25 vault.

19 Or di je dont que bien doit on honorer et les grans et les moyens en
qui ces biens sont. Hé Dieux! com c'est uns honorables et pesanz faiz a
porter, et bien doit estre en grant doubte qui tel faiz porte sur li qu'il ne li
chee; car a grant peine et travail, en grant paour et peril, en grant soing a
5 s'entente mise, et par long temps et par pluseurs annees, a chargier ce faiz
sur ces° espaules, et en petit lieu et pou de heure peut cheoir et tout perdre
cui Diex ne donne senz et aviz du savoir garder. Si doit sembler a un
chascun que tiex gens doivent mettre toute la bonne diligence qu'il peuent
afin que l'en ne leur puist rien reprocher ne reprover sur eulx ne sur les
10 bontez que Dieu leur a donnees. Et quant telx gens et de tel estat sont entre
autres genz, dont sont il plus regardé que autres. Lors les oit l'en plus
volentiers parler que autres, car ilz scevent parler de grans et de grosses
et de honorables besoignes. Et semble (f.94v) a un chascun que bien en
doivent et scevent parler. Et dont sont il regardés sur toutes bonnes ma-
15 nieres et contenances, tant en compaignie comme avecques les grans dont
ilz sont regardez, quant ilz sont avecques dames et damoiselles dont ilz sont
regardez, et demandent de leur estat mesmes et de leur vie et de leurs
gouvernemens. Or n'est ce pas dont tout le bien de ceulx qui se arment que
d'estre armez et de bien faire es armeures tant seulement. Mais convient
20 avecques ce que en tous les regars qui dessus sont nommez, que en nulle
maniere l'en ne puist chose deshonneste veoir ne dire sur eulx; car de leur
deffaute seroit le parler et la renommee plus grant que d'un autre qui n'aroit
pas si grant renommee de bonté. Et de telx gens qui sont ainsi faisanz et
faiz et parfaiz en tele bonté come dessus est dit, bien les doit l'en volentiers
25 oïr et escouter et raconter de grans biens, de bons faiz et de bonnes paroles
qui en celle maniere ont esté faiz et diz par pluseurs bons, tant par ceulx qui
sont trespassez de cest siecle come de ceulx qui encore vivent. Et pour ce
nous enseignent li bon chevalier et les bonnes gens d'armes dont vous avez

good lord gives new life to the territory under his command, and an unworthy lord reduces to nothing a great part of the resources of his territory, and the impoverished good companion cannot maintain anyone nor reward him. And not so much account is taken of being honored by a valiant poor man as of a valiant great lord. Nor are the valiant poor men as much respected and obeyed in time of action as are the great lords; but this does not mean that the good reputation does not belong to and remain with those who have earned it, whether rich or poor, and he who does most, the more lasting benefit there remains for him and the more worthy he is.

The Heavy Responsibilities of Men of Rank and Prowess

19   I say therefore that one should honor the great lords and those of middle rank in whom this prowess is to be found. Ah God! What an honorable and weighty burden to bear! And he who bears such a burden should fear lest he let it fall, for with great effort and endurance, in fearful danger and with great diligence, for a long time, stretching over a number of years, he has devoted himself to bearing this responsibility on his shoulders, and in one brief moment he may fall and lose everything, if God does not grant him the wisdom and good judgment to know how to keep it safe. So it must seem to everyone that such people should strive with the utmost diligence to ensure that they suffer no reproach against themselves nor against the bounties God has bestowed on them. And when men of such condition are in the company of other people, they are held in higher regard than the rest. Then men prefer to listen to them above all others, for they can talk of great, important and honorable affairs, and it seems to everyone that they should and can speak of such matters. Thus they are closely observed as examples of good manners and behavior, whether they are in the company of great lords who hold them in high regard or in the company of ladies and damsels who also hold them in high regard; and they are questioned about their situation, way of life, and conduct. It is not, therefore, the only virtue of those who bear arms that they carry weapons and perform feats of arms; but, in addition to this, it is necessary that in all the respects mentioned above, in no way can anything dishonorable be perceived nor said concerning them; for there will be much greater talk and notoriety about their shortcomings than there would be concerning some one without such a great reputation. And one should take pleasure in hearing about, listening to, and recounting the good deeds, the great feats, and the admirable utterances of such people who are thus striving to achieve, have achieved, and have perfected themselves in such knightly qualities, both those who have

oï ci devant retraire et parler et raconter les grans biens, honneurs, prouesces
et vaillances que ilz ont aquiz par leurs grans peines, travaulx et paours et
perilz de corps et perte de leurs amis mors que ilz ont veu (f.95r) mourir en
plusieurs bonnes places ou ilz ont esté, dont ilz ont eu mesaises et courroux
en leur cuer souvent. Et qui vourroient bien raconter leurs vies si dures
come elles ont esté et sont encores a ceulx qui ceste vie d'onnour veulent
mener, elles seroient trop longues a escripre. Mais de leurs enseignemens et
de leur doctrine veil je un petit retraire selon ce que eulx dient et commandent a toutes jennes gens qui tele vie d'onnour ont en volenté de querir,
qui Dieu et toute sa puissance aiment et doubtent souverainement, si se
doubteront et garderont pour celle amour et pour celle doubtance de faire
mauvaises oevres. Avecques ce enseignent li bon dessus dit que gens qui a
celle honnour veulent venir ne doivent mettre entente ou vivre de leur
bouche delicieusement, ne en trop bons vins, ne en trop delicieuses viandes,
car ces delices sont trop contraires ou temps que l'en ne les pouoit avoir ne
trouver a sa volenté, qui le plus de fois avient a ycelles gens qui tele honnour
veulent querir, si leur en est plus dur a soufrir et aussi n'en ont il mie les
cuers ne les corps si legiers de soufrir les dures vies des boires et des men-
giers que il faut avoir en ceste honnour acquerir. Et envis muert, ce dit on,
qui apris ne l'a, et envis aussi se tient l'en de telx delices de boire et de
mengier qui aprises les a. Si ne doit on avoir a telx delices nulle grant plaisance, ne ne t'entremettes* (f.95v) trop de savoir deviser bonnes viandes
ne bonnes saulces, ne les quelx des vins valent le miex ne n'i met trop ta
cure, si en vivras plus aise. Mais se d'aventure tu trueves bien a boire et
a mengier, si le pren liement et soufisamment et sanz grant outrage, que li
bon dient que l'en ne doit pas vivre pour mengier, mais l'en doit mengier
pour vivre, quar nulz ne doit tant menger qu'il soit trop saoul, ne tant boire
qu'il soit ivres Et toutes ces choses doit l'en faire moiennement, si puet on
vivre sanz trop grant grevance. Et vous avez oÿ dire moult de foiz que les
jeunes gens qui prennent leur nourreture es grans cours des riches hommes
pou* se travaillent en acquerir ces grans travaulx, quar quant ilz ont moillé
leurs doys en la saulce de la court et mengié les loppins, envis se peuent
retraire. Si ne se doit on mie si atruandir, quar qui pour sa gloute gorge pert
a faire son corps, l'en lui devroit traire les dens toute l'une aprés l'autre, qui
tel dommage leur font come de perdre si haulte honnour qu'ilz peussent
avoir acquise en leur jeunesce dont d'eulx . . . ° Ha! viellesce, bien dois estre
desconfortee quant tu te trueves es corps de ceulx qui peussent avoir fait
tant de biens en leur joennesce et qui rien n'en ont fait, de quelque estat
qu'ilz soient, selon ce que un chascun peut et doit faire (f.96r) selon leurs

now departed from this world and those who are still living. We therefore learn from the good knights and men-at-arms whose great achievements and honorable deeds of prowess and of valor have been related, described, and told above and which they have accomplished through suffering great hardship, making strenuous efforts, and enduring fearful physical perils and the loss of friends whose deaths they have witnessed in many great battles in which they have taken part; these experiences have often filled their hearts with great distress and strong emotion. If anyone might want to give an account of their lives, hard as they have been and still are, for the benefit of those who want to take up this honorable vocation, their adventures would take too long to record. However, I want to say a little about the advice they have to give us according to what they themselves recommend to young men who desire to seek such an honorable life, who love and fear God and His might, and because of this love and fear will beware of and refrain from evil deeds. In addition, the above-mentioned good men-at-arms teach that those who want to achieve this honor should not set their minds on the pleasures of the palate, neither on very good wine nor on delicious food, for these delights are very out of place at a time when they are not to be had nor to be found at will, as is usually the case for those who want to seek such honor; and desire for such things makes it more difficult for them to endure, and their hearts and bodies find it less easy to bear the lean fare in food and drink which the quest for such honor requires. A man will be reluctant to risk death who has not learned this, and also a man is reluctant to abstain from such pleasures of eating and drinking who has become accustomed to them. One should take no pleasure in such delights; do not concern yourself with being knowledgeable about good dishes and fine sauces nor spend too much time deciding which wines are the best, and you will live more at ease. But if it so happens that you find good food and drink, partake of them gladly and sufficiently but not to excess, for men of worth say that one should not live in order to eat, but one should eat in order to live, for no one should eat so much that he is too full, nor drink so much that he is drunk. And one should do all these things in moderation and so live without too much discomfort. And you have heard it said many times that the young men who are maintained in the great courts of powerful men make little effort to seek out these great trials, for when they have dipped their fingers in the sauce of the court, and eaten the choice morsels, they may be reluctant to give this up. Thus one should not grow sluggish in this way, for the man who for his greedy gullet fails to make a name for himself, should have all those teeth pulled out, one by one, which do him

estas. Et ceste viellesce doit estre tristre, doulereuse et honteuse en tous estas ou ilz se truevent avecques autres bonnes gens. Si s'en doivent bien
70 prendre en garde toutes joennes gens qui a tel estat d'onneur veulent venir. Si enseignent encore li bon dessus dit a tous ceulx qui a tel honnour ont volenté de venir que ilz ne se vueillent mie trop entremettre ne mettre leur entente en nul gieu la ou convoitise les sourpreigne, come gieu de dez, car le gieu n'i est plus puis qu'en le fait par convoitise de gaaigner. Et le plus
75 des fois y avient que l'en y cuide gaaigner l'autrui, que l'en y pert le sien, et mout en y a qui y perdent .CCC,V^e et mil livres et plus, dont il leur vaudroit miex a les donner pour Dieu, ou les donner par parties es bons chevaliers et escuiers qui bien l'ont deservi et qui le voudroient deservir avec la bonne renommee qui seroit de ceulx qui ainsi le voudroient faire, tant de grans
80 come de moyens; car se li grant et li moyen le vouloient ainsi faire, chascun selon son pouoir, il en seroit assez plus des bons qu'il n'est quant il verroient que leur volenté seroit cogneue; mais moult en y a qui par convoitise de gaaigner se mettent a juer ou pour deffaute de contenance ou de desplaisance d'estre en la compaignie des bonnes gens. (f.96v) Et aussi a un jeu
85 que l'en appelle le jeu de la paume l'ou maintes gens perdent et ont perdu de leur meuble et de leur heritage; et en jouant a telx geus, l'en ne vouroit veoir ne rencontrer nulles bonnes gens dont il l'en convenist laissier leur gieu pour eulx parler et tenir compaignie. Si doit on laissier le gieu des dez pour convoitise de gaigner aux houlliers, ruffiens et ribaux de tavernes. Et
90 se vous y voulés jouer, si n'i faictes force comment il vous en preigne, ne trop n'y mettez du vostre, que vostre gieu ne tournast a courrouz. Ne des gieux de la paume aussi; quar grant tort en a l'on fait aux femmes, que li gieux de la pelote souloit estre li gieux et li esbatemens des femmes. Et toutevoies devroit il sembler que li plus beaux gieux et li plus beaux es-
95 batemens que telles gens qui tel honnour veulent querre devroient faire seroient qu'il ne se doivent point lasser de jouer, de jouster, de parler, de dancer et de chanter en compaignie de dames et de damoiseles ainsi honorablement comme il puet et doit appartenir et en gardant en* fait et dit et en tous lieux leur honneur et leurs estas, que toutes bonnes gens
100 d'armes le doivent ainsi faire de droit; car en teles compaignies, en telx gieux et esbatemens prennent les bonnes gens d'armes (f.97r) leurs bons commencemens, que regars et desir, amour, pensee et souvenir, gayeté de cuer et joliveté de corps les met en la voie de l'encommencement et de l'encommencier a ceulx qui onques n'en avroient eu cognoissance de faire et parfaire
105 les grans biens et honnours dont li bon se sont fait. Iteulx gieux sont plus beaux et plus honorables et dont plus de biens pueent venir que des gieux

so much damage as to lose him the high honor he might have acquired in his youth.° Ah! old age, you should indeed be disconsolate when you find yourself in the body of one, of whatever rank he may be, who could have achieved so much in his youth, but has done nothing, in relation to what he can and ought to do according to his rank. And such old age must be sad, grievous, and shameful in the presence of other men of good standing. All young men who desire to attain such an honorable status should take note of this. In addition, the above-mentioned men of good standing tell all those who desire to achieve this honor that they should not concern themselves too much with nor devote too much attention to any game where greed might overcome them, such as the game of dice, for it is no longer a game when it is engaged in through greed for gain. And what usually happens is that when one thinks one will win another's money, one loses one's own, and there are many who lose three hundred, five hundred, a thousand *livres*, and more of their money. It would have been better for them to have given the money thus lost for the service of God or to have apportioned it to good knights and squires who have already merited such a gift or would like to merit it; those of high or middle rank who had the the will to give in this way would earn a good reputation. If those would each according to their power act thus, there would be more good fighting men than there are now, were they to see that their will for it would be recognized. However, there are many who take up gambling for greed of gain or through a fault in behavior or from a dislike of the company of men of good standing. There is also a game called real tennis at which many people lose and have lost some of their chattels and their inheritance; and while playing such games, one would not want to see nor meet any men of good standing for whom it would be necessary to leave the game and speak to them and keep them company. One should leave playing dice for money to rakes, bawds, and tavern rogues. And if you are determined to play, do not mind too much about winning, and do not stake too much of your money lest your game turn to anger. The situation is the same for real tennis; women have greatly suffered over this, for ball games used to be women's pastime and pleasure. Yet it should be apparent that the finest games and pastimes that people who seek such honor should never tire of engaging in would be in the pastimes of jousting, conversation, dancing, and singing in the company of ladies and damsels as honorably as is possible and fitting, while maintaining in word and deed and in all places their honor and status. All good men-at-arms ought rightly to behave thus, for in such society and such occupations and pastimes worthy men-at-arms

des dez dont on puet perdre le sien et son honnour et toute bonne com‑
paignie. Toutevoies li biaux gieux sont bons qui sont sanz corrocier, mais
quant courroux y vient et s'i met, l'en ne jeue plus. Et quant l'en ne peut
estre tousjours en tele et si bonne compaignie come j'ay dit dessus, qui a ce
mestier d'onnour ne puet durer tant comme l'en voudroit, si se doit l'en
aler jouer, bourder, parler et escouter et demander de ce que l'en ne scet
avecques les meilleurs que l'en puisse trouver; et en teles bonnes compaig‑
nies fait bon hanter souvent, que moult en y a qui pour les chetives com‑
paignies qu'ilz ont amees et pour les chetifs conseulx qu'ilz ont euz et creuz,
que li aucun grant homme en sont si achaitivez et de cuer et de maniere que
aucune foiz en perdent les corps ou honnour ou païs ou l'amour de leurs
subgiez, et autel est il des moiens a un chascun selon leurs estas. Dont doit
il sembler a un chascun que c'est le plus beau jeu qui soit que d'estre (f.97v)
souvent en bonne compaignie et loing des chaitis et des chaitives oevres
dont nulz biens ne peuent avenir. Encore nous enseignent li bon dessus dit
que combien que a toutes gens d'estat appartient bien a amer les deduiz des
chiens et des oiseaux, c'est a entendre que l'en ne laisse de riens a faire ne a
travailler en nulle chose qui a l'onneur de son corps faire puisse touchier en
la plus petite heure du jour ne de la nuit qui puisse estre; car la plus chiere
chose qui soit a perdre, c'est le temps qui passe, qui ne se puet recouvrer ne
plus retourner; et il puet escheoir en une heure d'acquerir telle honnour
que en pourroit bien faillir a le trouver en un an ou jamays. Et pour ce, vous
qui querez celui haut honnour, gardez que vous ne perdez temps, que ce
vous seroit trop grant perte. Et certes qui a cestui haut honnour veult ave‑
nir, il ne se puet ne ne doit excuser, que se li corps li demeure sain et il vit
son aage soufisamment qui ne le doie avoir puis qu'il vueille faire ce qu'il y
appartient et qui pourroit bien faire se en lui ne demeure; si n'en doit on
nulz avoir pour excusez sanz essoine*° de corps ou de mise ou de bonne
volenté. Et pour ce devez vous estre certains que il n'est nulz qui se puisse
ne doie excuser de faire bien s'il veult, un chascun selon son estat, les uns
(f.98r) selon les armes, les autres selon la clergie, les autres selon les choses
seculieres. Dont il appartient a un chascun de soy entremettre es choses et
besoignes neccessaires, que ceulx qui bien y font sont a prisier et a loer, un
chascun selon son estat et selon ce qu'il fait et qu'i° vaut. Et pour ce ne se
doit nulz esmaier de faire les biens, que li bon dessus diz nous ensaignent,
et par verité, que ceulx ont grant part en bonté qui veulent devenir bons. Et
ilz dient voir, quar pour le grant desir qu'ilz ont de venir et d'attaindre a
celui haut honnour, riens ne leur grieve qu'ilz aient a soufrir, mais leur
tourne tout a tres grant deduit. Certes c'est bele chose que de faire le bien,

make a good start, for glances and desire, love, reflection and memory, gaiety of heart and liveliness of body set them off on the right road and provide a beginning for those who would never have known how to perform and achieve the great and honorable deeds through which good men-at-arms make their name. Such pastimes are finer and more honorable and can bring more benefits than can games of dice, through which one can lose one's possessions and one's honor and all good company. Yet fine games are good where there is no anger, but when tempers rise, it is no longer play. And when one cannot always be in the kind of good company I have described above, which cannot in this honorable vocation last as long as one might wish, one should go and play games, jest, talk, listen, and ask about matters of which one is ignorant in the company of the best people to be found, and it is of benefit often to frequent such society, for there are many, among whom some great lords, who, for the poor company of which they have been fond, and for the bad advice which they have received and believed have thereby been so diminished in heart and in behavior that sometimes they lose their lives or honor or land or the love of their subjects, and it is the same for those of the middle degree, according to their rank. Thus it should appear to everyone that the best pastime of all is to be often in good company, far from unworthy men and from unworthy activities from which no good can come. The men of worth mentioned above also teach us that, although it befits all men of rank to enjoy the sport of hunting with hawk and hound, it is to be understood that one should not fail in any way to put great effort into anything which might improve one's chance of winning an honorable reputation at any moment of the day or night; for the most precious thing there is to lose is time which passes, and cannot be won back nor can it return; and it can happen that such honor is won in an hour which one might fail to find in a year or indeed ever. And for this reason, you who seek to attain this high honor take care that you do not waste time, for you would lose too much thereby. Indeed anyone who wants to attain this high honor, if he retains his physical health and lives for long enough, cannot and should not be excused from achieving it, provided he be willing to do what is required and could do well if he does not hang back; and no one should be held to be excused, unless physically prevented, whether for lack of funds or of the will for it. Therefore, you should know for certain that there is no one who can or should excuse himself from performing well according to his station, some in relation to arms, others in relation to the clerical vocation, others in relation to the affairs of the world. It therefore behooves each person to engage in the appropriate

que ceulx qui font le bien a droit ne s'en peuent lasser ne saouler; car quant plus en ont fait, adont leur semble qu'ilz en ont pou fait, de la grant plaisance qu'ilz ont et qu'il y prennent de en faire tous les jours de plus en plus. Et cilz biens sont bons a faire, quar quant plus en fait l'en, et moins s'en orgueillist l'en, et semble tousjours que l'en en ait fait le moins. Si doit on tenir moult pou de compte de tous ces autres chetifs deduiz qui si pou peuent valoir a l'encontre de telx biens honorables qui sont si publiez et tant cogneuz et tous temps durent. Et encore enseignent les bons a vous qui celi haut honneur voulez que en vos (f.98v) encommencemens n'aiez trop cures de vos besoignes demorer ou païs dont vous estes, especialment que elles se puissent faire par vos personnes, car il ne pourroit estre a ce que vous voulez faire et acquerir, mais les laissiez et commettez en la garde et gouvernement de vos plus especiaulx amis; et nulle melencolie ne vous en devez donner se vos besoignes ne sont si bien faictes, ne se portent si bien par autrui come par vous ou en vos personnes se vous y estiez, car en nulle maniere ne se pourroit faire, et c'est la coustume toute firtee;° car qui veult faire l'avoir avant que le corps, il puet bien faire l'avoir, mais du corps sera il pou de nouvelles. Et qui a volenté de faire le corps avant que l'avoir, et Dieu li donne vie et santé, il ne puet faillir, a l'aide de Dieu, de faire le corps, et en nulle maniere ne puet faillir qu'il n'ait de l'avoir et des biens assez, quoy qu'il demeure.° Si ne vous doit ja chaloir d'amasser grant avoir; car qui plus fait d'avoir, plus envis veult mourir et plus doubte la mort, et qui plus a d'onnour, moins doubte a mourir, que li bien et honnour lui demeure a tousjours, et li avoir s'en va, et en pou de heure ne scet on qu'il devient. Et de ce soiez certain que qui veult faire son corps par convoitise d'avoir, il pourra faire le corps une partie du temps, mais en la parfin la convoitise de l'avoir li (f.99r) deffera trestout, car grant convoitise fait faire moult de maulx; et tous maux faiz sont durement contraires au haut honnour dont vous avez et devez avoir si tres grant desir. Si vous devez bien garder de celle convoitise et de toutes autres oevres qui a si noble conqueste comme d'acquerir honnour vous y puissent empescher ne destourner si haute emprise comme d'onnour avoir. Encores vous enseignent icelles bonnes gens d'armes dessus diz a qui vous avez si grant desir de resembler, car combien que li mestiers d'armes soit durs et penibles et perilleux a l'endurer, leur semble il que bonne volenté et gayeté de cuer font toutes ces choses passer seurement et liement, et tout ce travail ne leur semble nient, que tout ce y peuent penser qui plus les puet tenir en liesce de cuer et de corps mais que bien soit quant il le doivent faire.° Si doivent icelles gens vivre loiaument et liement, entre les autres choses amer par amours hono-

affairs and undertakings, for those who do well in them deserve to be esteemed and praised, each according to his status and according to what he does. Hence no one should be dismayed at the thought of undertaking great deeds, for the above-mentioned men of standing tell us truly that those who have the will to achieve great worth are already on the way to great achievement. And they speak the truth, for because of their great desire to reach and attain that high honor, they do not care what sufferings they have to endure, but turn everything into great enjoyment. Indeed, it is a fine thing to perform great deeds, for those who rise to great achievement cannot rightly grow tired or sated with it; so the more they achieve, the less they feel they have achieved; this stems from the delight they take in striving constantly to reach greater heights. And great good comes from performing these deeds, for the more one does, the less is one proud of oneself, and it always seems that there is so much left to do. Little importance should be attached to those other paltry pastimes which are of so little worth in comparison with those honorable achievements which are so celebrated and renowned, and are of lasting value. And the men of worth also advise you who aim for this great honor that at the beginning of your career you should not, through your too great concern for your own affairs, remain in your own territory, especially as such matters can be dealt with by your own people, for to stay at home would prevent you from achieving your aim; you should hand these affairs over into the charge of your closest friends; and do not feel depressed if your affairs are not so well looked after and do not prosper as well in the charge of others as they would in your charge or that of your own men, if you were there, for this would not be possible; and it is the established custom,° for the man who wants to make a fortune before making his reputation may make the fortune, but there will be little heard of his reputation; and the man who desires to make his reputation before his fortune, and God grants him life and health, cannot fail, with God's help, to make his reputation and can in no way fail to get enough wealth, whatever the delay.° You should not care about amassing great wealth, for the more worldly goods a man acquires, the more reluctant he is to die and the greater his fear of death; and the more honor a man gains, the less he fears to die, for his worth and honor will always remain, and the worldly goods will disappear, and soon no one will know where they have gone. And be sure of this: whoever wants to establish himself through greed for wealth, he may in the short term make some kind of a name for himself, but in the end greed for wealth will destroy it utterly, for through great greed many evil deeds are committed, and all evil deeds will

rablement, que c'est le droit estat de ceulx qui celi honour veulent acquerir.° Mais gardez que les amours et li amers soient telement que vous gardez si cher come vous devez amer vos honnours et vos bons estaz que l'onnour de vos dames gardez souverainement et que tout le bien, l'onnour et l'amour que vous y trouverés, gardez le secretement sanz vous en venter en nulle maniere, ne faire aussi (f.99v) les semblans si tres grans qu'il conviegne que autres ne pluseurs s'en apperçoivent, que nul bien en la parfin, quant il est trop sceu, n'en vient mie volentiers, mais en peuent avenir moult de durs emcombriers qui puis tournent a grant ennui; et ce n'est mie le plus grant deduit que l'en en puisse avoir que de dire: "J'ayme celle la," ne de vouloir en faire telx semblans que chascun doie dire: "Celi aime trop bien par amours celle dame la." Et moult en y a qui dient qu'ilz ne vouldroient pas amer la royne Genyevre, s'il ne le disoient ou s'il n'estoit sceu. Ycelles gens aimeroient miex que chascun dist et cuidast qu'il amaissent trop bien par amours et ja n'en fust rien, que ce qu'il amassent et bien leur en deust venir et fust tenu bien secret. Et ce n'est mie bien fait, que plus parfaicte joie en a l'on d'estre en la compaignie de sa dame secretement que l'en ne pourroit avoir en un an la ou il seroit sceu et apparceu de pluseurs. Et devons savoir certainement que la plus secrete amour est la plus joieuse et la plus durable et la plus loyal, et tele amour doit l'en vouloir mener.° Mais ainsi come l'en doit vouloir garder l'onnour de sa dame en tant comme a lui touche et pour l'amour que l'on y a, l'en y doit garder son honnour mesmes pour l'onnour de sa (f.100r) dame et l'amour que elle lui monstre. C'est a entendre que de vos manieres, de vos estas et de la valeur de vos corps vous devez en telle maniere ordener que la renommee de vous soit tele et si bonne, si grant et si honorable que l'en doie tenir de vous grans comptes et de vos grans biens a l'ostel et aux champs et especialment des faiz d'armes de pays et des faiz d'armes de guerres ou les grans honnours sont congneuz. Et ainsi seront vos dames et devront estre plus honnorees quant elles avront fait un bon chevalier ou un bon homme d'armes. Et quant l'en pourroit dire que un bon chevalier ou un bon homme d'armes ayme une tele dame, ou cas la ou il pourroit estre sceu, certes plus grant honnour seroit a la dame que° ainsi aimeroit que de celles qui voudroient mettre leur temps [a]* un chaitif maleuré qui ne se voudra armer, ne pour armes de pays ne mesmement pour les faiz d'armes de guerres ne se voudroit entremettre la ou eulx le pourroient et savroient bien faire. Et ceulx qui ainsi aiment et veulent amer, quel honnour font il a leurs dames quant l'en pourroit dire qu'elles aiment un maleureux?

run counter to the great honor you should and do desire to win. You must guard against such greed and all other behavior which might stand in the way of and deflect you from such a noble achievement as winning honor. These above-mentioned good men-at-arms whom you are so eager to resemble have further lessons to give you, for although the practice of arms is hard, stressful and perilous to endure, it seems to them that strength of purpose and cheerfulness of heart makes it possible to bear all these things gladly and confidently, and all this painful effort seems nothing to them, for they can think of all that can keep them happy in mind and body, provided there are honorable deeds to be done when they should do them.° And these people should live loyally and joyfully, and, among other things, love a lady truly and honorably, for it is the right position to be in for those who desire to achieve honor.° But make sure that the love and the loving are such that just as dearly as each of you should cherish your own honor and good standing, so should you guard the honor of your lady above all else and keep secret the love itself and all the benefit and the honorable rewards you derive from it; you should, therefore, never boast of the love nor show such outward signs of it in your behavior that would draw the attention of others. The reason for this is that when such a relationship becomes known, no good is, in the end, likely to come of it; great difficulties may arise which then bring serious trouble. The greatest pleasure to be derived from love is not to be found in saying "I love so and so" nor in behaving in such a way that everyone will say: "That man is the lover of that lady." And there are many who say that they would not want to love Queen Guinevere if they did not declare it openly or if it were not known. Such men would prefer it to be said by everyone that they were the accepted lovers of ladies, even if this were not true, than to love and meet with a favorable response, were this to be kept secret. And this is ill done, for there is more perfect joy in being secretly in the company of one's lady than one could have in a whole year, were it to be known and perceived by many. And we should know for certain that the most secret love is the most lasting and the truest, and that is the kind of love for which one should aim.° But just as one should want to protect the honor of one's lady concerning one's relationship with her for the sake of the love one has for her, one should also protect one's own honor for the sake of the honor of one's lady and for the love she shows to oneself. That means that by your manners, your behavior, and your personal bearing you should so present yourself that your renown may be so good, so noble, and so honorable that you and your great deeds are held in high esteem in your quarters and on the field, espe-

20 Laquelles° des deux dames doit avoir plus grant joye de son amy quant elles sont a une feste en grant assemblee de gens (f.100v) et elles scevent la couvine l'une de l'autre, ou celle qui ayme le bon chevalier et elle voit son amy entrer en la salle ou l'en menjue et elle le voit honorer, saluer et festier de toutes manieres de gens et tirer avant entre dames et damoiselles, chevaliers et escuiers, avecques le bien et la bonne renommee que un chascun lui donne et porte, dont icelle tres bonne dame s'esjoist en son cuer si tres grandement de ce qu'elle a mis son cuer et s'entente en amer et faire un tel bon chevalier ou bon homme d'armes. Et encores, quant elle voit et cognoist que avecques les amours qu'elle y a, chascuns l'ayme, prise et honoure, dont elle est tant liee et tant aaise de cuer du grant bien qu'elle voit et cognoist, qui est en celui qui l'aime, dont tient elle son temps a bien emploié. Et des autres dames, s'aucune en y avoit qui aymast le chaitif maleureux qui ne se veult armer et sanz nulle essoine, et elle le voit entrer en celle sale mesme, et elle voit et cognoist que nulz n'en tient compte de lui, ne on le festie,° ne fait semblant, et pou de gens le cognoissent, et ceulx qui le cognoissent n'en tiennent nul compte, et demeure derriere les autres, que nulz ne le trait avant. Et certes, se il en y avoit aucunes de telles, bien devroient avoir le cuer a malaise quant elles verroient qu'elles ont mis leur temps et leur entente en amer et (f.101r) prisier ceulx que nulz ne prise, ne honoure, ne riens n'en oyent recorder ne raconter de nul bien qu'il feissent oncques. Hé Dieux! come c'est petit confort et petit soulaz a ycelles dames se aucunes en y avoit qui voient leurs amis a si petit d'onnour sanz avoir essoine fors que de bonne volenté! Comment osent teles gens amer par amours quant ilz ne scevent, ne veulent savoir le bien qu'il convient qu'il cognoissent et

cially in feats of arms in peace and in feats of arms in war where great honor wins recognition. Thus your ladies will and should be more greatly honored when they have made a good knight or man-at-arms of you. And when one could say that a good knight or a good man-at-arms loves a certain lady, where it might be possible for this to be known, greater honor would indeed come to the lady who might have such a love than to those who might choose to waste their time on a paltry wretch, unwilling to take up arms, neither for deeds of arms in peace nor even for deeds of arms in war, when he would have had the physical strength and skill to perform them. And those who love thus and want to love, what honor do they confer on their ladies when it could be said that each one of these loves a miserable wretch?

The Lady Who Sees Her Knight Honored
20   Which one of two ladies should have the greater joy in her lover when they are both at a feast in a great company and they are aware of each other's situation? Is it the one who loves the good knight, and she sees her lover come into the hall where all are at table and she sees him honored, saluted, and celebrated by all manner of people and brought to favorable attention before ladies and damsels, knights and squires, and she observes the great renown and the glory attributed to him by everyone? All of this makes the noble lady rejoice greatly within herself at the fact that she has set her mind and heart on loving and helping to make such a good knight or good man-at-arms. And when she also sees and understands that, in addition to the true love for one another which they share, he is in addition loved, esteemed, and honored by all, this makes her so glad and happy for the great worth to be found in the man who loves her, that she considers her time to have been well spent. And if one of the other ladies loves the miserable wretch who, for no good reason, is unwilling to bear arms, she will see him come into that very hall and perceive and understand that no one pays him any attention or shows him honor° or notices him, and few know who he is, and those who do think nothing of him, and he remains hidden behind everyone else, for no one brings him forward. Indeed, if there is such a lady, she must feel very uneasy and disconsolate when she sees that she has devoted time and thought to loving and admiring a man whom no one admires or honors, and that they never hear a word said of any great deed that he ever achieved. Ah God! what small comfort and solace is there for those ladies who see their lovers held in such little honor, with no excuse except lack of will! How do such people dare to love (*amer par amours*)

doivent faire, especialment ceulx qui par droicte raison s'en doivent entremettre. Et certes celle amour ne puet rien valoir ne durer longuement, que les dames ne s'en repentent et retraient d'une part; et li chaitifs de droicte honte et pour ce que eulx n'oseront dire ne poursuir leurs dames qu'il ne
30 soit mie ainsi, si s'en retraient; et les en convient retraire a leur grant honte et mesaise de cuer, ne nulle bonne raison n'ont il de dire le contraire que elles ne le doient ainsi faire. . Et pour ce est il que l'en doit bien amer, celer, garder, servir et honorer toutes dames et damoiselles par qui sont fait et se font les bons corps des chevaliers et des escuiers et les bonnes gens d'armes,
35 dont tant d'onnour leur vient et leur acroist leur bonne renommee. Et aussi icelles tres bonnes dames doyvent et sont bien tenues d'amer et honorer ycelles bonnes gens d'armes qui, pour deservir d'avoir (f.101v) leur tres bonne amour et leur bon acueil, se mettent en tant de perilz de corps comme li mestiers d'arme[s] desire, quant pour avenir et attaindre a celui
40 hault honnour pour lequel haut honnour ilz pensent a deservir d'avoir l'amour de leurs dames.° Et li enseignemens d'icelles tres bonnes dames si est telx: "Ayme loyalment se tu veulx estre amez." Et ainsi devez amer loyaument et vivre liement et faire vos oevres honorablement et en bonne esperance, que tous les estaz d'amours et d'armes se doivent mener de droicte
45 pure gayeté de cuer, qui fait venir la volenté de venir a honnour.

21 Aprés toutes ces manieres d'amer ci dessus, vous enseignent li bon dessus dit que vous gardez que en nulle maniere vous n'ayez trop grant amour en vos corps nourrir, car c'est la plus mauvaise amour qui soit. Mais ayez grant amour en vos ames et en vos honnours bien garder, qui plus longue-
5 ment durent que ne fait le corps qui aussi tost muert gras comme maigre. Et li trop amer son corps a nourrir est moult contraires a tout bien. Premierement, quant vous avriez ycelle mauvaise volenté de trop amer a nourrir ces chetifs* corps en vostre jonesce, vous voudrés dormir tost et esveiller tart, et s'en vous entrebrise vostre heure de dormir longuement, il vous en
10 sera trop mal; et tant come (f.102r) vous dormirés plus longuement et souvent, de tant perdrez vous temps de trouver savoir et d'aprendre aucun bien. Et ceste vie de longuement dormir est moult contraire a ceulz qui veulent attaindre au haut honnour, car moult des foys les convient dormir tart et esveillier matin, et ainsi l'ont acoustumé, si leur en est de miex et de santé
15 de corps et d'onnour acquerir. Si faut encores a ces chaitis corps nourir, qu'il aient touzjours blans draps et lit mol, et se aucunefoys y faillent, les

when they do not know nor do they want to know about the worthy deeds that they should know about and ought to perform, especially those who for good reason should undertake them? And indeed this love can be worth nothing, nor can it last for long without the ladies wanting to have no more of it and withdrawing, and the miserable wretches, through well justified shame, dare not protest, nor insist that their ladies should not treat them thus; instead they themselves retreat, and they have to do so in great shame and discomfort, nor can they put forward any arguments to persuade their ladies to behave differently. Therefore men should love secretly, protect, serve, and honor all those ladies and damsels who inspire knights, men-at-arms, and squires to undertake worthy deeds that bring them honor and increase their renown. And these noble ladies should, as is their duty, love and honor these worthy men-at-arms who, in order to deserve their noble love and their benevolence, expose themselves to so much physical danger as the vocation of arms requires from those who aim to reach and achieve that high honor through which they hope to deserve to win the love of their ladies.° And the advice of these noble ladies is as follows: "Love loyally if you want to be loved." Thus you should love loyally and live joyfully and act honorably and in good hope, for these activities of love and of arms should be engaged in with the true and pure gaiety of heart which brings the will to achieve honor.

A Good Man-at-Arms Should Not Pamper His Body
21   Having examined all these different ways of loving, the aforementioned men of worth tell you that you must in no way indulge in too great fondness for pampering your body, for love of that is the worst kind of love there is. But instead direct your love toward the preservation of your soul and your honor, which last longer than does the body, which dies just as soon, whether it be fat or lean. Too great a desire to cosset the body is against all good. In the first place, if you have this bad tendency for being excessively fond of cosseting this wretched body in your youth, you will want to go to sleep early and wake up late, and if your long hours of sleep are interrupted, you will suffer greatly from this, and the longer you sleep the less time you will have to acquire knowledge and to learn something of value. And this life of long sleeping will stand in the way of those who want to attain high honor, for they have often to go to sleep late and rise early, and they have accustomed themselves to doing so, and this helps them to achieve physical fitness and honor. The pampering of these wretched bodies also requires white sheets and soft beds, and if these are

reins et les costes leur deulent tant qu'il ne se peuent aidier de tout le jour. Et cil bon lit leur attraient le repos et la foison dormir qui leur fait perdre tant de bien ouir. Est ce bien le contraire a ceulz qui honour quierent, quar
20 le plus de foys ont mauvais lis, et moult de fois dorment sanz lis et touz vestus, et si leur souffist mielx cil repos et cilz gesirs, que eulz ne le voudroient mie ne prendroient en grey autrement pour le grant bien et honnour qu'il y attendent a avoir. Et encores, pour nourir ces chietiz corps qui n'ont nulle heure de vivre, faut il qu'il soient pehu et abevrez des meilleurs
25 vins et viandes que l'en puet trouver ne avoir et mengier a heure, ou autrement leur en seroit trop en mal pour les tres grans deliz qu'il y prennent. Et pour ycelles glout[o]nnies doubtent travail de bien faire. Et certes ytelz delices sont moult contraires a yceus qui ce haut honneur vont querant, car il ne regardent point ne ne se (f.102v) delitent a teles delices, mes boivent et
30 menjuent et le po et l'auques tout ainsi come il le treuvent, et tout leur souffist; et liement, pour l'onnour qui leur en rent si tres grans guerredons, et trop joyeusement font, et prennent li bon les biens et les honnours que Dieux leur a donnés et donne, pour les chaitifz qu'il voient qui n'en ont point. Et pour ce vous enseignent li bons dessus diz qu'il n'est pas bien de
35 vivre mais de bien vivre. Encores faut il en soustenir et a nourir ces chaitis corps que en hiver soient fourrez et vestuz chaudement et en chaudes maisons, et en esté legierement vestuz et en freiches maisons et es plus froides caves, ou autrement il ne pourroient vivre par leur chaitives coustumes.

22   Or est ce bien au contraire de ceuls qui a honnour veulent venir, car il se gouvernent selon le temps, quar quant il fait froit, il endurent le froit, et quant il fait chaut, il seuffrent aussi et endurent le chaut. Et tout leur est bon pour la grant plaisance qu'il ont de venir a honnour et de vivre hono-
5 rablement. Et a ce vous enseignent li bon dessus diz que, pour trop longuement aaisier vos corps delicieusement, vous n'aquerrez ja grant honnour. Et sur toutes ces choses avient encore pour ces chaitiz corps gouverner que, pour ce que il ont grant paour et grant doubte qu'il n'aient deffaut de leurs aises qu'il ont acoustumez, sont convoiteux de prendre partout l'ou il en
10 peuent prendre ne avoir, et (f.103r) aussi eschars de le despendre qu'il n'en mettent, ne despendent fors que en leurs corps aaisier, dont li diable en feront leur feste. Et tout ce est contraire a yceus qui veulent despendre le

sometimes lacking, such men's backs and ribs ache so much that they can do nothing all day. And these good beds encourage rest and an abundance of sleep, which prevents them from hearing much that would be of profit to them. The contrary is true of those who seek honor, for more often than not they have poor beds and many a time they sleep without beds at all and with their clothes on; and this rest and repose is quite enough for them, for they would not want it otherwise for the great profit and honor they expect to have from it. And in addition, to sustain these wretched men's bodies, which have little time to live, they have to be provided with the best food and wine that are to be found, and require to eat at the right time, or otherwise they will be in too great distress because of the great delight they take in such things. And because of this gluttony, they dread the hardship associated with deeds of arms. And indeed such delights are rejected by those who go in search of this high honor, for they have no regard for and do not indulge in such pleasures, but drink and eat whatever small amount they find and are quite satisfied; they do so gladly and joyfully for the sake of the honor which brings them such a great reward; and the men of worth accept the benefits and the honors which God has bestowed and continues to bestow on them instead of on the miserable wretches who, as they see, receive nothing. Hence we can learn from the above-mentioned men of worth that it is not good just to live, but to live in a good way. Furthermore those wretched men have to be sustained and pampered so that in winter they are wrapped in furs and warmly clad and live in warm houses, and in summer are lightly clad and live in cool houses or in the coldest vaults, otherwise they cannot survive because of their decadent habits.

Good Men-at-Arms Have No Fear of Discomfort

22 It is quite the opposite for those who want to win honor, for they adapt to the seasons: when it is cold, they endure the cold, and when it is hot, they put up with the heat. And they are prepared to accept all this for the great pleasure they experience in winning honor and in living honorably. And in relation to this we learn from the above-mentioned men of worth that honor is not achieved through spending much time in keeping the body delightfully comfortable. And on top of all these things, it also arises that in order to maintain these wretched bodies, because of their great fear lest they lack their accustomed comforts, they are eager to grab whatever they can whenever they can, and are so miserly in spending that they will only shell out to maintain their bodies in comfort, at which the devils will rejoice. And this is quite the opposite to those who want to

leur en acquerir honnour; car il amassent du leur ce qu'il peuent et empruntent assez, tant qu'il doivent de retour, et leur tarde qu'il soient briefment an lieu la ou il le puissent briefment despendre en travaillant pour acquerir honnour. Et li bon dessus dit vous enseignent que touzjours les armes rendent ce qu'en y met, quoy qu'il demeure.° Et encores ont cilz chaitiz corps si tres grant doubte de mourir qu'il ne se peuent asseurer. Si tost comme il saillent hors de leurs maisons que il voient une pierre en un mur qui saille avant un pou hors des autres, jamais n'y oseroient passer, car il leur semble touzjours qu'elle leur doie cheoir sur les testes. S'il passent une riviere un pou trop grant ou trop roide, il leur semble, de la grant paour qu'il ont de mourir, qu'il doyent touzjours cheoir dedens. S'il passent sur un pont qui soit un po trop haut ou trop bas, il descendent a pié et ont encores grant paour que li pons ne fonde* desous eulz, tant ont paour de mourir. S'il voient un pas qui soit un po trop mol, il se tordroient bien demie lieue pour trouver le dur pour la paour qu'il ont de cheoir dedens. S'il ont un po de maladie, il cuident tantost estre mors. Se aucuns les manacent, il ont grant paour de leurs chetiz corps et tres grant paour de perdre leurs avoirs qu'il ont si chaitivement amassez. (f.103v) Et s'il voyent plaies sur aucuns, il ne l'osent regarder du chaitif cuer qu'il ont. Et encores cilz treschaitis ne savront ja gesir en si fort maison, car quant il vente un po trop, qu'il n'aient grant paour que la maison ne chee sur eulz. Et encores ycelles chietives gens, quant il montent a cheval, n'osent il ferir des esperons pour ce que leurs chevauls ne queurent, tant ont paour de cheoir, que leurs chevaux ne cheent, ne eulz aussi. Or poués veoir que ycelles chaitives gens qui ont ces chaitifs cuers ne seront ja asceur qu'il ne vivent en plus grant paour et doubte de perdre ces chaitis corps que n'ont ycelles bonnes gens d'armes qui en tant de perilz et en tant de dures aventures mettent leurs corps pour acquerir honnour; car il ont tant acoustumé et cogneu que de teles chaitives paours, dont cilz chaitis ont et si souvent, ne leur en chaut il de nient. Et la ou li chaitis ont grant envie de vivre et grant paour de mourir, c'est tout au contraire des bons; car aus bons ne chaut il de leur vie ne de mourir, mais que leur vie soit bonne a mourir honorablement. Et bien y pert es estranges et perileuses aventures que il querent. Et pour ce dient li bon dessus dit que adonques est bon a homme de mourir quant sa vie lui plaist, que Dieux fait belle grace a ceulz a qui leur vie est tele que le morir est honnorable; car li bon dessus dit vous enseignent que il vault miex mourir que laidement vivre.

spend what they have in winning honor; for they gather together as much as they can of what they have and they make considerable borrowings, so that they owe a great deal on their return, and they are eager to come quickly to a place where they can quickly spend what they have in striving to win honor. And we learn from the above-mentioned men of worth that the practice of arms always gives back what is put in it whatever the delay.° And these wretched people are so afraid of dying that they cannot overcome their fear. As soon as they leave their abode, if they see a stone jutting out of the wall a little further than the others, they will never dare to pass beneath it, for it would always seem to them that it would fall on their heads. If they come to a river which is a little big or too fast flowing, it always seems to them, so great is their fear of dying, that they will fall into it. If they cross a bridge which may seem a little too high or too low, they dismount and are still terrified lest the bridge collapse under them, so great is their fear of dying. If they see before them a boggy stretch, they will go a good half league out of their way to find some firm ground for fear of sinking into the mud. If they suffer from a slight illness, they think they are about to die. If they are threatened by anyone, they fear greatly for their physical safety and dread the loss of the riches they have amassed in such a discreditable way. And if they see anyone with a wound, they dare not look at it because of their feeble spirit. What is more, no matter how strong the place these poor wretches may find in which to spend the night, if there is a little too much wind, they will be greatly afraid that the roof will come down on them. Furthermore, when these feeble wretches are on horseback, they do not dare to use their spurs lest their horses should start to gallop, so afraid are they lest their horses should stumble and they should fall to the ground with them. Now you can see that these wretched people who are so fainthearted will never feel secure from living in greater fear and dread of losing their lives than do those good men-at-arms who have exposed themselves to so many physical dangers and perilous adventures in order to achieve honor; for they are so accustomed to and familiar with such things that they are quite unaffected by such pathetic fears to which these wretches are so often subject. And while the cowards have a great desire to live and a great fear of dying, it is quite the contrary for the men of worth who do not mind whether they live or die, provided that their life be good enough for them to die with honor. And this is evident in the strange and perilous adventures which they seek. For this reason the above-mentioned men of worth say that a man is happy to die when he finds life pleasing, for God is gracious toward those who find their life of such quality

23 (f.104r) Or convient il avoir un estat souverain en ycelles bonnes gens d'armes, si comme li bon dessus dit dient et enseignent qu'il soient humbles entre leurs amis, fiers et hardiz contre leurs ennemis, piteux et misericors sur ceulz qui le requierent par amandement, cruelz vengeur sur ses ennemis, cointes, aimables et de bonne compaignie avecques touz fors avecques ses ennemis; car li bon vous enseignent que vous ne devez pas parler longuement ne tenir parole avecques voz ennemis, que vous devez penser qu'il ne parolent pas a vous pour vostre bien, fors que pour traire de vous dont il se puissent aviser de vous porter plus grant domage. Si devez estre large de donner au miex emploié, et tant eschars comme pourrés de laissier rienz du vostre a vous° ennemis. Amez et servez vos amis, heez et grevez vos ennemis, reposez vous avecques vous amis, travaillez vous contre vous ennemis. Vous devez conseillier voz emprises doubteusement et les devez parfournir tres hardiement. Et pour ce vous enseignent les bons dessus diz que nulz ne se doit trop desesperer pour couardise ne trop affermer en sa hardiesce; car trop desesperer par couardise fait a homme perdre son fait et son honnour, et trop affier en sa hardiesce fait a homme perdre le corps folement, mes puis que l'en est en besoigne, l'en doit plus doubter laide couhardise que la mort. Gardez que convoitise ne soit en vous pour tolir ne pour avoir l'autruy sanz (f.104v) cause. Et gardez sur tant comme vous vous amez que vous ne vous laissiez rienz tolir du vostre. Dites et racontez le bien des autres et le vostre non, et n'aiez envie* sur autruy. Et sur toutes choses fuyez tençon, quar doubteuse chose est a tencier a son pareil, et forsenerie est de tencier a plus haut de luy, et laide chose est de tencier a plus bas de luy, et tres laide chose est de tencier a fol et a yvre. Encore vous asseignent° les bons dessus diz que vous vous gardez de dire laides paroles, mais gardez que vous paroles soient plus profectables que courtoises. Et gardez que vous ne loez vostre fait, ne ne blasmez trop l'autruy. N'aiez envie d'oster l'onnour d'autruy, mais gardez le vostre souverainement. Gardez que vous n'aiez en despit nulles povres gens ne nulz mendre de vous, que moult en y a des povres qui valent miex que ne font li riche. Gardez vous de trop parler, car en trop parler convient que l'en die folie, et par exemple li fol ne se peuent taire, et li saige se taisent juques a tant qu'il aient temps de parler. Et vous gardez de trop grant simplece, quar qui riens ne scet, ne bien ne mal, son cuer est aweugle et non voyant, ne il ne scet conseillier

that death is honorable; for the said men of worth teach you that it is better to die than to live basely.

Advice on Conduct Toward Friends and Enemies
23   There is a supreme rule of conduct required in these good men-at-arms as the above-mentioned men of worth inform us: they should be humble among their friends, proud and bold against their foes, tender and merciful toward those who need assistance, cruel avengers against their enemies, pleasant and amiable with all others, for the men of worth tell you that you should not converse at any length nor hold speech with your enemies, for you should bear in mind that they do not speak to you for your own good but to draw out of you what they can use to do you the greatest harm. You should be generous in giving where the gift will be best used and as careful as you can that you let your enemies have nothing that is yours. Love and serve your friends, hate and harm your enemies, relax with your friends, exert yourself with all your strength against your foes. You should plan your enterprises cautiously and you should carry them out boldly. Therefore the said men of worth tell you that no one should fall into despair from cowardice nor be too confident from great daring, for falling into too great despair can make a man lose his position and his honor, and trusting too much in his daring can make a man lose his life foolishly; but when one is engaged on an armed enterprise, one should dread vile cowardice more than death. Take care not to be so greedy as to take what belongs to others without good cause. And be sure that, as you value yourself, you do not let anything of yours be taken from you. Speak of the achievements of others but not of your own, and do not be envious of others. Above all, avoid quarrels, for a quarrel with one's equal is dangerous, a quarrel with some one higher in rank is madness, and a quarrel with some one lower in rank is a vile thing, but a quarrel with a fool or a drunk is an even viler thing. The aforesaid men of worth also tell you to refrain from saying unpleasant things and to make sure that what you say is of some profit rather than merely courteous. And make sure that you do not praise your own conduct nor criticize too much that of others. Do not desire to take away another's honor, but, above all else, safeguard your own. Be sure that you do not despise poor men or those lesser in rank than you, for there are many poor men who are of greater worth than the rich. Take care not to talk too much, for in talking too much you are sure to say something foolish; for example, the foolish cannot hold their peace, and the wise know how to hold their peace until it is time to speak. And be careful not

ne lui ne les autres; que se un aweugles veult mener un autre, certes il meismes chiet en la fosse premiers et li autres amprés luy. Or vous gardez encores de chastier les folz, que vous y perdriez voz poines, et si vous en herront, mes chastiez les sages qui vous en ameront mieulx. N'aiés ja grant
40 (f.105r) esperance en gens qui en brief temps seurmontent les autres par grant fortune sanz desserte, car il ne peuent durer; car aussi tost sont il prestz de descendre comme il sont monté. Et li bon dessus diz vous enseignent que fortune essaie les amis; car quant elle s'en va, elle vous laisse les vostres et en maine ceuls qui vostres n'estoient. Encores vous di je que de
45 largesce que vous faciez ne de dons bien emploiez ne vous devez repentir, car li bon dessus dit vous enseignent qu'il ne doit souvenir a bon homme de ce qu'il a donné, fors tant seulement quant cilz a qui il l'a donné l'en fait souvenir pour le bon guerredon qu'il en rent. Encores vous devez garder d'estre mal renommés en vos viellesces d'escharceté, car quant plus avrez
50 donné, donnez encores plus, que quant plus avrez vescu, moins avrez a vivre. Et vous gardez souverainement de vous enrichir du domage des autres, mesmement de la povreté des povres, que mieulx vault nette povreté que desloyal richesce. Encores vous enseignent li bon dessus dit que vous devez tenir voz amis en tele maniere que vous ne doiez doubter qu'il ne devieng-
55 nent vostre ennemi, que vous devez penser que tant comme vous tendrez vostre secret en vous, il est touzjours en vostre puissance; et si tost comme vous l'avrez descouvert, vous demourrez en son dengier. Et se descouvrir le vous convient, si vous en descovrez a vostre loyal ami, et vostre maladie descouvrez au loyal mire. Encore vous enseignent li bon dessus dit que en
60 alant dessus voz ennemis et pour eulz encontrer, que (105v) en voz cuers n'aiez jamaiz pensee que vous doiez estre desconfit, ne comment vous serez pris, ne comment vous vous enfuirez, mes aiez les cuers fors et fermes et sceurs et touzjours en bonne esperance de vaincre et non mie estre vaincus, soit au dessous ou au dessus, que comment qu'il soit, ferez vous tousjours
65 bien pour la bonne esperance que vous avrez; car moult en y a qui se retraient, que s'il demourassent et en feissent ce qu'il peussent, ce pourroit estre a la desconfiture de leurs ennemis, et d'aucuns qui sont pris assez legierement que, se il feissent ce qu'il peussent bien faire, que ce fust a la grant perde de leurs ennemis. Et pour ce devez vous avoir touzjours en touz estas
70 ferme volenté de faire le meilleur, et souverainement droite, ferme esperance que de Dieu viengne et que Dieu vous aide, non mie de vostre force ne de vostre sens ne vostre puissance, fors que Dieu tant seulement, que vous veez assez souvent que par les moins vaillans sont vaincu li meilleur, et par le moins de gens sont vaincu* li plus, et par les plus foibles de corps

to be too guileless, for the man who knows nothing, neither of good nor of evil, is blind and unseeing in his heart, nor can he give himself or others good counsel, for when one blind man tries to lead another, he himself will fall first into the ditch and drag the other in after him. Refrain from remonstrating with fools, for you will be wasting your time, and they will hate you for it; but remonstrate with the wise, who will like you the better for it. Do not put too much faith in people who have risen rapidly above others by good fortune, not merit, for this will not last: they can fall as quickly as they rise. And the aforementioned men of worth tell you that fortune tests your friends, for when it abandons you, it leaves you those who are your friends and takes away those who are not. I repeat that you should never regret any generosity you may show and any gifts well bestowed, for the above-mentioned men of worth tell you that a man of worth should not remember what he has given except when the recipient brings the gift back to mind for the good return he makes for it. You must avoid acquiring a bad reputation for miserliness in your old age, for the more you have given, the more you should give, for the longer you have lived, the less time you will have yet to live. And above all refrain from enriching yourself at others' expense, especially from the limited resources of the poor, for unsullied poverty is worth more than corrupt wealth. The aforementioned men of worth also tell you that you should treat your friends in such a way that you have no need to fear lest they become your enemies, for you should consider that as long as you keep your secret to yourself, it is always within your control, but as soon as you have revealed it, you are at its mercy. And if you have to reveal it, only disclose it to your loyal friend, and disclose your illness only to a loyal doctor. The aforementioned men of worth also tell you that when moving against your enemies to meet them in battle, never admit the idea that you might be defeated nor think how you might be captured or how you might flee, but be strong in heart, firm, and confident, always expecting victory, not defeat, whether or not you are on top, for whatever the situation, you will always do well because of the good hopes that you have. Indeed, many retreat when, if they had stayed and done what they could, their enemies might have been defeated; and some who have been easily taken prisoner, if they had resisted as well as they could, their enemies would have suffered great losses. You should, therefore, always and in all circumstances be determined to do your best, and above all have the true and certain hope that comes from God that He will help you, not relying just on your strength nor your intelligence nor your power but on God alone, for one often sees that the best men are defeated

75 desconfis les plus fors, et par les plus folz et en fole ordenance desconfis pluseurs sages sagement ordenez. Si poués assez veoir et cognoistre que de vous n'avez riens fors ce que Dieu vous donne. Et ne vous fait Dieu grant grace et grant honnor, quant il vous donne grace de vaincre vos ennemis sanz domage de vostre corps? Et se vous estes desconfis, ne vous fait Dieu
80 grant grace se vous estes pris honnorablement et au los de voz amis et de voz ennemis? Et se vous estes en bon estat et vous y (f.106r) mourez honnorablement, ne vous fait Dieu grant grace quant il vous donne si honorable fin en ce siecle et vostre ame anmoine avec luy en celle joye qui tousjours durera? Et poués veoir que nulz ne doit trop doubter ne trop
85 esjoïr ne trop couroucier de teles aventures quant elles aviennent, mes tout regracier et remettre a celui qui les donne plus debonnairement que l'en ne lui scet requerir. Et li bons dessus diz vous enseignent que, se vous voulez estre fors et de bon courage en ces choses, gardez que vous prisiez moins la mort que la honte. Et ceulz qui mettent leurs corps en peril pour droite
90 cognoissance de honte eschiver sont fort en tout. Encores vous enseignent li bon dessus dit que vous devez pensser en voz cuers les choses qui avenir vous peuent, et les bonnes et les mauvaises, si que vous puissiez souffrir paciamment les males et attemprer les bonnes. Et en toutes vos adversitez soiez tousjours fermes et sages. Et aussi bien avez vous mestier de penser
95 comment vous pourrez et devrez soustenir aucuns biens ou honnours, quant Dieux les vous donne, que vous ne les perdez par mauvaise garde, comme de vous oster et de partir des mals quant il vous aviennent. Si en devez mercier et loer premierement celui qui les vous donne, et les garder sanz orgueil, que vous devez savoir que la ou orgueil est, la maint tout
100 courrous et toutes folies, et la ou humilité maint, la est sens et liesce. Et aussi comme li bon dessus dit vous enseignent et vous dient pour verité que, se orgueil estoit si haut qu'il fust jusques aus nues et (f.106v) la teste li venist jusques au ciel, si convendroit il qu'il cheist et fondist a perte et a nient. Et vous devez savoir que d'orgueil naist moult de branches dont assez
105 de malz viennent et tant comme pour perdre ame et corps, honnour et avoir. Si devez garder ce que vous savez et l'onneur que vous avez sanz orgueil. Et ce que vous ne savez, requerez humblement qu'il vous soit apris. Encore vous enseignent li bon dessus dit que vous ne vous affiez trop en ce que fortune vous baille, que ce sont choses qui doivent perir, ou par perdre
110 ou par maladie ou par force ou par mort, que la mort n'espargne nulluy, ne les haus ne les bas, mes hingale tout. Et pour ce ne se doit nulz remiser° en soy, que ce n'est chose qui puisse longuement durer, mes tantost s'en peut aler et sanz nulle heure attendre. Et qui parfaitement penseroit en ce, jamés d'orgueil ne seroit souspris.

by lesser men, and a greater number of people may be defeated by a smaller, and the strongest in body may be overcome by the weakest, and the wisest and best ordered in battle by the most foolish and worst ordered. You can see clearly and understand that you on your own can achieve nothing except what God grants you. And does not God confer great honor when He allows you of His mercy to defeat your enemies without harm to yourself? And if you are defeated, does not God show you great mercy if you are taken prisoner honorably, praised by friends and enemies? And if you are in a state of grace and you die honorably, does not God show you great mercy when He grants you such a glorious end to your life in this world and bears your soul away with Him into eternal bliss? And you can see that no one should be too afraid or too overjoyed or too disturbed at such happenings when they occur, but should give thanks and commit everything into the hands of Him who gives graciously more than one can ask for. And the aforesaid men of worth teach you that if you want to be strong and of good courage, be sure that you care less about death than about shame. And those who put their lives in danger with the deliberate intention of avoiding shame are strong in all things. The aforesaid men of worth also tell you that you should reflect in your hearts on the things which may happen to you, both the good and the bad, so that you can suffer the bad patiently and treat the good with restraint. And in all adversity be always steadfast and wise. And you also need to consider how you can and must maintain any benefit or honor which God may bestow on you, so that you do not lose them through negligence such as by removing yourself and distancing yourself from trouble when it comes upon you; and you should first thank and praise Him who gives you these things and preserve them without arrogance, for you must understand that where there is arrogance, there reigns anger and all kinds of folly; and where humility is to be found, there reigns good sense and happiness. And as the aforesaid men of worth teach you and tell you truly, if arrogance were to be so high that it towered up into the clouds and its highest point reached the heavens, it would have to fall and would crumble and be reduced to nothing. And you should know that from arrogance grow many branches from which many evils come, so many as may cause the loss of soul and body, honor and wealth. You should preserve what you know and the honor you have without arrogance. And what you do not know, you should ask with due humility to be taught it. The aforesaid men of worth also tell you not to put too much trust in the gifts of fortune, for they are things which are destined to come to an end, whether through loss or illness or force or death, for death spares no one, neither the high nor the low, but levels all. And no one

24   Et pour ce que l'on a parlé cy dessus des biens de fortune, et li aucun n'entendroient pas bien quelz il sont, les convient il un po plus d'esclarcir pour en avoir plus grant cognoissance et pour miex cognoistre les estaz de fortune en ce mestier. Et a ce pourroit on dire que l'en ne se doit point fier es biens de fortune qui viennent sanz desserte, que elle est muable et doit perir. Mais se vous avez volenté de estre sages et vous y travailliez, et par vostre travaille Dieux vous fait celle grace que vous le soyez et par cela vous soiez eshauciez, ycilz biens n'est mie de fortune: il vous doit durer, mes que vous le sachiez garder honestement en gouvernant vous premierement (f. 107r) et autres se besoings estoit. Quar se vous estes sages, vous ne ferez fors bien et ne vous devez excuser de estre preudoms et loyaulx, car c'est le plus grant bien et le plus souverain qui soit. Car il n'est mie sages qui veult, ne n'est pas preux qui veult, ne si n'est mie riches qui veult; mais nulz ne se doit ne ne peut excuser qu'il ne soit preudome et loyaulz qui veult. Et se vous avez renommee d'estre bons homs d'armes, et dont vous soiez enhauciez et honorez et vous l'aiez desservi par vostre grant travaille, peril et hardiesce, et Nostre Sires vous a fait telle grace qu'il vous ait ce laissié faire dont vous avez tele renommee, ycilz biens ne sont mie biens de fortune, mais sont biens qui par raison doivent durer, mes que l'en les sache garder humblement et honorablement. Et moult de foys avient, ainsi comme par avant est dit, en fait d'armes de batailles que li moins desconfisent le plus, et moult de fois avient que li pis ordenez sur les champs desconfisent ceulz qui sont en bon ordenance,° et moult de fois est avenu que les moindres et foibles ont desconfis les plus grans et les plus haus en touz estaz qu'il ne estoient. Yceste fortune est bonne, que pour les grans biens et hardiesce qui en ycelles [journees] sont es vainqueeurs, et par la chaitiveté des vaincus et des desconfis dont il sont venu en leur dessus d'ycelles journees bien se peut appeller dure fortune sur les vaincus et plus male fortune sur ceulz qui sont causes des desconfitures. Mes toutevoies se li moins encontrent le plus, et les plus febles encontrent les plus fors, et les mal ordenez encontrent ceulz qui sont en bonne ordenance, (f. 107v) et ainsi le vouloient faire et continuer longuement, ne leur pourroit durer ceste fortune que elle ne deust cheoir par droite cognoissance de la raison; car la raison est touzjours plus segure et plus ferme et longue duree que les fortunes ne sont qui touzjours

therefore should delay,° because such gifts do not last for long, but can vanish at any moment, without waiting for the hour. And the man who perfectly understands this will never be overcome by arrogance.

The Role of Fortune

24 And because the benefits of fortune have been discussed above, and some may not understand what these are, it is necessary to give a brief explanation of them so that people have a better knowledge of them and understand better the position of fortune in this calling. And in relation to this, it could be said that one should not put trust in the benefits of fortune, which are not earned, for fortune is fickle and is destined to come to an end. But if you have the will to be wise and you strive at it, and in return for your efforts God, through His grace, grants you wisdom, and through this you are exalted, this benefit does not come from fortune: it should last, provided you know how to preserve it honestly, in controlling yourself first, and then others if necessary. For if you are wise, you will only do good and ought not to excuse yourself from being a man of worth and loyal, as it is the greatest and most supreme good there is, for a man may want to be wise and fail, and want to be valiant and fail, and want to be rich and powerful and fail, but no one should or can excuse himself from being a man of worth and loyal, if he has the will. And if you have the reputation of being a good man-at-arms, through which you are exalted and honored, and you have deserved this by your great exertions, by the perils you have faced and by your courage, and Our Lord has in his mercy allowed you to perform the deeds from which you have gained such a reputation, such benefits are not benefits of fortune, but are benefits which by right should last, provided that one knows how to conserve them humbly and honorably. And it often happens, as has been said earlier, that in armed encounters in battle the smaller number defeats the greater, and many a time the worst marshaled on the field defeat those who are well marshaled, and many a time the lesser and weaker have defeated those who were in every respect greater and the nobler in rank. This fortune is good, for the great prowess and valor which in those battles is to be found in the victors; and for the faintheartedness of the conquered and defeated whom they have overcome in relation to these battles, it could be called ill fortune for the vanquished and worse fortune for those who themselves caused the defeat. Nevertheless if the lesser number encounter the greater number, and the weaker the stronger, and the ill marshaled those who are well marshaled, and they wanted to continue thus for some length of time, this run of good fortune would not last long

35 sont appareilliez de cheoir. Et s'il est ainsi que par vostre grant bien et de vostre bon sens vous aiez fait services ou de vostre bon travail honorablement, combien que vous soiez de bas estat, que vous soiez enhauciez en grant et en haut estat de possessions et d'autres biens de ce monde, ycilz biens qui par la grace de Dieu sont ainsi venus ne sont mie bien de fortune.
40 Il vous doivent valoir et durer ainsi comme peuent durer les biens de ce monde, mais que vous les gardez, mettez et usez convenablement et sanz grant gloire fors que a Dieu qui les vous a donnez. Ycilz biens, ainsi bien desserviz et bien gouvernez et en bon usage mis sanz orgueil, ne a la grevance d'autruy, ne pour trop grant convoitise, ne pour trop grans delices,
45 ne sont fors biens de raison; mais ceulz qui sont renommez de sens, et il ne le sont mie, et ceulz qui sont renommé d'estre preudomme, et il ne le sont mie, et ceulz qui sont renommez d'onnour de fait d'armes, et il ne le vaillent mie, et ceulz qui ainsi sont seurmontez en grans hautesces et en grans richesces et es grans estas et sanz nulle deserte, quant ycelles gens sont
50 seurmontés et de tele fortune, si n'en scevent user fors si desmesureement que par les degrez dont il sont monté l'un aprés l'autre en celle hautesce de fortune, pour le (108r) foible fondement sur quoy elle est fondee, convient qu'elle chee, fonde et descende desordeneement par ces mesmes degrez a perde et a nient, dont il ont pis assez de la descendue que ce qu'il y fussent
55 onques euz montez° en celle hautesce. Et pour ce est li proverbes des anciens veritables que qui plus haut monte qu'il ne doit, de plus haut chiet qu'il ne vourroit.° Or veez vous donques que les biens qui sont bien comparez et bien deservis sont cil qui par raison doivent venir et durer a plus grant perfection tant de l'ame comme du corps; et ceulz qui veulent avoir
60 les grans biens et honnours sanz poine, et sanz travaulx en prennent toutes leurs aaises et leurs delices, iceles gens le peuent assez attendre, mais ja n'en n'avront nul. Et pour ce n'est il nulz, tant soit petit ou de petit estat, que se il veult desservir et traveillier a faire le bien, que li bien ne li viengne si marveilleusement qu'il ne le savroit souhaidier mieux, ne que Diex li donne
65 avecques la bonne renommee. Ne aussi n'est il nulz si grant ne de si haut estat que se par leurs chaitivetés il n'endurent a traveillier ne a deservir d'avoir le bien, qu'il en aient ja nul, ainçois demourront en leurs chaitivetez et en la male grace du peuple et en tres mauvaise renommee, que quant plus est uns homs de grant et de haut estat, et plus ait grant renommee en plu-
70 seurs parties du monde ou de sa bonne renommee ou de la mauvaise (f.108v) que de pluseurs autres moiennes gens ne pourroit estre; car qui bien savroit pourquoy et comment les empereurs, les roys, les princes des terres furent eslevez et faiz pour estre seigneurs sur leur peuple, les causes

without changing for the worse, and this is according to reason. Reason is always more certain and assured and long lasting, for there is no good fortune which may not at any moment be changed and brought down to earth. And if, by your great worth and your good sense or by your strenuous efforts, you have done good and honorable service, however low you may be in rank, if you are raised to a noble and high rank in possessions and other advantages of this world, these benefits which have come to you by the grace of God are not the gifts of fortune. They should retain their value and last as long as the benefits of this world can last, provided you safeguard them and put them to proper use, finding no great glory in them except in relation to God who has given them to you. These benefits, thus well merited and put to good and careful use, without arrogance, without damage to others, without indulgence in greed or excessive pleasure, are all benefits that can be justified. But those who are reputed to be wise and are not, and those who are reputed to be men of worth and are not, and those who are reputed to have won honor through deeds of arms and are unworthy of this renown, and those who have been raised up to noble rank and great wealth and high estate, when people of that kind are elevated to such good fortune, they know no better than to exploit this with very little restraint. As a result, the foundation on which their height of fortune is based is so weak that it must crumble and collapse so that they come tumbling down those very steps which they had earlier mounted; they, therefore, suffer more from the descent through having mounted so high. Hence the proverb of the ancients is true: "He that climbs higher than he should falls lower than he would."° You see, therefore, that the benefits which are well earned and well deserved are those which, according to reason, should reach the greatest perfection and last, be they of the soul or of the body; and those who want to have the great benefits and honors without painful effort, and in idleness take all their ease and pleasure, such people, however long they wait, will get nothing. And because of this, there is no one, however humble or of however low a rank, if he is willing to strive for and deserve honorable achievement, to whom the benefits may not come in such abundance that he could not ask for more and to whom God may not grant together with these things an honorable reputation. Nor are there any men so important or of such high rank that they will win any of the rewards if they cannot endure the great effort required from those who would deserve to have such benefits; rather they will remain inadequate, out of favor with the people and with a bad reputation, for the more a man is of high and noble rank, the more his reputation, whether

et maniere de le faire et avoir fait furent moult bonnes, sainctes et justes, car les plus convenables personnes de corps et les plus parfaiz en toutes bonnes meurs, esleus en trestout leur peuple, il les eslisoient et esleurent a celui temps, dont sont venus depuis et sont encores les empereurs, roys et princes qui a present sont.° Et pensez vous que les premiers* esleuz dessus diz fussent esleuz a seigneurs pour avoir tous leurs aises et leurs delites? Certes nennil. Furent il esleuz pour ce qu'il n'amassent Dieu ne ses oeuvres ne Saincte Eglise? Certes nennil. Furent il fait pour faire le domage du commun peuple et faire leur profit singulier? Certes nennil. Furent il fait pour apovrir leur peuple et pour eulz enrichir sanz autre bonne cause? Certes nennil. Furent il faiz pour avoir les richesces et les mal emploier? Certes nennil. Furent il fait pour non faire raison et justice autant au petit comme au grant? Certes nennil. Furent il fait pour estre cruels sanz pitié et sans misericorde? Certes nennil. Furent il fait pour sejourner assez et pour po traveillier? Certes nennil. Furent fait pour touzjours boire et mengier le plus delicieusement qu'il peuent? Certes nennil. (f.109r) Furent il fait qu'il ne se deussent point armer, ne mettre leurs corps en peril de batailles a la deffension de leurs terres et de leur peuple? Certes nennil. Furent il fait pour estre couhart? Certes nennil. Furent il fait pour estre eschars et non donner du leur a ceulz a qui il est bien emploié? Certes nennil. Furent il fait pour mener vies deshonestes et diffamees? Certes nennil. Furent il fait pour estre larges et donner le leur aus chaitiz et en mal emploié? Certes nennil. Furent il fait pour amer et croire les chaitis et les flateurs? Certes nennil. Furent fait pour alongier les bons d'entour eulz? Certes nennil. Furent il faiz pour estre enfermez en leurs maisons, dont nulz ne puisse parler a eulz? Certes nennil. Furent il faiz pour mentir et faire contre leurs promesses, seremens ou seellez? Certes nennil. Furent il fait pour faire, ne faire faire, ne consentir nulz mauvais fait? Certes nennil. Furent il fait pour avoir nulle plaisance ne amistié a genz de mauvaise vie? Certes nennil. Furent* il fait pour oïr voulentiers paroles deshonestes et pour veoir chaitis jeux? Certes nennil. Furent il fait pour oïr volentiers vilaines paroles d'autrui en leur presence? Certes nennil. Furent il fait que quant adversitez leur viennent, qu'il ne les sachent endurer ne soustenir? Certes nennil. Furent il fait pour estre fiers et orgueilleux et cruelx a leur servans?* Certes nennil. Furent il fait pour aler prendre leurs deduis en boys et en rivieres et pour en laissier a faire leurs grans besoin(f.109v)gnes? Certes nennil. Furent il fait pour estre bordelier ne aler es tavernes? Certes nenil. Furent il fait pour avoir en despit n'en desdaing povres genz? Certes nennil. Furent il fait pour jurer ne malgroyer villainement Dieu ne la Virge Marie ne sains ne

good or bad, will spread throughout the world, more than would be the case for many of middle rank. If anyone would like to know why and how the emperors, kings and princes of lands were raised up and made lords over their people, the reasons for doing this and the way it was done were good, holy and just; for the persons with the best physical qualities and the highest standard of moral conduct, selected from among all the people, these men chose them at that time; from these descended the emperors, kings, and princes of today.° And do you think that those above-mentioned who were the first to be selected, were chosen to be lords to take their ease and their pleasure? Indeed no! Were they chosen because they did not love God and his works and the Holy Church? Indeed no! Were they chosen to harm the common people and to obtain profit for themselves? Indeed no! Were they created to impoverish their people and enrich themselves without good cause? Indeed no! Were they created to have power and riches and to make ill use of them? Indeed no! Were they created not to maintain justice for the humble as well as for the great? Indeed no! Were they created to be cruel, without pity and without mercy? Indeed no! Were they created to linger for a long time in idleness and to make little effort? Indeed no! Were they created so that they might eat and drink as luxuriously as they could? Indeed no! Were they chosen in order to refrain from taking up arms and from exposing themselves to the perils of battle in the defense of their lands and people? Indeed no! Were they chosen in order to be cowards? Indeed no! Were they chosen to be miserly and not give to those who deserve it? Indeed no! Were they chosen to lead dishonest and ill famed lives? Indeed no! Were they elected to be generous to the unworthy and to bestow gifts on wastrels? Indeed no! Were they chosen to cherish and believe in the unworthy and the flatterers? Indeed no! Were they chosen in order to send away from their company men of worth? Indeed no! Were they chosen to shut themselves up in their houses where no one can speak to them? Indeed no! Were they chosen to lie and to break their promises, oaths, and sealed agreements? Indeed no! Were they chosen to commit, have others commit, or give consent to any misdeed? Indeed no! Were they chosen to have any pleasant relations or friendship with those who lead a wicked life? Indeed no! Were they chosen in order to take pleasure in listening to dissolute conversation or in watching worthless pastimes? Indeed no! Were they chosen in order to take pleasure in listening to malicious comments on others in their presence? Indeed no! Were they chosen so that when they meet adversity they cannot endure it or bear it? Indeed no! Were they chosen in order to be proud, arrogant, and cruel to

saintes? Certes nennil. Furent il faiz pour estre oyseux et nient faire? Certes nennil. Furent il faiz pour ce qu'il ne sceussent ou voussissent parler a ceulz qui viennent vers eulz? Certes nennil.

25   Or convient il donques aprés toutes ces demandes et responses venir a la verité pour quoy telz empereeurs, roys et princes de grans peuples et terres furent eslevez et faiz. Or devez savoir que en celi temps il eslisoient entre eulz ceulz que il veoient qui avoient bon corps, fort et bien taillié de souffrir paine en touz estaz et pour travaillier ou bon gouvernement de leur peuple, tant en temps de leurs guerres comme en temps de paiz.° Ycelles genz ne ycelz seigneurs n'estoient mie eslevez pour avoir les grans repos ne les grans deduis ne les grans delices, mes pour avoir plus grans paines et travaulx que nulz des autres. Et avec les personnes esleues teles comme j'ay dit dessus, regardoient il et demandoient et enqueroient diligenment de toutes leurs condicions afin qu'il fussent souffisans de gouverner li° peuple; adonc les eslisoient il. Si devez savoir qu'il estoient esleuz et faiz pour avoir plus de paines de travaulx de corps et de mesaises en leurs (f.110r) cuers que nulz autres de leur peuple pour la grant charge qu'il prenoient et avoient ou gouvernement dont il estoient esleuz et chargiez.° Adonc il avoient tres grant diligence de bien gouverner leur peuple, si estoient esleuz et faiz pour amer, doubter et servir Dieu et toutes ses oevres.° Dont furent il faiz pour faire le proffit du peuple avant que le leur singulier. Dont furent il faiz pour garder leur peuple sanz rienz prendre du leur fors que teles droitures comme il estoient tenuz a leurs seigneurs, et non mie les seigneurs eulz enrichir sur la povreté de leurs peuples sanz causes raisonnables. Dont furent il faiz pour despendre leur richesces en toutes bonnes euvres, si qu'il ne soient repris de les mal emploier. Dont furent il faiz pour fair[e] raison et justice autant au petit comme au grant et tout droit.° Dont furent il faiz pour estre piteus et plains de misericorde la ou elle doit appartenir. Dont furent il faiz pour po sejourner et assez travaillier pour le bien de leur commun peuple.° Dont furent il faiz pour eulz armer les premiers et travaillier et mettre leurs corps es aventures de batailles pour la deffension de

those who serve them? Indeed no! Were they chosen in order to go and take their pleasure in sports of the woods and rivers instead of undertaking their great tasks? Indeed no! Were they chosen to be whoremongers or frequenters of taverns? Indeed no! Were they chosen so that they could despise and disdain poor men? Indeed no! Were they chosen in order to curse or blaspheme wickedly against God or the Virgin Mary or the saints? Indeed no! Were they chosen in order to be idle and to do nothing? Indeed no! Were they chosen so that they could not and would not speak to those who approach them? Indeed no!

The True Function for Which Rulers Were Created

25 Now, after all these questions and answers, we must come to the true explanation for the creation of such emperors, kings, and princes of great lands and peoples. You should know that at that time were chosen those who were seen to have good physique, strong, and well equipped to endure hardship of all kinds and to strive for the good government of their people, whether in time of war or of peace.° These personages and these lords were not raised up to have great periods of rest nor great pleasures nor great delights, but to endure more and to strive harder than any of the others.° And in relation to the persons chosen as explained above, they were examined and questioned and interrogated diligently concerning their qualities in order to discover whether they were fit persons to govern the people, and then they were chosen. You should know that they were chosen in order to endure and withstand greater physical hardship, painful exertions, and mental anxiety than any of their people because of the heavy responsibility they had taken on in the task of government for which they had been chosen and with which they had been entrusted.° They showed then great diligence in giving their people good government, and they were chosen that they might love, fear, and serve God and all his works.° They were, therefore, chosen so that they might place the people's profit before their own. They were, therefore, chosen that they might protect their people without taking anything from them apart from those dues the people owed to their lord, and it was not for the lords to enrich themselves at the cost of impoverishing the people without reasonable cause. They were, therefore, chosen to spend their wealth on all kinds of good works so that they were not reproached for making ill use of it. They were, therefore, chosen to administer justice and to maintain the rights of the humble as well as of the mighty.° They were, therefore, chosen that they might show pity and mercy where appropriate. They were, therefore, chosen that they might avoid

leur peuple et de leurs terres. Dont furent il faiz pour estre hardiz et de bon courage a l'encontre de leurs ennemis et de touz ceulz qui rienz leur voudroient oster du leur ne de leur honnour. Dont furent il faiz pour donner du leur et estre larges envers les bons qui bien l'avoient deservi et a ceulz qui taillié estoient du desservir et es povres pour eulz soustenir.° Dont furent il faiz pour estre eschars et garder le leur sanz le donner ne departir a (f.110v) malvaises gens ne de chetif estat, ne pour faire mauvaises oeuvres. Dont furent il faiz pour mener vies teles et si honestes que nulz mauvais reproches ne fust en eulz ne nuls diffamez de mauvaises vies ne deshonestes et que touz devoient prendre exemple a leur bonne et honeste vie. Dont furent il faiz pour chacier et eslongier fors de leur* compaignie toutes chetives genz, bourdeurs et flateurs et touz autres de chetifs courages. Dont furent il faiz pour amer, honorer et tenir chier et croire les bons et les sages et preudommes et amer leur compagnie et tenir pres de eulz. Dont furent il fais pour eulz monstrer souvent et estre entre la gent pour souvent oïr et respondre des choses qui peuent toucher a eulz et a autruy et a aucune foiz eulz jouer entre les leur. Dont furent il faiz pour tenir ce qu'il promettoient et disoient de leur bouche veritablement, dont par plus forte raison devoient il tenir leurs seremens et seellez sanz corrumpre. Dont furent il faiz pour eulz garder que en nulle maniere nul consaintement ne fust en eulz de faire ne faire faire ne de souffrir a faire nulz mauvais faiz ne mauvaises oeuvres. Dont furent il faiz pour eslongier d'entour eulz et de leur compaignie toutes gens de mauvais estat et de malvaise vie et de en avoir nulle plaisance. Dont furent il faiz pour ce qu'il ne deussent avoir nulle plaisance de oïr paroles deshonestes ne de jouer ne veoir jouer a nulz chietiz jeux. Dont furent il faiz que pour leur noblece ne devoient souffrir de mesdire (f.111r) d'autruy ne d'ommes ne de femmes ne d'en parler vilainement sanz cause. Dont furent il faiz que quant adversitez leur avenoit ou aucunes persecucions, qu'il les sceussent souffrir et soustenir sagement et vassement et de fort courage. Dont furent il faiz, quant il sont en leur grans poissances et en leurs grans hautesces et seignouries et a leurs grans victoires dessus leurs ennemis, que il les sachent avoir et demener humblement et sanz orgueil, et [estre] misericors, sanz desmesuree fierté, et en regraciant et rendant touz les biens qu'il ont a celui de qui il les tiennent et qui leur a donnez et qui tout leur peut retolir toutes foiz qu'il li plaist. Dont furent il faiz que pour prendre ne veoir les deduis des chiens ne des oyseaus en boys ne en rivieres que tant les deussent amer ne avoir plaisance qu'il en deussent delaissier a faire ne jour ne heure de leurs besoingnes neccessaires a leur bon gouvernement pour eulz ne pour leur peuple. Dont furent il faiz que en nulle place

long stays in one place° and to exert themselves for the good of their common people. They were, therefore, chosen to be the first to take up arms and to strive with all their might and expose themselves to the physical dangers of battle in defence of their people and their land. They were, therefore, chosen to be bold and of good courage against their enemies and against all those who seek to deprive them of possessions or honor. They were, therefore, chosen to give of their own freely and generously to men of worth who had well deserved it and to those likely to deserve it and to the poor to sustain them.° They were, therefore, chosen to be careful and to conserve what they have without giving or distributing it to unworthy people nor to those of poor standing nor for the committing of evil deeds. They were, therefore, chosen so that they might lead lives of such integrity that no reproach could be levelled against them, nor could they be held in ill repute for any unworthy or shameful behavior; for their good and honest way of life should set an example for others. They were, therefore, chosen so that they might drive away from their company all worthless people, all liars and flatterers, and all others of a base disposition, and to avoid all association with them. They were, therefore, chosen to love, honor, and hold dear the good and the wise and the men of worth, to pay heed to their words, to associate closely with them and enjoy their company. They were, therefore, chosen to show themselves often and to move among the people, to listen often and to give replies concerning matters which may affect themselves and others, and sometimes to disport themselves with their own men. They were, therefore, chosen in order to keep their spoken promises, and so, for even stronger reasons, they should keep their sworn and sealed undertakings and never declare them null and void. They were, therefore, chosen that they might keep away from themselves and their company all men of ill repute and evil way of life and to take no pleasure in them. They were, therefore, chosen that they might take no delight in hearing any shameful words or in playing or watching any worthless games. They were, therefore, chosen so that their nobility would not tolerate the slandering of others, neither men nor women, nor the speaking ill of people without good cause. They were, therefore, chosen so that when they encountered adversity or persecution, they should know how to endure and bear them wisely and valiantly and with great courage. They were, therefore, chosen, so that when they are at the height of their power and lordship and at the time of their great victories over their enemies, they would know how to behave in this position, with due humility and without arrogance, and showing mercy, without excessive pride and ferocity, giving thanks and ac-

deshoneste ne deussent aler ne repairier come es bordeaux et es tavernes, que ce ne sont mie lieux ne places la ou nulz grans seigneurs doient monstrer qu'il y aient ne doient avoir nulle plaisance, tant pour leurs bons estaz garder comme pour la deshonesteté, dont li pluseurs voudroient faire autretel a l'exemplaire des grans seigneurs qui ainsi le feroient. Dont furent il faiz que nulles povres gens, homes ne fames, ne deussent avoir en desdaing ne en despit d'eulz oïr et delivrer benignement et plus que le plus riches;° car il n'ont mie si bien le dequoy pour (f.111v) poursuigre leurs besoingnes comme les plus riches, dont maintes povres genz en ont perdu a avoir leur raison par longuement poursuivre et par deffaute de mise. Dont furent il faiz que en nulle maniere ne deussent villainement parler ne jurer Nostre Seigneur ne la Vierge Marie ne les sains et saintes, que quant plus sont grans et plus doivent garder que Dieux soit doubtez, amez, serviz et honorez en faiz et en parler partout la ou il sont. Dont furent il faiz pour ce que nulle oisiveté ne deust estre en eulz, que il ne deussent touzjours penser et labourer ou bien d'eulz et de leur peuple. Dont furent il faiz pour ce que il sceussent parler et respondre souffisaument selon ce que l'on leur requiert ou dit ou demande.

26 Or pouez vous veoir et cognoistre par les condicions dessus dites les bons princes et les chetiz princes; car ceulz qui sont mieux condicionnez sont meilleurs des autres, et ceulz qui moins en ont tant valent il moins, et ceulz qui ont plus de mauvaises condicions que de bonnes ne sont dignes de terre tenir ne de peuple gouverner. Et tout autretel est il a parler sur les autres seigneurs comme dux, contes, barons et autres seigneurs de grans terres et peuples a gouverner, de quelque estat qu'il soient, et aussi touz autres seigneurs, tant soient de moyen estat: que touzjours qui miex fait qu'il ne soit li miex louez, prisiez et honnorez entre touz autres. Et n'est ce

knowledging their indebtedness for all that they have to God from whom they hold it and who gave it to them and who can take everything away from them again whenever it may please Him. They were, therefore, chosen so that, when participating in or watching the pleasure of the chase, with hawk or hound, in the woods or by the river, however much they might enjoy these sports and take delight in them, that this should not lead them to neglect neither for a day nor even an hour the duties required to maintain good government both on their own behalf and on that of their people. They were, therefore, chosen so that they should not visit nor frequent disreputable places such as brothels and taverns, for they are not places in which great lords should let it be seen that they take pleasure, for the sake of their own good reputation and in order not to incite disreputable behavior, for many might want to follow the example set by the great lords in relation to such places. They were, therefore, chosen so that they should not despise any poor people, whether men or women, nor disdain to listen to them, and should treat them more benevolently than they would treat richer men; for they have not the same means to carry on their affairs as have the richer men, and as a result, many poor men, on account of their lack of financial means, have failed to achieve by their lengthy endeavors what by right they should have done. They were, therefore, chosen so that they should in no way use bad language nor curse in the name of Our Lord or that of the Virgin Mary or those of the saints, for the higher their rank the more they should make sure that God be feared, loved, served and honored in word and deed wherever they are. They were, therefore, chosen that there might be no idleness in them, lest they might not always devote all their thoughts and efforts to striving on behalf of themselves and their people. They were, therefore, chosen so that they might know how to speak and respond adequately in relation to what is asked or requested of them.

The Good Rulers Contrasted with the Unworthy

26   Now you can perceive and know by the qualities set out above which are the good and which are the unworthy princes, for those who have more of these qualities are superior to the others; and those who have less are to that degree inferior; and those who have more bad characteristics than good are not worthy to hold land or govern people; and the same can be said of other lords such as dukes, counts, barons, and others of whatever rank, in relation to ruling over great lands and peoples. And it can also be said of all nobles, be they only of middle rank: he who does best will he not always be the most praised, esteemed, and honored? And is it not

10 dont grant merveille de ceulz qui miex aiment faire le mal et mener les chietives vies et faire les cheitives oeuvres que (f.112r) les bonnes? Car les mals a faire sont honteux, doubteux et perilleux a faire; et les chietives vies sont de grant diffame et blasme et acroissement de pechiez; et les chietives oeuvres sont pour estre avec les bons deshonestement et deshonorablement et pour
15 venir a tres malvaise fin. Or est ce donques a cognoistre fermement et seurement que les bons faiz, les bonnes vies, et les bonnes oeuvres sont plus plaisans a faire et a mener que ne sont les malvaises dont dessus est dit; car ceulz qui font les bons faiz, il les font liement et seurement et sanz nulle doubte de malvaise reproche. Et ceulz qui mainnent les bonnes vies peuent
20 aler bonnement partout et plainement et sanz nulle doubtance. Et ceulz qui font les bonnes oeuvres, yceulz ne doivent tenir nul compte d'envie ne de haynne que l'on ait sur eulz ne de nul mal que l'on en die ne que on leur veille faire; car leurs bons faiz, leurs bonnes vies et leurs bonnes oeuvres les porteront, gouverneront et sauveront seurement partout. Et tout en autele
25 maniere pouroit l'en parler sur les princes et prelaz de Sainte Eglise qui voudroit, comme sur papes, cardinaux, patriarches, arcevesques, evesques, abbez et autres ministres de Sainte Eglise et qui ont cures d'armes; mais a gens laïcs n'en appartient mie a tant parler, si s'en doit l'en taire le miex que l'en peut.

27   Or pour ce que vous avez cy devant oÿ parler des (f.112v) meurs*, des condicions et des estas des grans princes et autres seigneurs et moyens dont uns chascuns, de quelque estat qu'il soient, se doivent travaillier de avoir en eulz le plus des bonnes, que quant plus en avront, et miex vaudront et plus
5 liement et plus honorablement en vivront; si en y pourroit avoir aucuns qui pour une ou deux bonnes condicions qu'il pourroient avoir penseroient et cuideroient que pour ycelles se deussent passer et du remenant ne pourroit chaloir; et pour ce est il donques raison que les biens que peuent et doivent faire ycelles gens qui honnour d'armes veulent avoir et acquerir, soient un
10 po escharciz° a la fin de en avoir cognoissance. Si pouez et devez savoir assez que les meilleurs condicions que nulz puisse avoir, si est d'estre preudoms, comment ainsi qu'il appartient entierement de le estre. Et a dire que l'en soit preudoms, en y a d'aucuns que l'en peut bien tenir a preudommes pour la grant simplece qui est en eulz, et a grant paine savroient il faire le mal, se
15 tout le vouloient il faire, tant sont simple d'eulz mesmes. Et pour ce que les biens sont plus aaisiez a faire et a gouverner que les mals ne sont, pour ce ycelles simples genz si se prennent a les faire, et toutevoies font il que saiges,

very strange that there are those who prefer to do evil and lead vile lives and do vile deeds rather than good ones? Surely, ill deeds are shameful, fearful, and dangerous to commit, and unworthy ways of life bring shame, blame, and an increase of sin, and unworthy acts lead to behaving in a shameful and dishonorable way in relation to worthy men, bringing one to a bad end. It should, therefore, be recognized firmly and with certainty that deeds of valor, a good way of life, and good undertakings are more pleasant to carry out than are the above-mentioned bad ones; for those who perform deeds of valor do so gladly, confidently and without fear of reproach; and those who lead a good life can fittingly go anywhere freely and without fear. Those who carry out noble undertakings should take no account of envy or hatred of which they may be the object or of any ill which may be said of them or which people may want to do to them; for their deeds of valor, way of life and noble undertakings will bear them along, direct them, and keep them safe everywhere. And the same could be said by anyone who might want to speak of the princes and prelates of the Holy Church such as popes, cardinals, patriarchs, archbishops, bishops, priests, and other ministers of the Holy Church who have the care of souls, but it does not befit lay people to speak more of this, rather they should hold their peace as best they can.

The Scale of Qualities in a Man of Worth: Simplicity of Heart
27 Now I have described to you above the way of life, the qualities and conduct of great princes and other lords, including those of middle rank, in which each person of whatever degree should strive to achieve the very highest standard so that they will be of greater worth and will live more happily and honorably. There might, then, be some persons who, for one or two good qualities which they might have, might think and believe that these will suffice for them and that it would not matter about the rest, and it is therefore right that the good exploits that should be performed by those people who want to achieve honor at arms should finally be described a little more clearly° in order that it should be known what they are. You can and ought to know that the best qualities that anyone can aim for and achieve is to be a man of worth, according to what is required to attain this completely. As for declaring some one to be a man of worth, there are some whom one can well hold to be men of worth for their pure simplicity of heart, and they would scarcely know how to do wrong, even if they wanted to do so, for they are themselves so innocent. And because good actions are easier to do and to control than are evil ones, these simple people set out to

que les biens sont les meilleurs a tenir. Et encores peut il avoir en aucuns plus de biens que ces simples genz n'en ont, que j'ay dit devant. (f.113r)

28   En autre maniere peut l'en tenir les aucuns a preudommes qui font des ausmosnes assez et volentiers sont es eglises et oyent des messes assez et moult dient de paternostres et autres oroisons et jeunent les caresmes et les autres jeunes commandees. Mais peut estre que en aucuns d'iceulz a condicions contraires a celles et que chascuns n'apperçoit mie si plennement comme les biens que j'ay dit dessus, comme de convoitise en leurs cuers couvertement ou d'envie sur autrui ou de hayne et male volenté ou de plusers autres choses qui leur amaindrissent, quant a Dieu, une grant partie des biens devant diz. Et si les tient l'en a preudommes pour les biens qui en eulz s'apparissent; mais toutevois pourroit l'en miex faire quant a estre preudoms.

29   Se*° y sont ceulz que un chascuns doivent tenir a preudommes. Ce sont ceulz qui ayment Dieu, servent et honorent, et sa tres douce mere et toute sa poissance, et se gardent de faire les oevres dont il les doient courroucier, et qui ont en eulz teles condicions et si seures que leurs vies ne soient reprouvees de nulz vilains pechiez ne de malvais reproches, et ainsi vivent loyaument et honestement. Et ceulz doit l'en tenir a preudommes. Et ainsi pourroit l'en tenir les aucuns a saiges, dont les uns ont sens assez, mais il tournent leurs sens en si tres grant malice que il en deperdent (f.113v) le droit bon sens naturel dont il deussent et sceussent bien user, s'il eussent voulu, mais il le attournent et mettent leur sens plus a mal que a bien, et toutevois convient il sans en faire le mal, mais il n'est mie bon de savoir ne de avoir tel veus.

30   Se* en y a d'autres que li aucuns tiennent a saiges, mais il mettent leur sens et leur entente en si subtilz engin que les grans subtillitez les destour[n]ent* aucunes fois de venir a droit sens loyal, et ainsi yteles subtilles genz sont descordans en toutes besoingnes. Ainsi comme ceulz qui se departent d'un bon grant chemin pour aler les santiers et puis se forvoient, tout autretel est il que de leur grant subtilleté perdent a ouvrer du droit bon

perform them all; all the same, in doing this they behave wisely, for it is better to hold to the good. Yet there may be greater virtues in some than are to be found in these aforementioned simple people.

Those Who Present Themselves Outwardly as Generous and Devout
28   Some may be held to be in a different way men of worth, that is those who give alms freely and like to be in church and attend mass frequently and say many paternosters and other prayers and fast in Lent and other recommended fasts. But perhaps there are in some of those men less obvious characteristics opposed to the good qualities mentioned above: for example, there may be concealed in their hearts greed or envy of others or hatred or ill will or many other things that detract from a great part of the good characteristics mentioned above. They are held to be men of worth for the characteristics which are apparent in them, but nevertheless one can do better as far as being a man of worth is concerned.

Those Who Act Loyally and Serve God
29   And° there are those who should be held to be men of worth by everyone. That is those who love, serve, and honor God and His gentle Mother and all His power, and refrain from actions by which they might incur Their wrath, and who have within them such steadfast qualities that their way of life cannot be criticized for any vile sins nor for any shameful reproach, and they thus live loyally and honestly. And these should be held to be men of worth. Thus some could be considered wise who are very clever, but they direct their intelligence to such malicious ends that they lose the true and natural good sense which men ought and should know how to use were they to have the will to do so, but they set their intelligence to work toward evil rather than good; nevertheless intelligence is needed to perform such evil deeds, but it is not good to have knowledge combined with such intentions.

Those Who Are Too Ingenious and Over Subtle
30   And there are others whom some consider to be wise, but they put all their intelligence and concentrated effort into such cunning schemes that their great subtlety sometimes turns them aside from reaching a true, loyal, and sensible conclusion, so that these subtle people are out of step in all undertakings. Like those who leave the good main road to follow minor paths and then get lost, in the same way, through their great subtlety they

sens naturel. Et pour ce n'est ce mie tout le bien de sens que l'en pourroit bien avoir que de mettre s'entente en tres grans subtillitez.

31   Se en y a d'aucuns lesquelz un chascun doivent tenir a saiges: ce sont ceulx qui a leurs commancemens mettent paine et diligence de cognoistre qu'est miex a faire, et le bien et le mal, et ce qui est a faire de raison, et pour ce qu'il ont cognoissance qu'est a faire au contraire de la raison, se prennent
5 eulz a gouverner eulz mesmes sagement, loyaument et seurrement et tout droit. Et s'il ont a faire a autruy, ytelles gens ne demandent point le droit d'autruy, mais le leur veulent garder souverainement et leur honnour (f.114r) aussi. Et encores ycelles gens scevent bien conseillier autruy loyaument et sagement. Et ycelles genz euvrent partout de bon sens sanz nul
10 mauvais malice et non pas par ses tres grans subtilletez et sanz nul malvais reproche. Yceuls doit l'en tenir vrais saiges, et telx sens est bon de quoy l'en use bien en tout.

32   Or vient a parler de celles bonnes genz d'armes que l'on tient a preux, dont il en y a d'aucuns qui sont bons de la main, hardis et apers, mais leur maniere de besoingner ou mestier d'armes est touzjours tele* que quant il sont sur les besoignes faire, il n'y regardent profit, ne avantage pour leurs
5 amis, ne a la grant grevance de leurs ennemis, mais sanz conseil donner ne prendre fierent des esperons et a po d'arroy, et font d'armes assez de leur main et moult de fois plus a leur domage que a leur profit, mais de l'onneur de la main font il assez, et en ceste maniere se sont il trouvez en pluseurs bonnes journees sanz autre estat ne maniere de le faire; mais contre
10 l'onnour de hardiesce ne leur peut l'en rienz reprouver; et a ceuls qui tant de bonnes journees ont veues et esté aidant de si bon ouvrage de la main et de leurs corps comme il y ont fait, l'en les doit bien appeller preux, combien que, quant a estre preus a droit, l'en y pourroit encores miex faire.

33   Si en y a encores d'autres bonnes gens d'armes et que l'en doit bien tenir a preux. Ce sont ceulz qui en maintes places et lieux et en lointains païs estran(f.114v)ges vont querir et ont trouvees les besoignes et en conduit d'autruy et sanz autre gouvernement avoir, et po s'en sont entremis de gou-

fail to act according to natural good sense, and therefore they will not profit fully from their natural intelligence through setting their mind to such great subtlety.

Those Who Are Truly Wise

31   And there are some whom everyone should consider to be wise. It is those who, from their youth, strive diligently to learn what is best to do, to distinguish good from evil, and to know what is reasonable to do; and because they recognize what course of action would be against reason, they endeavor to behave loyally, confidently, and according to what is right. And in their dealings with others, such people do not seek to take away the rights of others, but want above all to protect such rights for them and their honor as well. And in addition, these people know well how to advise others honestly and wisely, without any evil malice, not using excessive subtlety, and without incurring shameful reproach. These should be held to be truly wise, and such power of reasoning is good if it is always put to good use.

Those Who Have Courage and Skill But Are Thoughtless

32   Now it is time to speak of those good men-at-arms who are held to be valiant, of whom there are some who are skilled in handling weapons, brave, and adept, but their way of pursuing a career in arms is always such that when they are in action, they do not consider the benefit or advantage for their friends or the harm done to their enemies, but, without giving or taking advice, they spur forward in a disorderly way and perform personally many feats of arms. This is often more to their disadvantage than to their advantage, but they achieve many striking deeds of arms, and in this way take part in many good battles without attempting to contribute in any other way, but they cannot be reproached in relation to the honor earned through bravery; and these men, who have seen so many great days of combat and made such a fine contribution by their physical exploits, should indeed be called worthy, although as for being worthy in the truest sense, it would be possible to do better.

Those Who Perform Great Deeds But Do Not Lead or Advise

33   There are yet other good men-at-arms who should be held to be worthy. That is those who have gone in search of military undertakings in many places, in distant lands and foreign parts, and have found them where another is in command, so that they have no responsibilities of leadership,

vernement ne de conseil donner, mais ont prises les besoignes ainsi comme il les ont trouvees a leur honneur et sanz nul reproche. Et toutevoies, quant Dieu leur a donné tele grace de tant travaillier et trouver tant de bonnes journees d'armes a leur honneur, l'en les doit bien tenir a preux, combien que, quant a tel estat de prouece, l'en puisse encore miex faire.

34 Encores en y a d'autres qui° souverainement l'en doit plus tenir a preux. Ce sont ceulz qui en leur joennesce ont mis es places et journees qu'il ont trouvees leurs corps en aventure baudement et hardiement et sanz nulle doubtance ne pensee de mort, de prison ne de mise pour querir teles aventures, car trop grant sens n'est mie bon a jones genz en leur commancement d'estre es faiz d'armes. Et quant ycelles jeunes gens ont cognoissance a quoy li faiz des armes peuent monter ne a quoy il peuent valoir tant de l'onne[u]r comme du peril, si se met en ycelles bonnes gens d'armes sens et cognoissance de tout cognoistre. Et pour la grant cognoissance que il en ont, ycelles genz, pour les aventures ou il se sont trouvez en leur joennesce, et il s'en avisent et leur en souvient, dont se prennent il en ouvrer sagement en leur fait, quant il leur en avient le besoing de leurs guerres mesmes, et bien leur en chiet pour leur bon sens et gouvernement qu'il y scevent faire, et aussi scevent il bien aidier et con(f.115r)seillier autruy de l'autruy guerre. Et celles bonnes genz dont l'en voit tant de cognoissance et de hardement es faiz d'armes, a yceulz baille l'en les gouvernemens des gens d'armes et pour les mener et gouverner en faiz d'armes comme chevetaines, connestables, mareschaux ou en autres estaz de gouvernemens des faiz des armes. Et quant yteles bonnes gens d'armes sont ainsi approuvez de leur bon ouvrage de leur main et de leur corps, de leur bon travail et de leur bon sens, de leur bon avis, de leur bonnes hardiesces asseurees et de leurs bonnes paroles qui y sont bien seans en telx fais et de bonnes contenances que l'en voit en eulx sur les durs partis que l'on peut trouver es faiz d'armes, tant a leur dessus comme a leur dessous, et du bon reconfort qui en eulz est et doit estre en touz estaz, ne de nulle taiche ne sont entoichiez dont l'en doie dire nulle vilennie sur euls en nulz estat. Et ycelles bonnes genz d'armes qui assez de bonnes aventures et bonnes journees ont trouvees et veues et dont touzjours se sont passé si tres honorablement comme a la bonne louange de touz, et de leurs amis et de leurs ennemis, ycelles genz sont ceulz de quoy l'on fait les preus qui passent ceulz dont est devant parlé; car li assez

and they have not involved themselves much in leading or in giving advice, but have undertaken whatever fighting has presented itself to them in an honorable way and without reproach. Nevertheless, when, through God's grace, they have been given the opportunity for so much strenuous effort and for so many good days of combat where they can win honor, they should be held to be worthy, although in relation to such a standard of prowess, one might do better.

The True Men of Worth, Brave and of Good Counsel
34   There are yet others who should above all men be held to be of great worth. That is those who in their youth, in the places and the battles in which they have taken part, have risked their lives gladly and boldly and without any thought or fear of death, of prison, or of the expense which might be incurred in seeking these adventures, for too much good sense is not right for young men at the beginning of their career in arms. And when these young men learn what the practice of arms involves or what it can mean in terms of both honor and danger, these good men-at-arms acquire wisdom and understanding which lead to full knowledge. And through the great knowledge that these men have gained from the adventures they encountered in their youth and through what they learned and remembered from their experiences, they begin to act wisely on their own behalf when the need arises in their wars, and all goes well for them because of their good sense and the way they know how to conduct themselves; they also know well how to help and counsel others in their wars. And these good men in whom is to be found so much experience and bravery in the practice of arms are entrusted with the command of men-at-arms to lead them in combat as captains, constables, and marshals or in other offices concerned with the direction of the practice of arms. The quality of these good men-at-arms has been thus fully proved through their great physical exploits, through their strenuous efforts of endurance, through their good sense and wise counsel, through their great acts of true valor and their fine words, which are indeed fitting in relation to such deeds, through their splendid bearing, to be seen under the very difficult conditions often to be encountered in the practice of arms, whether winning or losing, through the great support which should and is to be found in them in all situations, and finally through the absence of any characteristics which could under any circumstances be criticized or condemned. And these are the good men-at-arms who have sought out and experienced many fine adventures and battles, in which they always acquit themselves with great honor, receiving

trouver des bonnes journees et li souvent y faire son tres grant honour fait a cognoistre l'espreuve de ceuls qui y deviennent preus; car les bonnes espreuves que celles bonnes gens d'armes ont faites en assez et pluseurs bonnes journees d'armes leur font avoir celle renommee de proesce dont chascuns les doivent tenir et tiennent a preux, qui est uns tres haut noms en armes, et ycelles genz sont (f.115v) entre touz autres preus dessus diz a prisier, loer et honnorer souverainement.

35 Or appartient, aprés touz ces biens dessus diz, que il soit parlé d'unes autres manieres de gens qui sont et doivent estre les plus souveraines qui soient entre toutes gens laycs et seculiers. Ce sont et doivent estre unes genz qui sont appellez villanz° hommes, et ycelles villans genz si sont li plus honnorez, plus amez et plus prisiez que nulles autres genz d'armes qui soient. Et pour ce que l'en puisse miex avoir la cognoissance des villans hommes est il assavoir comment ne pourquoy l'en les doit et devroit tenir a telx. Si devez savoir que se uns homs avoit sens assez et il ne fust preudoms, cilz deus[t] se convertir* du tout en mal. Et se uns homs estoit preudoms et ne fust mie assez saiges, tele preudommie est bonne mais non mie tant vallable ne de si grant merite comme li saige de droit sens naturel qui sont vrai preudomme. Et quant a avoir le nom de proesce, et l'on ne soit preudoms ne sages, en tele prouesce n'attendez ja a la fin nulle grant perfection. Et pour ce est il que se vous avez cognoissance que sur aucune personne ait tele grace de avoir et de user de tel sens comme le meilleur de trois manieres de sens dessus devisiez, et vous aiez cognoisance que en celui mesmes ait toutes condicions de preudomm[i]e*, mesmes la meilleur condicion des trois manieres et de preudommie° dont il est fait mencion ci dessur, et en celi meismes vous aiez cognoissance qu'il a en li droite loyal prouesce et tele comme la (f.116r) meilleur des trois manieres et de preuesce° dont dessus est dit, yceli ou ceulz en qui touz les trois souverains biens sont enz* et sont et demeurent et perseverent jusques au mourir, certes tenez fermement ycelles genz a* villanz, car il ont en volenté de valoir, si ont il valu et si valent et que touz au miex mettent paine de valoir enjusques a la mort. Et pour toutes ces valours sont il tenuz a villans hommes, et a teles genz fait* bon prendre exemplaire et mettre paine de faire les ouvres pour eulz resembler. Si devez savoir que en nulle maniere nul qui soit en cestui monde, ne qui

universal praise from friend and foe alike. It is from such as these that those men of worth are made who surpass those who have been spoken of before, for often to seek out good days of battle and often to perform with great honor serve to provide evidence for all to see of the valor of those who prove their worth there, for the fine proofs of valor which these excellent men-at-arms have furnished in many good days in the pursuit of arms give them this renown for prowess, for which everyone should consider them to be men of worth, the most glorious name to win in the practice of arms. And these men are to be prized and honored above all the other men of prowess described above.

The Men-at-Arms of Supreme Worth
35   After this examination of all these good qualities and achievements described above, it is now time to speak of another category of men who are and ought to be supreme among all lay people. These are men who are rightly said to be of high merit, and are more honored, better loved and prized than any other men-at-arms. And in order better to learn about the men of high merit, one needs to know how and why they should be held in such high esteem. You should know that if a man were sufficiently intelligent but not a man of worth, his intelligence would be turned wholly to evil. And if a man were of worth and had not enough wisdom, he would still be of merit, but not of such value and of such merit as the wise men of natural good sense who are true men of worth. And as for having a reputation for prowess without being a man of worth or wise, do not expect in the end any great perfection in such prowess. For this reason, if you know of some one who is endowed with the gift of the kind of intelligence presented as the best of the three kinds of intelligence described above, and you know that in this person is also to be found all the qualities of a man of worth, the very best of the three kinds of worth, as mentioned above, and you know that in addition there is in this man true and loyal prowess, of the best of the three kinds described above, so that this man and others like him combine within themselves throughout their lives these three supreme qualities, if you find such a man or men, consider them to be most assuredly of high merit. You should indeed do so because they had the will to be of high merit, and indeed they have been and are of high merit, and they strive to their utmost to be of high merit until death. And it is good to take such men as examples and to strive to act in such a way as to resemble them. You should know that in no way can anyone in the world, now or in the past or the future, ever have such a complete set of good qualifications

onques y furent, ne que jamais y soient, ne peuent avoir eues, ne n'ont, ne jamais n'avront teles antieres bonnes condicions comme dessus est dit pour ces villans, se ce n'est purement de la droite grace de Nostre Seigneur et de sa tres douce mere et de sa glorieuse court. Et pour ce est il que ycelles genz a qui Nostre Sires a donné de sa grace tant de bontez ne doivent tenir ne penser ne cuidier que en nulle maniere nul de ces biens dessus nommez dont il sont tant amé, loé et honnorez que il leur soient venuz de leur mesmes. Nennil voir, que s'il avoient ceste tres oultrecuidiee pensee, certes tout autresi comme la noif se deffait par la poissance de la chaleur que le soleil li met sur, tout autretel est il des biens, des graces, des honnours, des hautesces, des poissances, des beautez, des sens, des preudomies, des prouesces et autres vertus qui pourroient estre sur aucuns. Et yceulz appliqueroient a leurs personnes, en pensant et cuidant que d'eulz vien(f.116v)gnent et leur soit venu, et ne rendent mie le grey ainsi comme il doivent et il sont tenu, a ce haut soleil, a ce tres haut Seigneur de qui il les ont et tiennent et n'en ont cognoissance, dont cilz tres haus Sires si fait decheoir et fondre tous ytels biens si mal desservis et si mal cogneus en pluseurs manieres come par maladies dont il endurent* tout leur temps et en perdent les gloires qu'il en avoient, tant des biens, des graces et des honnours qui tantost et en po de heure sont oublié et po ramenteu, et les hautesces et poissances sont tantost confondues par force d'anemis qui leur croissent, dont il sont abaissié de celle hautesse et amaindri durement de celle poissance. Et quant de la beauté de legier est effaciee et tantost passee, et pour ce donne Nostre Sires beauté es malvais pour ce que les bons ne cuident que ce soit trop grant chose. Et du sens vous devez estre certains que quant Nostre Sires veult grever les saiges qui ne le recognoissent, il leur oste le sens comme poissans de l'oster ainsi comme il est poissans de le donner. Et des preudommies dont li aucun pourroient avoir celle fol[e] creance qu'il ne pechassent ne peussent pechier, yceste fole creance les fait cheoir de leur entencion, car a eulz ne doivent il mie appliquier ceste grace*, mais a Dieu le tout poissant qui les donne et a qui l'en les doit regracier et requerir. Et se autrement le font, il cheent ou gouvernement et en la poissance du dyable, qui les maine a pechié et a dempnacion. Et des prouesces qui a grant paine et a grant peril sont acquises et par pluseurs (f.117r) annees, et en un[e] seule heure les peut l'en toutes perdre et a l'on perdues pour deffaute de recognoissance de celi qui les avoit donnees. Mes honte est si acoustumee et honnour si po cogneue ou temps de maintenant que l'on n'y fait compte, mais ceulz qui mettent paine de acquerir cestes honorables proesces et ceulz que Dieux a donné grace de les avoir acquises bien doivent tout leur temps re-

as have been described above as possessed by men of high merit, except purely by the grace of God and of His gentle Mother and of His heavenly court. And thus it is that these people whom Our Lord has of His grace endowed with so many gifts should not maintain nor think nor believe that in any way do any of these virtues listed above, for which they are so much loved, praised and honored, come from themselves. Indeed no, for if they had such an overweaningly proud thought, just as certainly as snow melts away through the powerful heat directed on it by the sun, so would it be for all the good things, the favors, the honors, the high estate, the power, the beauty, the intelligence, the worth, the prowess, and the other strengths which might be found in some one. Were these men to claim the credit for all these qualities, believing that they all stem from themselves, and were they not to give thanks as they should and it is their duty to do to this mighty sun, to this Almighty Lord from whom they have received them and hold them and do not acknowledge this, then this Almighty Lord would cause all these benefits, so ill merited and unacknowledged, to crumble and collapse in various ways, as, for example, by chronic illness through which they would lose the glory they had won. Thus many of the benefits, the favors, and the honors which in such a short time are forgotten and lapse into oblivion, and the high position and power are soon reduced to nothing by the force of their enemies, which increases so that they are brought down from this high position and their power is greatly diminished. As for beauty, it soon fades and vanishes, and because of this Our Lord grants beauty to the unworthy so that the worthy may not attach too great importance to it. As for intelligence, you can be certain that when Our Lord wants to harm the wise who do not acknowledge Him, He takes away their intelligence, as One who has the power to take away just as He has the power to give. And as for the reputation for worth on account of which some might have the foolish belief that they were not and could not be guilty of sin, it is this very belief which makes them fail in their intention, for they should not attribute this grace to themselves but to Almighty God who gives such gifts; it is He to whom thanks should be given and to whom entreaties should be made. And if these men do otherwise, they fall under the dominion and power of the devil who will lead them into sin and damnation. And as for the skills and achievements of prowess which are acquired through great effort and danger over a number of years, in one hour they can be and have been lost for lack of gratitude towards Him who granted them. But nowadays shame is so familiar and honor so unfamiliar that little account is taken of them, but those who put great effort into

gracier et mercier, loer et honorer Nostre Seigneur, prier et requerir humblement que ainsi comme il leur a donnees et faiz, que il ne leur veille retollir ne deffaire pour leurs dessertes. Et pour ce que vous aiez cognoissance
70 certaine et ferme es choses dessus dites, que nul ne se doit tenir fermes ne seurs de bien qu'il ait en soy qu'il en puisse bien user se par Nostre Seigneur ne l'a et de li li demeure, pouez vous prendre par exemple vray des anciens temps passez que Sanses li fors qui fu si tres fors, comme les anciennes ystoires le racontent, que par deseperance et par haynne arracha la cou-
75 lonme d'une maison pour tuer soy et les autres qui estoient dedens, et par ainsi mesusa il de sa force moult durement.° Et de Absalon qui fu si tres beaus comme nulz pouoit estre, et les plus beaus cheveux que nul peust porter, que pour la delectacion qu'il post° avoir de sa beauté, ainsi comme il chevauchoit dessouz un arbre, si cheveux s'athacherent a celli arbre, et
80 demoura penduz par ses beaux cheveux et la morust.° Et de Salomon qui fu si tres sages, si comme il est raconté es anciennes ystoires, il mesusa de son sens par tele (117v) maniere que pour l'amonestement de sa fame il se mist a aourer les ydoles en samblance de soy delaissier de la foy de Dieu, et ainsi failli a son sens tres villainement.° Et quant a parler de preudommie, mes-
85 sieres sains Pierres, qui tres fermement amoit et creoit Nostre Seigneur comme ses vrais disciples et apostres, ne le renoya il trois foiz en une nuit de sa bouche mais non mie de cuer? Et toutes les trois foiz pecha mortelment, dont moult tost se repenti et par la grace de Nostre Seigneur, comme vrais disciples, et toutes fois pecha il.° Dont fort chose seroit es preudom-
90 mes de maintenant qu'il peussent estre si fermes en la foy de Nostre Seigneur comme estoit cils sains preudoms messires sains Pierres qui ainsi sainctement vesqui et qui tant est honorez pour sa tres sainte vie. Et quant a parler de prouesce, Jullius Cesar,° qui si tres bon chevalier fu et tant fist et fu en tres grans et merveilleuses batailles et tant fist de belles conquestes
95 pour ceulz de Romme, et pour ce que a son retour de toutes ses honorables batailles et de toutes ses belles et profitables conquestes que il revint a Romme, il vit et cognust que par envie ceulz de Rome ne li firent mie tele honour comme il avoient a coustume de faire a ceulz et autres qui avoient conquesté et combatu pour l'onnour et prouffit de Rome et qui tant n'en
100 avoient mie fait, ce li sembloit, comme il avoit fait, en prist il en son cuer grant courrous et grant hayne encontre ceulz de Romme, dont il (f.118r) meismes estoit, et tant que depuis il les guerria et fist de grans domages et les conquist et se fist couronner empereur de Romme; et moult gouverna fort et fist deffendre que nulz ne portast coutel ne espee en son consistoire
105 pour doubte qu'il ne le tuassent, qu'il ne se pouoit fier en eulz. Si avint que

acquiring these honorable skills and achievements of prowess and those to whom God has by His grace granted that they should acquire them should indeed spend all their time giving thanks, praising and honoring Our Lord, praying and entreating humbly that as He has given and granted to them, so He will not take away and withdraw according to what they deserve. And so that you may have sure and certain knowledge of the things said above, that is, that no one should be confident concerning any good within him, that it can be put to any good use unless it be acknowledged that it comes from the Lord and depends upon Him, you can take Samson as a true example from ancient times: he was so strong, as the old accounts tell us, that through despair and through hatred he tore down the pillar of a building to kill himself and all the others who were inside, and through this he greatly misused his strength.° And there was Absalom, who was as handsome as anyone could be and had the most beautiful hair in the world; through the delight he took in his beauty, as he rode beneath a tree, his hair became entangled in that tree and he remained hanging by his beautiful hair and died there.° And there was Solomon, who was so very wise; as it is told in the ancient accounts, he made such ill use of his intelligence, that because of his wife's admonitions he began to adore idols, and in this way seemed to abandon the worship of God; he therefore failed most shamefully in relation to his wisdom.° And when one speaks of great worthiness, St. Peter, who steadfastly loved and believed in Our Lord as His true disciple and apostle, did he not deny him thrice in one night with words from his lips but not from his heart; on each of these three occasions, he committed mortal sin, for which he soon repented, by the grace of Our Lord, as His true disciple; nevertheless he sinned.° Therefore it would be a great thing for men of worth, if they could be as steadfast in the faith of Our Lord as was this holy man of worth, St. Peter, who lived in such a holy way and who is so honored for his saintly life. And as for military achievement, there was Julius Caesar,° who was such a very good knight and engaged in so many great and wonderful battles and made so many fine conquests for those of Rome. On his return from all his glorious battles and all his fine and rich conquests, when he came back to Rome, he saw and understood that through envy the people of Rome did not show him as much honor as they were wont to do to other men who had conquered and fought for the honor and profit of Rome and who had not done as much as he had, so it seemed to him. Then his heart was filled with great anger and hatred against the people of Rome, the city from which he himself came, so much so that after that he waged war on them and inflicted great losses and overcame

li mauvais, qui grant haynne et envie avoient sur lui, se pourpenserent de porter greffes en leurs tables pour semblance d'escrypre, et de ce le devoient tuer. Si avint que a l'eure* que Julius Cesar li emperieres ala en consistoire, et li uns de ceulz qui savoit ceste malvaise emprise l'en voult aviser, se li bailla en alant une lettre ou ceste emprise malvaise estoit contenue, mais il ne la lut point, ançois l'emporta en sa main, dont ce fu ses domages. Quant il fu en consistoire et les huis furent fermés, adonques li malvais traitours prindrent chascuns son greffe et de ces greffes le mistrent a mort moult douleureusement et cruelment, dont d'un si tres bon chevalier si preux et si vaillant fu tres grant pitié et domages. Mes pour ce ne se doit nuls donner mal cuer ne male volenté se l'en ne li porte l'onnour que l'on li devroit porter pour telz faiz d'armes, especialment contre son seigneur ne contre les siens, ne que l'on en doie vouloir nulluy grever ne avoir haynne qu'il ot encontre ceulz de Romme, dont il meismes morust si estrangement et douleureusement comme dessus est dit. Et peut estre que, se il ne se fust tournez contre ceulz (f.118v)de Romme, que il eust vescu plus longuement et bien honorablement entre toutes manieres de gens comme tres parfaitement bons chevaliers que il estoit. Dont ne se doit nulz trop loer en soy ne trop vouloir que il soit trop loez ne avoir trop grant gloire de ce que l'en le loe, que les biens et honnours de ce monde ne sont point ferme fors tant seulement comme il plait a Dieu qui les donne et de qui l'on les tient. Et bien doivent savoir ceulz qui les biens font que nulz bienfaiz ne peut estre perdus ne recelez, et qu'il ne soit sceu et ramenteu, mais covient qu'il soient dit et cogneu par les amis et ennemis de ceulz qui les font et par pluseurs autres. Si n'en doit chaloir a nulz de ceulz qui font ces grans biens, fors que Dieu regracier et celli Seigneur qui les donne en tele maniere qu'il en doie savoir gré a ceuls a qui il les a donnez pour les bonnes recognoissances et services qu'il li en rendent et desservent, et de plus ne leur doit chaloir, mes que il facent touzjours bien; et le die qui veult, et qui veult, si s'en taise, que touzjours sont les bons les plus avanciez. Or pouez chascun savoir et cognoistre fermement qu'il n'est sens, preudommie, force, beauté, proesce ne vaillance qui en nulle personne puisse estre, demourer ne perseverer se ce n'est purement de la grace de Nostre Seigneur. Et pour ce que aucun voudroient dire que en un homme seul ne pourroient estre toutes ces graces et ces vertus dessus dites, et bien pour(f.119r)roient dire voir selon le temps et condicions qui a present sont et regnent; mais, se toutes gens qui veulent mettre leur entente de venir et de acquerir ycelles tres hautes honnours qui par force d'armes et de bonnes euvres les convient acquerir, il devroient mettre leur entente de savoir et de aprendre commant les meilleurs cheva-

them and had himself crowned emperor of Rome. He gave them strong government and forbade the bearing of any knife or sword in his Senate House for fear lest they might kill him, for he could not trust them. What happened then was that the evil men who so hated and envied him had the idea of carrying styles with their tablets, apparently for writing, and by this means they were to kill him. When the emperor went into the Senate House, one of those who knew about this wicked enterprise wanted to warn him of this and gave him, as he walked alone, a letter in which this plot was set out; but he did not read it, rather he carried it away in his hand, from which great harm came to him. When he entered the Senate House and the doors were shut, then the wicked traitors took their styles and with these stabbed him to death very painfully and cruelly, and this was a grievous loss of such a good knight, so worthy and so valiant. But no one should become so annoyed and full of such ill will if he is not given the honor he should receive for such feats of arms, especially not against his lord or his own men; nor ought one to want to harm nor show hatred as Caesar did to the men of Rome, for which he himself died so strangely and painfully as has been told above. And perhaps, if he had not turned against the men of Rome, he might have lived longer and with great honor among all kinds of people as the very perfect knight that he was. Therefore no one should have too high an opinion of himself nor should he expect too much praise nor place too much value on it, for the good things and honors of this world are not certain and constant except insofar as it may please God who grants these benefits and from whom they are held. And those who perform great deeds should know that no great deed can be lost or hidden so that it is unknown and forgotten, but such deeds should be talked of and made known by the friends and enemies of those who perform them and many other people besides. And those who have performed these great deeds should not be concerned with this but only with thanking God, that Lord by whose grace these deeds can be achieved, in such a way that He should regard with favor those to whom He has granted these achievements for the true acknowledgment and service they give Him in return; nothing else should matter to them provided they continue to perform great deeds. And may he who wishes say it, and he who wishes remain silent about it: the men of worth are always those who get furthest. Now each of you can know and be certain that there is no wisdom, worthiness, strength, beauty, prowess, or valor that may be found in anyone and may remain and endure save only by the grace of Our Lord. And some might say that all these above-mentioned graces and virtues cannot be found in one man alone, and

liers qui onques furent eurent et acquirent les hautes bontez et honnours dont il est tant parlé et si veritablement, comme la Bible le tesmoingne. Et pour ce que de touz yceulz ramentevoir seront trop lonc, si pourroit l'en parler briefment et veritablement du tres bon chevalier Judas Machabeus,° de qui l'en peut bien dire et raconter que en li seul furent comprises toutes les bonnes condicions cy dessus escriptes, que il fu saiges en touz ses faiz; il fu preudoms et de saincte vie; il fu fors, appers et penibles; il fu beaus entre touz autres et senz orgueil; il fu preux, hardis, vaillans et bien combatens et par les* plus belles, grandes et fortes batailles et aventures et plus perilleuses qui onques furent, et en la fin il morust en bataille saintement comme sains en paradis. Et ainsi est voir, car en touz ses faiz et en tout son temps se gouverna cilz bons chevaliers en la bonne creance, fiance et esperance de Nostre Seigneur et en li regraciant et merciant devotement de touz les biens et honnours qui li avenoient. Et Nostre Sires, pour la grant foy et cognoissance que cilz bons chevaliers avoit en li, le conforta, gouverna et aida (f.119v) en touz ses faiz si tres grandement, hautement et honorablement; come la Bible le tesmoigne, qui est veritez, que touz ses faiz furent sanz orgueil et sanz envie et sanz convoitise, fors que de touz biens faire, et en desconfisant ses ennemis pour la foy Nostre Seigneur soustenir et maintenir, le voult Nostre Sires prendre en sa glorieuse compaignie et mettre en la compaignie et ou nombre des sains et en grant memoire a touzjours de sa tres haute chevalerie. Hé Diex! comme c'est uns tres beaus exemplaires a toute chevalerie et a genz d'armes qui ont volenté de venir a celle tres haute prouesce et vaillance, dont tant de biens sont faiz et recordez en leur vie et tant longuement aprés leur mort. Et qui bien aviseroit et penseroit a la vie es biens et es bons faiz de ce bon saint chevalier dessus dit et que l'en vousist retraire et resembler le plus pres que l'en pourroit de sa tres bonne vie et condicions, seurement pourroit l'en tenir et fermement que yceus qui ainsi voudroient leur vie et leurs estaz gouverner ne pourroient ne devroient faillir de venir a tres haute honnour de chevalerie, tant de l'ame comme du corps tout ensemble, que moult en y a qui peuent avoir grant renommee du corps, que puis sont les armes) perdues. Et de aucuns autres en y a qui po sont renommez de ces hautes honnours, que leurs arme sont et vont en sauvement en la compaignie de Nostre Seigneur. Mais cui Dieux donne grace de tres haute (f.120r) honnour en ce siecle et a la fin l'ame en paradiz, ainsi comme il fist a ce tres bon cheuallier dessus dit et a pluseurs autres, plus ne li pourroit demander. Et pour ce que li aucuns pourroit dire que es mestiers d'armes l'en ne pourroit sauver l'ame, il ne savroient qu'il diroient, que entre touz bons mestiers neccessaires et acoustumez peut l'en perdre ou

they might well be speaking the truth according to the time and the circumstances to be found today; yet all those who were willing to devote themselves entirely to winning these high honors, which they must achieve by force of arms and by heroic deeds, should be intent on learning how the best knights there ever were came by and won the noble qualities and high honors of which there is so much and so truly said, as the Bible testifies. And as it would take too long to recall all these knights, a brief and true account could be given of the excellent knight Judas Maccabeus,° of whom it can be said that in him alone were to be found all the good qualities set out above. He was wise in all his deeds, he was a man of worth who led a holy life, he was strong, skillful, and unrelenting in effort and endurance; he was handsome above all others, and without arrogance; he was full of prowess, bold, valiant, and a great fighter, taking part in the finest, greatest, and fiercest battles and the most perilous adventures there ever were, and in the end he died in a holy way in battle, like a saint in paradise. And this is true, for in all his deeds and throughout his life this good knight conducted himself according to the true belief, trust, and hope in Our Lord, thanking Him devoutly for all the benefits and honors which came to him. And Our Lord, for the great faith that this good knight had in Him and the understanding he had of Him, comforted, guided, and helped him in all his great, noble, and honorable deeds; and the Bible, in which lies the truth, bears witness that all his actions were without pride, envy, or greed, and directed only toward performing great deeds and defeating his enemies in order to uphold and maintain belief in God. For all this it was the will of Our Lord that he should be accepted into His glorious company and numbered among the saints and that the memory of his great chivalry should be celebrated for ever. Ah God! what a splendid example is this for all knights and all men-at-arms who aim to attain these heights of prowess and valor whereby so many good deeds are performed and win recognition during the lifetime of such men and for so long after their death. And in relation to those who might reflect on and consider the life devoted to good and to great deeds of this fine and saintly knight described above, whom one would like to resemble as closely as possible in his good way of life, it could be maintained confidently and firmly that such people who would thus desire to conduct their way of life and behavior could not and should not fail to attain the high honor of chivalry, in terms of both soul and body. There are indeed many, who can achieve much renown for physical achievement, whose souls° are afterward lost; and there are others who have won little renown for these high honors while their souls have gone to their

sauver l'ame qui veult. Mais quant es mestiers d'armes, dont l'en peut et doit acquerir ces tres hautes honnours, l'on y peut bien faire les corps honoreement et vassaument et a sauver les ames, que quant les fais d'armes des guerres deuement encommanciees et les batailles qui s'en ensiuent, ainsi come se lurs seigneurs ont guerres, leurs subgiez peuent et doivent guerrier pour eulz et entrer seurement et hardiement pour cestes causes en batailles, que se l'en le fait bien, les corps sont honorez, et se l'on y meurt, les anmes sont sauvees se autre pechié ne les en destournent. Et en oultre, se aucun de son sanc l'on vouloit desheriter ou pour grant neccessité de leur honnour garder, encores en tele neccessité peut l'on entrer en guerres et en batailles seurement pour les corps et pour les ames, car li cas loist de le faire et est de neccessité. Encores, se aucun vouloient oster l'onnour ne l'eritage de povres pucelles ne de povres femmes vesves, et autrement ne les peust l'en destourner de ce sanz guerre ou bataille, l'en y doit entrer seurement (f.120v) et pour les corps et pour les ames sauver, et tout en autele maniere pour povres orphelins et orphelines. Et encores par meilleur raison peut l'on guerroier et entrer* en batailles, un chascun endroit soy, pour son honnour deffendre et pour son heritage, qui autrement ne s'en pourroit deffendre, et seurement pour les corps et pour les ames. Encores pour les droiz de Sainte Eglise garder et maintenir, l'on n'y doit espargnier a y mettre les corps pour les deffendre par guerres et par batailles, se autrement ne les peut l'on avoir. Et qui ainsi le fait, il fait l'onnour de son corps et le sauvement de s'ame grandemant. Encores qui fait guerre contre les ennemis de la foy et pour la crestienté soustenir et maintenir et la foy de Nostre Seigneur, ycelle guerre est droite, sainte, seure et ferme, que les corps en sont sainctement honorez et les ames en sont briefment et sainctement et senz paine portees en paradis. Ceste guerre est bonne, que l'on n'y peut perdre ne les corps ne les armes. Si ne doit l'on rienz doubter ycelles guerres dessus dites qui de grant neccessité et a leur droit garder sont encommanciez, mes que elles soient maintenues et gouvernees en tele maniere que l'on soit touzjours en tel estat de concience que l'on ne doubte point ne doie doubter a mourir pour toutes hontes eschever, qui a ces mestiers d'armes peuent avenir moult de foys a qui Dieux ne donne grace de les en garder. Et pour ce doit chascuns (f.121r) bien savoir et penser que en touz les mestiers qui en ce monde sunt, ne de* quoy nul se doient ne puissent mesler, ne religieux ne autres, n'ont tant besoing de estre net de conscience comme genz d'armes doivent estre; et bien peut apparoir que ainsi soit; que qui veult penser et considerer en l'ordre de chevalerie comment elle fu ordenee et faite et coment l'en y devoit entrer devotement et sainctement, l'en pourroit dire que ceste ordre, la ou

salvation in the company of Our Lord; but the man to whom God by His grace grants high honor in this world and in the end the soul's acceptance in paradise, as He did to this excellent above-mentioned knight and to a number of others, such a man could not ask for more from God. Were anyone, therefore, to say that those who are engaged in a career of arms would not be able to save their souls, they would not know what they were saying, for in all good, necessary, and traditional professions anyone can lose or save his soul as he wills. But when in the profession of arms, in which one can and should win these high honors, one can indeed make one's personal career honorably and valiantly and save one's soul, as for example in the practice of arms in wars which have been begun in the proper manner and in due form and in the battles which ensue. This is the case when lords have wars, and their men can and should fight for them and move confidently and bravely into battle for such causes, for if one performs well there, one is honored in life, and if one dies there, one's soul is saved, if other sins do not stand in the way of this. In addition, if someone is intent on disinheriting a man's kinsman or if there is a need to defend their estate, when under such compulsion, men can embark on wars and battles without fear for body and soul, for the circumstances make this legitimate and of necessity. And again, if some people wanted to seize the land and inheritance of defenseless maidens or widows and could not be dissuaded from this except by war or combat, one ought to embark on this confidently in regard to one's personal reputation and the saving of one's soul, and the same is true in relation to the defense of orphans. And for even better reason, one can wage war and embark on battles on one's own account to defend one's land and inheritance when it cannot be defended in any other way, and this can be done without endangering one's personal honor or soul. And again, to preserve and maintain the rights of the Holy Church, one should not hold back from committing oneself to their defense by war and battle, if they cannot be maintained in any other way. And the man who acts thus wins in noble fashion personal honor and the salvation of his soul. Moreover, the man who makes war against the enemies of religion in order to support and maintain Christianity and the worship of Our Lord is engaged in a war which is righteous, holy, certain, and sure, for his earthly body will be honored in a saintly fashion and his soul will, in a short space of time, be borne in holiness and without pain into paradise. This kind of war is good, for one can lose in it neither one's reputation in this world nor one's soul. Nor ought one to fear those wars mentioned above which are started from great necessity and to protect one's rights,

elle seroit bien menee et gouvernee au propos et en la maniere que li ordre de chevalerie se doit gouverner, que l'on pouroit dire que entre toutes autres ordres ce seroit la souveraine, excepté le service divin. Que vous devez savoir que les autres ordres de religion furent et sont faites et ordenees pour servir et prier Nostre Seigneur pour eulz et pour les trespassez et en vie, et sanz avoir regart ne delit es choses mondaines; et bien le peuent et doivent faire quant leur demourance est toute ordenee et est taillie de demourer es abbayes, es cloistres, es maisons et liex ordené pour faire les services de Nostre Seigneur et les prieres, oroisons et abstenances teles conme il y sont tenuz et obligiez par les veuz et promesses, un chascun selon les poins de leurs religions, et sanz nul peril de leurs corps ne a grant travail d'aler aval les champs pour eulz armer ne en doubte d'estre tuez. Et pour ce le font il bien et doivent faire ce a quoy leurs vies et leurs estaz sont establiz et ordenez si paisiblement. Mais quant a l'ordre de chevalerie, pour (121v) bien dire et monstrer veritablement que c'est la plus perilleuse et d'arme et de corps et la ou il appartient plus et mieux gouverner nettement conscience, ceste° ordre de chevalerie, que nulle autre ordre qui soit en ce monde.

36 Et pour ce que l'on entende miex et pour quoy, et les bonnes raysons, l'orde° de chevalerie fu faite et establie, est il bon du retraire pour en avoir miex la cognoissance. Si devez savoir que quant l'en veult [faire] chevalier nouvel,° il convient tout premierement que il soit confés et repentans de touz ses pechiez et qu'il se mette en tel estat qu'il doie recevoir le corps Nostre Seigneur. Et puis quant vient la veille dont l'en doit estre chevalier le landemain, il se doivent mettre en un bain et y demourer une longue piece en pensant que il doient laver et nettoier d'illec en avant leurs corps

provided they are carried on and conducted in such a way that one is always in such a state of purity of conscience that one does not and should not fear to die in order to avoid all shame, which in this pursuit of arms can often happen to those whom God does not graciously protect from such things. And because of this each person ought to be aware and bear in mind that in all the callings there are in the world, whether religious or secular, in which anyone should or might be engaged, no men have so great a need for a clear conscience as is required of men-at-arms. It can indeed be shown that this is so, for if anyone will reflect and consider how the order of chivalry was founded and established and how it should be entered devoutly and in a holy manner, one might say that this order, when it is well conducted for the purpose and in the manner that the order of chivalry should be conducted, might of all orders be the supreme order, except for the divine service. For you should know that the other orders, that is the religious orders, were and still are established and ordained to serve God and to pray to Him on behalf of themselves and of others, whether living or dead, and to take no account of nor delight in worldly things; and they can and indeed ought to conduct themselves in this way, when their manner and place of living is ordained and laid down: to dwell in abbeys and in cloisters, in the places ordained for the service of Our Lord and for such prayers, orisons, and fastings that they are bound and obliged to perform by their vows, each one according to the articles of their religious rules; they are spared the physical danger and the strenuous effort of going out onto the field of battle to take up arms, and are also spared the threat of death. Therefore they do and should do that for which their way of life has been established and ordained in such peaceful terms. But as for the order of chivalry, it can truly be said and demonstrated that it is the most dangerous for both soul and body, and the one in which it is necessary to maintain a clearer conscience than in any other order in the world.

The Knighting Ceremony
36   And in order that it should be better understood why and for what good reasons the rite of entry into the order of chivalry was established, it is best to describe how it is performed and thus give a greater knowledge of it.° You should know that when a new knight is to be made, first of all he must confess, repent of all his sins, and make sure that he is in a fit state to receive the body of Our Lord [the Host]. On the eve of the ceremony, all those who are to be knighted the next day should enter a bath and stay there for a long time, reflecting on the need to cleanse their bodies henceforth

de toute ordure de pechié et de deshonestes vies. Et toute celle ordure doivent laissier dedanz celle eaue. Adont se doivent partir tout net de conscience de celle eaue et de ce bain et se doivent aler gesir en un lit tout neuf
et les draps blans et nez; et la se doivent reposer comme ceulz qui [sont
issu]* du grant travail de pechié et du grant peril du tourment des deables.
Et segnefie le lit repos, comme repos de bien, de conscience, de soy apaisier
envers Nostre Seigneur de tout ce de quoy l'on l'avroit courroucié ou temps
passé. Puis doivent venir les chevaliers au* lit pour vestir yceulz et les
doivent vestir (f.122r) de neufs draps, linges et toutes choses neuves qui y appartiennent en segnefiant que, ainsi comme le corps de celli doit estre nettoiez de toute ordure de pechié, le revest l'on des draps blans et neufs et nez
en segnefiance que des lors en la se doivent tenir nettement et sanz pechié.
Puis les doivent vestir li chevalier de cotes vermeilles en segnefiant que il
sont tenus d'espendre leur sanc pour la foy de Nostre Seigneur defendre et
maintenir et les droiz de Sainte Eglise et toutes autres droitures dessus dites
que chevalier soit tenu de faire. Et puis leur apportent les chevaliers chauces
noires et les enchaucent en segnefiance que il leur doie remembrer que de
terre soient venu et en terre doivent retourner pour la mort que il doivent
attendre, dont il ne scevent l'eure, et pour ce doivent mettre tout*° orgueil
dessouz leurs piez. Et puis leur apportent les chevaliers une courroie toute
blanche et l'en seignent et mettent entour de lui en seignefiance que il soient
environné en tout entour leurs corps de chasteté et de netteté de corps.
Dont leur apportent les chevaliers un manteu vermeil et li mettent sus les
espaules en signe de tres grant humilité, que mantiaus ainsi faiz furent faiz
anciennement par droite humblesce. Puis les mainnent les chevaliers a grant
joie en l'eglise, et en l'eglise doivent demourer et veillier toute nuit jusques
au jour en tres grant devocion en priant a Nostre Seigneur qu'il leur veille
pardonner les mauvais dormirs et (f.122v) veilliers qu'il ont faiz ou temps
passé et qu'il leur doint veillier en sa grace et en son service d'illeuc en avant.
Et l'andemain les ammainnent les chevaliers a la messe et pour la oïr tres
devotement en priant a Nostre Seigneur qu'il li donne grace de entrer et de
gouverner ceste ordre en son service et en sa grace. Et quant la messe est
chantee et dite, dont les chevaliers les amainent a celli ou a ceulz chevaliers
qui leur doivent baillier l'ordre. Dont li chevaliers qui baille l'ordre baille
deux esperons dorez a deux chevaliers, a un chascun le sien; et cil duy chevalier li mettent en chascun pié le sien en segnefiance que l'or est le plus
convoiteux mettail qui soit, et pour ce les y met l'en es piez qu'il oste de
son* cuer toute mauvaise convoitise d'avoir. Dont cilz chevaliers qui leur
doit baillier l'ordre de chevalerie prent une espee; pour ce que l'espee tran-

from all impurities of sin and dishonorable ways of life; they should leave all such impurities in the water. Then they should come out of the water in the bath with a clear conscience and should go and lie in a new bed in clean white sheets; there they should rest as those who have emerged from a great struggle against sin and from the great peril of the devils' torment. The bed signifies repose, stemming from virtue, from a clear conscience, from making one's peace with God with regard to all past actions that might have angered Him. Then the knights should come to the beds to dress those to be knighted; the stuff in which they dress them, the linen and all that goes with it should be new: this signifies that just as the body of each one should be cleansed of all the impurities of sin, so should it be clothed in new, white, and clean material, signifying that they should all from henceforth keep themselves pure and free from sin. Then the knights should robe them in red tunics, signifying that they are pledged to shed their blood to defend and maintain the faith of Our Lord and the rights of the Holy Church and all the other just rights set out above which it is the knight's duty to protect. Then the knights bring black hose and put them on those to be knighted; this signifies that they should remember that from the earth they have come and to the earth they must return for the death which awaits them, they know not at what hour; therefore they should put all pride beneath their feet. Then the knights bring them white belts with which they gird them, signifying that they should surround their bodies with chastity and purity of the flesh. After that the knights bring them red cloaks and place them on their shoulders as a sign of great humility, for cloaks in this form were made in ancient times in all humility. Then the knights bring them joyfully into the church, and in the church they must remain and keep vigil all night until dawn, praying very devoutly to Our Lord that it may please Him to forgive the unworthy sleeping and watching of which they have been guilty in the past and that He grant them to keep vigil henceforth in His grace and in His service. The next day, the knights bring them to mass, to hear it devoutly, praying to Our Lord that He may grant them grace to enter and maintain this order in His service and His grace. When mass has been sung, the knights lead them to the person or persons destined to confer the order. For each one to be knighted he gives two gilded spurs, one to each of two knights; these two knights each fasten one to a foot, signifying that gold is the most coveted of all metals and is placed on their feet as a sign that they should remove from their hearts all unworthy covetousness of riches. Then the knight who is to confer the order of knighthood takes a sword; as the sword cuts on both sides of the blade, so should they defend and maintain

che de deux pars, ainsi doivent garder et soustenir et maintenir droiture, raison, et justice de toutes pars sanz fausser pour nulz a la foy crestienne et
50 les droiz de Sainte Eglise. Et puis li chevaliers qui leur baillent l'ordre les doivent baisier en signe de confermer l'ordre qu'il leur baillent et que eulz recevoient et que pais et amour et loyauté soit en eulz, et ainsi la doivent il pourchacier et mettre partout la ou il pourront bonnement. Et puis ycilz chevaliers leur doivent donner la colee en signe que a touzjours mais leur
55 doie souvenir de celle ordre de chevalerie qu'il ont receue et de y faire les oeuvres qui a cest ordre de chevalerie (f.123r) peuent appartenir; et ainsi se font et doivent estre faiz. Et ceulz sont bien eurez qui en tele maniere et en tele guise se gouvernent et maintennent ainsi comme li estaz le desire. Et qui feroit le contraire, mieux leur vaudroit qu'il ne l'eussent onques esté.
60 Et en l'estat de chevalerie pourroit l'en tenir que en trois manieres pourroient prendre les aucuns l'ordre de chevalerie. Les uns la veulent prendre joennes pour plus longuement travailler es estaz que a chevalerie appartient, peut et doit appartenir, sanz y rienz redoubter, ne espargnier ne corps ne avoir. Les autres si veulent avoir l'ordre de chevalerie pour ce que l'on die
65 qu'il soient chevalier et qu'il soient plus trait avant et honorez qu'il n'estoient devant, mais po se veulent entremettre des droiz estaz de chevalerie. Et pour ce pourroit l'en bien dire sur yceulz qu'il pourroient bien avoir l'ordre de chevalerie mais non mie le nom d'estre chevaliers, que tieux peut avoir l'ordre qui ne sont mie chevaliers. Si en y a aucuns preudommes an-
70 ciens qui veulent user leur viellesce et finer leurs jours en l'ordre de chevalerie; si se veulent mettre en cel aige de viellesce, et tres bien le peuent faire et doivent selon l'estat de chevalerie, car il doivent plus avoir de sens et de raison en eulz que les jeunes n'ont, et touz estaz de meurté et de bonne vie doit estre en eulz. Si peuent aidier et conforter en moult de bonnes mani-
75 eres neccessaires pour leur bon senz, et les bons (f.123v) jeunes par leurs espees, en soustenant et en gardant la foy, raison et droiture. Si peuent et doivent vivre li bon chevalier loyaument et honorablement.

37 Mais aprés ceste ordre de chevalerie est il bon de ramentevoir l'orde° de mariage. Dont en mariage pourroit on prendre trois manieres d'y entrer. Li aucun hommes et femmes si se marient en tel temps dont il n'ont point de cognoissance eue de pechié a autre famme, ne la fame a nul autre
5 homme, et plus par amour que par convoitise; et ainsi est bon le mariage

right, reason, and justice on all sides without being false to the Christian faith or to the rights of the Holy Church for anyone. Then the knights who confer the order on them should kiss them as a sign of confirmation of the order conferred on them and received by them, and that peace, love, and loyalty may be in them; thus should they strive on behalf of and uphold the order with all their hearts wherever they can. Then these knights should give them the *collee* [a light tap, probably here with sword] as a sign that they should for ever more remember this order of knighthood which they have received and carry out all the activities that may pertain to this order. And thus are these things done and so should they be done. Those are blessed by fortune who conduct themselves in such a manner as the estate requires. If anyone does the contrary, it would have been better for him never to have been made a knight. It can be held that there are three different ways of entering the order of knighthood. Some may choose to enter it when young, so that they can strive longer without fear and without sparing their bodies or possessions in all the services and conditions which pertain, can and should pertain to knighthood. Others want to have the order of knighthood so that people will say that they are knights and so that they will receive greater attention and honor than they did before; but they do not want to fulfill the true conditions and services of knighthood. For that reason it might be said of these men that they may well have the order of knighthood but not the reputation of being a knight, for men may have the order who are not real knights. There are also some ancient men of worth who want to spend their old age and end their days in the order of knighthood; they want to enter at this advanced age and they can indeed do so in keeping with the estate of knighthood, for they should have more sense and judgment than the young, and all the qualities of maturity and of virtuous living ought to be in them. Thus they can give help and comfort in many good and needful ways through their good sense, and the good young knights can do their part with their swords, maintaining and protecting the faith, reason, and justice. Good knights can and should live loyally and honorably.

The Order of Marriage

37 Having considered the order of knighthood, it is appropriate to turn our attention to the order of marriage. There are three possible ways of entering into marriage. Some men and women marry when the man has no carnal knowledge of a woman, nor a woman of a man, and they do it more for love than for greed for riches; such a marriage is good in that

pour avoir hoirs et pour eulz garder de pechié. Et d'aucuns en y a qui de rienz ne regardent es personnes a eulz marier fors que a la convoitise de l'avoir, et ceulz qui plus se marient par convoitise que par autre plaisance, soit homs ou femme, a envis en pourroit bien venir, que certes li dyables doivent estre a leurs noces. Si en y a d'aucuns qui sont vesves et ont des enfanz et sont enciens et se marient pour eulz garder de pechié plus que pour avoir enfanz ne lignié, et leur aaige ne leur donne de l'avoir, et se peuent bien vivre deuement en ceste ordre de mariage. Et ceulz qui mieux se gouvernent en l'ordre de mariage vivent liemant et plaisanment.

38   Or pourroit l'en parler ensivant des saintes ordres de religion, que en trois manieres y pourroit l'en entrer. Premierement, quant l'on y entre si joennes (f.124r) que l'on n'ait encores nulle cognoissance de pechié ne du monde; et l'on y entre de ce temps et de cel aaige, si se nourrissent en l'ordre et mieux le doivent prendre en gré, et par raison se doivent miex porter et selon les poins de religion et les garder. Si en pourroit avoir d'aucuns qui longuement se sont tenuz et cogneu le monde et mené des honestes vies et moult de foiz et longuement, et puis si se veulent mettre en religion et de legiere volenté, sanz avoir grant devocion. Dont leur est il moult grief chose a tenir et mener les droites [voies] et les poins et les regles qui es religieux appartiennent de mener, et a envis le veulent faire. Et bien en a l'on veu de telx et pluseurs qu'il vausist de mieux es religions que teles genz n'y fussent ja entrez, que telx religieux font et donnent grans diffames es religions et es bons religieux par les tres deshordenees vies et deshonestes que telz tres desordenez religieux mainent. Yceus ont l'ordre, mais ne sont mie religieux. Si en y a d'aucuns, quant il sont sur leur aaige et qu'il ne peuent plus travaillier au monde, si se mettent et rendent en religions pour y finer leurs jours plus sainnement pour les corps et pour les armes, et ainsi est bien. Dont peuent et doivent les bons religieux vivre ordeneement et saintement. Si pourroit l'en bien et devroit tenir que es trois ordres dessus dites pourroit et devroit appartenir et pour le meilleur a y entrer joennes en religion, jeunes en mariage et joennes en l'armeure et en chevalerie.

39   (f.124v) Si pourroit l'en encores parler briefment de la plus digne ordre qui soit: c'est ordre de prestre. Et en cest ordre est au contraire des autres

it provides heirs and saves the man and woman from sin. There are some who pay no regard to the person when entering into marriage, but do so out of greed for riches; in the case of those who marry more for gain than for any other pleasure, it is unlikely that any good will come of it, for indeed the devils must be at their wedding. Then there are some who are widowers, have children, are old, and marry more to keep themselves from sin than to have descendants, nor could they because of their age; these can live fittingly within the order of marriage. It is those who conduct themselves most properly in the order of marriage who live joyfully and pleasantly.

The Monastic Orders

38   Then one can consider the holy monastic orders, which can be entered in three different ways. First, when one enters so young that one has no knowledge of sin nor of the world; those who enter at such an age are brought up in the order and should accept it more willingly; they should, therefore, conduct themselves better and adhere more closely to the rules of the religious order. There might also be some who, after having for a long time lived in and known the world and after having committed dishonorable deeds often and over a lengthy period, want to enter a religous order, lightly and without being truly devout. Then it is very hard for them to keep to and follow the right paths and the precepts and rules to which religious are required to adhere, and they are very reluctant to do so. It has all too often been seen that as far as a number of such people are concerned, it would have been better for the religious orders if they had never entered them, as shame is brought to the monastic orders and to the good religious by the disordered and dishonorable lives led by such unruly brothers. Such men belong to the order but are not religious. Then there are some who have reached old age and are no longer capable of striving in this world, and they leave it to enter religious orders so that they can end their days in a more salutary way, for both their bodies and their souls; and this is right. Therefore good religious can and should live in an orderly and holy way. It is, therefore, possible and right to maintain that for the three orders considered above it can and should be most fitting and best to enter a religious order when young, marriage when young, and arms and knighthood when young.

The Order of Priesthood

39   We could also speak briefly of the worthiest order of all, that of priesthood. In this order, unlike those considered above in relation to entry when

dessus dites pour y entrer joennes, que nulz n'y doit entrer se en sa joennesce n'aprent son service que il convient qu'il aprengne et sache tres bien, que moult en y a qui s'i mettent si joenne [qu'il ne] scevent riens, ne ne s'entendent, dont c'est moult de foiz tres grant perilz. Et moult en y a qui bien s'entendent, mais il font mal l'estat qui y appartient; dont il leur avient moult mal quant il ne se gouvernent deuement selon le digne estat qu'il ont et qu'il prennent. Mais ceulz qui bien s'entendent et bien font et scevent leur service et devotement chantent et sonnent, et en cel estat se scevent et veillent gouverner ainsi come a ce digne estat d'estre ordenez a prestre peut et doit appartenir, ycelz prestres peuent faire moult de biens en trois manieres par leurs bonnes prieres envers ce tres haut Seigneur que tant de foiz tiennent entre leurs mains, premierement pour eulz, secondement pour les ames des corps trespassez, tiercement pour ceulz qui sont en vie, dont il ont memoire. Si peuent et doivent vivre ytelx bons prestres justement et devotement. Si peut l'en assez savoir que en l'orde de mariage, la ou elle se gouverne bien si comme a la dite ordre peut et doit appartenir, l'on y puet et doit vivre aaise de cuer et de corps et pour l'ame aussi. Et quant aus saintes (125r) ordres de religion, li bons religieux scevent les heures la ou il doivent faire le service Nostre Seigneur d'aler en l'eglise, les heures la ou il doivent boir[e] et mengier et dormir et po curer du monde. Si doivent et peuent vivre en paiz en leurs cuers de conscience les bons prestres seculiers qui ont si digne office a faire. Il ne leur appartient de chargier d'autres affaires que de celli, et se ainsi le veulent faire, il font selon leurs bons estaz et ce qui a eulz doit appartenir. Si ne doivent avoir a faire fors tant seulement dire leur service et les messes tres diligenment et tres devotement, et cest office doit bien souffire sanz aprendre nul autre.

40 Si pourroit l'en aprés toutes ces ordres parler de la bonne ordre de chevalerie qui entre toutes autres ordres pourroit l'en et devroit tenir la plus dure ordre de toutes, espeuciaument a ceulz qui bien la tiennent et s'i gouvernent selon ce que la dite ordre fu ordenee et faite. Et trop bien peut apparoir que es ordres de religion, combien qu'il leur soit dit a l'entrer, quant l'en cuidera mengier, l'en jeunera, quant l'on voudra jeuner, lors convendra mengier, et quant l'en cuidera dormir, il convendra veillier, et moult de teles autres choses, n'est ce mie comparasons d'assez souffrir comme en l'ordre de chevalerie. Que qui voudroit considerer les paines, travaux, douleurs, mesaises, grans paours, perilz, froisseures et bleceures que li bon chevalier, qui l'ordre de chevalerie maintiennent ainsi (f.125v) comme il doivent, ont a souffrir et sueffrent mainte foiz, il n'est nulle reli-

young, no one should enter it unless he learns as a youth his service, which he must study and know very well; for there are many who begin so young that they know nothing of it and have no understanding of it, and this can give rise to great dangers. There are also many who do have an understanding of it, but they do not conduct themselves as befits their office; it ill behooves them not to behave properly, in accordance with the worthy office which they have entered upon and which they have undertaken. But there are those who have set their minds to it and know and perform their service well and sing and chant devoutly and know how to behave in a manner befitting the noble estate of an ordained priest. Such priests can do much good in three ways by their devout prayers to that very high Lord whom they so often hold in their hands: first, they can pray for themselves, second, for the souls of the departed, third, for those who are still living whom they remember. These good priests can and should live righteous and devout lives. It is also true that in the order of marriage, where it is well conducted as is befitting and should befit the said order, one can and should live at ease in heart, body, and soul. And as for the holy religious orders, the good brothers know the hours when they should serve Our Lord by going into church, they know the hours when they should eat, drink, sleep, and care little for the world. These good secular priests who have such a noble office to perform should and can live at peace in heart and good conscience. It is not for them to undertake other duties, and if they behave in this way, they act in keeping with their position and as befits their office. They should not have anything to do except say their masses with diligence and devotion, and this office should suffice without learning any other.

The Rigors of the Order of Knighthood

40   After speaking of all these orders, it is now time to return to the good order of knighthood, which should be considered the most rigorous order of all, especially for those who uphold it well and conduct themselves in a manner in keeping with the purpose for which the order was established. It will indeed be apparent that, however much it may be said to those entering the religious orders that when they want to eat, they will fast, and when they want to fast, then they will have to eat, when they want to sleep, they will have to keep vigil, and many other such things, this is all nothing in comparison with the suffering to be endured in the order of knighthood. For, whoever might want to consider the hardships, pains, discomforts, fears, perils, broken bones, and wounds which the good knights who uphold the order of knighthood as they should endure and have to suffer fre-

gion ou l'en en sueffre tant comme font cil bon chevalier qui les faiz d'armes vont querant justement ainsi comme il est dessus dit*, ne nulz ne s'en puet
15 ne doit excuser de soy armer et justement ou pour son seigneur ou pour son lignage ou pour soy meismes ou pour Sainte Eglise ou pour la foy deffendre et soustenir ou pour pitié d'ommes et de fammes qui ne peuent leur droit deffendre. Et en tel cas doivent il mettre baudemant, hardiement et liement leurs corps en telx faiz d'armes et en teles aventures sanz y re-
20 doubter rienz. Et pour ce est il bien assavoir que a ces bons chevaliers peut avenir assez des dures vies et aventures, que l'en leur peut bien dire que quant il cuident dormir, il les convient veillier, et quant il voudront mengier, il les faut jeuner, et quant il ont soif, il n'ont rienz a boire moult de foiz, et quant il se cuident reposer, lors les convient travaillier et a tresnui-
25 tier, et quant il cuident estre asseur, lors leur viennent il de grans paours, et quant il cuident desconfire leurs ennemis, aucune fois se treuvent desconfiz ou mors ou pris et bleciez et [en] la paine de garir, sanz les perilz et aventures qui leur peuent avenir es chemins et voiages d'aler querir tel fait d'armes, comme en peril de mer, de rivieres, et passer de mauvais paz et
30 pons, de rimours, de robeurs. Et tous telz perilz leur convient avoir et passer quant il peuent, et Dieux leur en donne grace. Et ou (f.126r) sont les ordres qui tant pourroient souffrir?. Certes en ceste ordre de chevalerie peut l'on tres bien les aumes sauver et les corps tres bien honorer. [Toutesvoies qui fait les faiz d'armes plus pour la gloire de ce monde]° que pour l'ame
35 sauver, yteles genz peuent avoir aucune foiz d'onnour la renommee, mais les ames y ont petit proffit et les renommees en sont plus courtes. Et qui fait les faiz d'armes plus pour avoir la grace de Dieu et pour les ames sauver que pour la gloire de ce monde, les ames dignes sont mises en paradis et sanz fin, et les corps touzjours mais honorez et ramenteuz en touz biens. Et
40 ainsi est il de touz ceulx qui tielx justes faiz d'armes vont querant, ja ne soient il chevalier; que maintes bonnes genz d'armes sont ainsi bon comme li chevalier, et ausi d'aucuns seculiers comme d'aucuns bons religieux.

41 Et quant a parler d'une maniere de gens qui se arment et ne sont mie gens d'armes, ne raison n'est qu'il le soient pour les tres deshonestes et desordenees vies qu'il maintiennent en celle armeure, ce sont ceulz qui veulent guerroier sanz nulle raison de guerre, qui prennent les uns et les autres sanz
5 deffiance et sanz nulle bonne cause, et les robent et raimbent, blecent et

quently, there is no religious order in which as much is suffered as has to be endured by these good knights who go in search of deeds of arms in the right way as has been set forth above. No one can and should excuse himself from bearing arms in a just cause, whether for his lord or for his lineage or for himself or for the Holy Church or to defend and uphold the faith or out of pity for men or women who cannot defend their own rights. In such cases they should commit themselves eagerly, boldly, and gladly to such deeds of arms and adventures, fearing nothing. Hence it should be understood that good knights may have to undergo hard trials and adventures, for it can truly be said to them that when they want to sleep, they must keep vigil, when they want to eat, they must fast, and when they are thirsty, there is often nothing to drink, and when they would rest, they have to exert themselves all through the night, and when they would be secure from danger, they will be beset by great terrors, and when they would defeat their enemies, sometimes they may be defeated or killed or captured and wounded and struggling to recover; this is not to speak of the perilous adventures they may encounter on their journeys in search of deeds of arms, such as the danger of crossing sea or river, of passing over treacherous places or bridges, of encountering riots or robbers. All these dangers must they endure and come through safely when they can and God grants them grace. And where are the orders which could suffer as much? Indeed, in this order of knighthood, one can well save the soul and bring honor to the body. [Nevertheless those who perform deeds of arms more for glory in this world]° than for the salvation of the soul, may sometimes gain honor and renown, but the souls will profit little, and the renown will be the briefer for it. And for those who perform deeds of arms more to gain God's grace and for the salvation of the soul than for glory in this world, their noble souls will be set in paradise to all eternity and their persons will be for ever honored and well remembered. Thus it is for all those who go in search of deeds of arms in support of the right, whether or not they be knights, for many fine men-at-arms are as good as knights, and this is true also of some seculars as it is of some good religious.

Those Unworthy To Be Men-at-Arms
41   And as for those men who take up arms, but are not men-at-arms, nor is it right that they should be because of their very dishonest and disordered behavior under these arms, it is these men who want to wage war without good reason, who seize other people without prior warning and without any good cause and rob and steal from them, wound and kill them.

tuent. Ceulz qui en ceste maniere le font deshonoreement, le font mauvaisement et en traïson, ne autrement ne l'osent entreprendre de faire. Si vont encores courre sur es uns et es autres en prenant proies, prisons et autres biens, s'il les treuvent, et sanz nulle bonne cause. Si en y a d'aucuns
10 autres qui veulent faire entendant que teles mauvaises oeuvres (f.126v) ne feroient jamais, mais il les font faire par leurs genz meismes. Et encores d'autres qui dient que de teles mauvaises oevres ne s'entremettroient jamais, mais il receptent touz ceulz qui teulz mauvais faiz font, et les soustiennent et mieux les en aiment et les en prisent. Et pour ce dit l'on mout de foiz que
15 bien escorche qui le pié tient.° Certes toutes ytelles genz ainsi faisans, consentans et receptans ne sont digne de vivre ne d'estre en la compagnie des bons; car il n'aiment mie eulz: comment ameroient il autrui? Il n'ont nulle volenté de faire bien: comment le loeroient il de le faire a autrui? Il n'ont cure que l'on die bien de eulz: comment le diroient il d'autrui? Il n'ont nulle
20 volenté de faire oeuvres dont biens leur viengne: commant le pourchaceroient il pour autrui? Il ne veulent mie faire de quoy il soient honorez: comment honoreroient il autrui? Il n'ont nulle raison en eulz: comment la voudroient il faire a autrui? Si peut l'on bien dire de teles mauvaises genz qui se arment en tant de malvaises manieres, que il sont entechiez de quatre
25 tres mauvaises taches. La premiere si est de roberie sur les chemins, mauvaisement robee et sanz nulle bonne cause. La seconde si est de murdrir autrui pour mauvaise cause. La tierce si est que pour prendre, raimbre et rober autrui sanz deffiance ne sanz meffait, c'est traïson mauvaise. Et la quarte, prendre sur les eglises les biens dont Nostre Sires est serviz et mal
30 faire es personnes qui a si digne service sont orden[e]z comme de Dieu servir, et dont par teles males façons (f.127r) cilz dignes services en demouroit a faire. Ainsi pourroit en tenir qu'il sont fors comme mauvais crestien, et maudit soient les corps qui a tel usage mettent leur temps de faire telz mauvais faiz pour acquerir tele deshonnoree fame et renomee. Et certes ne
35 plus ne sont nulz seigneurs dignes de vivre qui teles genz ont en leur puissance et avecques ce ont la cognoissance de leurs males façons se il ne font tele justice que tuit autre qui avroient volenté de mal faire s'en retraissent et deussent retraire. Et n'est ce grant marveille quant teles genz mettent leurs corps en durs travaux d'armer, de travaillier, tresnuitier, chevauchier de jour
40 et de nuit, mal dormir, mal mengier et boire, mout de foiz en grans paours et perilz et dures aventures, et pour perdre les corps deshonoreement et dampner les ames perpetuelment? C'est grant penitance pour eulz en cest siecle et trop plus grant en l'autre a touz temps et sanz fin.

Those who use arms in this dishonorable way behave like cowards and traitors, nor would they dare to bear arms in any other way. They attack anyone, taking booty, prisoners, and other valuables, if they find them, and without any justification. There are some who want people to believe that they themselves would never commit such wicked deeds, but they have them done by their own men. There are others who say that they themselves would never engage in such evil works, but they receive those who commit such ill deeds and support them and like them and value them the better for it. Hence it is often said that he does mischief enough who helps mischief.° Indeed all such people who are thus doers or consenters or receivers in relation to such deeds are not worthy to live or to be in the company of men of worth; for they have no regard for themselves: how could they hold others in regard? They have no desire to live a valiant and good life: how could they advise others to do so? They do not care whether people speak well of them: how could they speak well of others? They have no desire to perform deeds which will bring them worthy benefits: how could they achieve this for others? They are not willing to act in a way which will bring them honor: how are they going to honor others? They lack all power of judgment: how could they behave reasonably to others? It could be said that such wicked men who practice arms in so many evil ways are characterized by four very bad forms of ill doing. The first is that of robbery on the highway, treacherously stealing and for no good reason. The second is to murder others in a bad cause. The third is to commit a treacherous deed by seizing, plundering, and robbing others without any challenge and without any wrongdoing on the part of the persons attacked. And the fourth is to take from the churches the wealth through which Our Lord is served and to harm those persons who are ordained to perform such a noble office as to serve God, and by such evil deeds this noble service will not be carried out. Thus they could be held to be nothing more than bad Christians. And cursed be these persons who devote their lives to committing such evil deeds in order to acquire such dishonorable ill fame! And indeed any lords who have such men under their control and have knowledge of their ill doings are no longer worthy to live if they do not inflict such punishment on them that would persuade anyone else who might have a desire for wrongdoing to draw back. And is it not greatly to be wondered at that such people should subject themselves to the great physical trials of enduring great hardships and exertions throughout night, of riding night and day, of sleeping little and having poor food and drink, of being often in fear and peril, at the mercy of all kinds of hazards, all this,

42 Si est bon que aprés ceste chetive matiere l'on se remette a parler des bons chevaliers et des bonnes genz d'armes qui ne se arment ne voudroient armer pour nulles chetives oeuvres ne pour nulz chetiz faiz, fors que pour touz les bons faiz, justes et honorables, sanz avoir nul reproche. Si est bien assavoir que a ycelles tres bonnes genz d'armes peut et doit appartenir de prendre et vestir leurs armeures aussi nettement et devotement et par tres bonne conscience come nul prestre doivent prendre pour eulz vestir les armes de Nostre Seigneur, pour chanter (f.127v) la messe et faire le service de Dieu. Et pour miex en avoir la cognoissance qu'il soit ainsi, devez vous savoir que a touz prestres qui a si haut service sont ordenez de faire, appartient a mener honestes vies; et quant il veulent venir en l'eglise pour chanter la messe, il y doivent venir nettoiez de touz leurs pechiez et en tres grant devocion, et de tres pure et devote conscience doivent prendre les armes de Nostre Seigneur contre les ennemis d'enfer qu'il ne leur puissent empeschier de faire leur devoir de ce tres digne service, dont Nostre Sires leur a donné tele poissance comme de faire venir et consecrer son propre corps entre leurs mains, lequel* de sa grace nous est monstrez et par eulz en Sainte Eglise touz les jours. Ytelles genz si doivent estre de nette vie et de sainte qui a tel saint service sont ordenez de faire. Si le peuent et doivent faire saintement et seurement, que, se il veulent estre net de consciance et sanz pechié, il n'ont doubte de nul, que tant comme il soient en tel estat, il n'ont doubte des dyables qui sont li plus fort ennemi a qui il aient a faire, que des ennemis de ce monde ne doivent il avoir nulle doubte, ne il ne doivent deservir qu'il aient nulz ennemis, ne il ne sont ne doivent estre tenuz de eulz mal vouloir ne d'eulz faire nulz maulx. Si peuent faire leur service seurement, que en cest estat Dieux est avecques eulz visiblement. En gardant ce glorieux service es eglises, la ou il le font, sont il seurement. Et touz ceulz qui y viennent, il y doivent venir devotement et (f.128r) obeïsseument de oïr et veoir le service et de obeïr aus sains comande[me]ns de nostre foy et de les avoir en memoire et de en faire les oeuvres, et de honnorer yceulz par qui telz services sont faiz et telz biens annonciéz. Or pouez veoir que telz bons prestres si se peuent armer des armes Nostre Seigneur pour faire ce tres gloriex service saintement, seurement et sanz doubte de nul, s'en eulz ne demeure. Mais les bons chevalliers

only to lose their lives and their honor and to damn their souls for ever? It means great penance for them in this world and even greater in the next for all eternity.

The Orders of Priesthood and Knighthood Compared

42 It is right that after treating such wretched subject matter we should resume our discussion of good knights and good men-at-arms who do not and would not take up arms for any unworthy undertaking nor in order to commit base deeds but only to perform deeds that are good, just and honorable, free from all reproach. It is certain that it can and should be fitting that all these good men-at-arms don their armor in as pure and devout a way and with as good a conscience as should priests don the armor of Our Lord to sing the mass and conduct the divine service. And in order to have a better understanding of this, you should know that it behooves all priests who are ordained for such a high service to lead honest lives; and when they come into the church to sing the mass, they ought to come there cleansed from all their sins and very devout, and in a pure and holy state of mind should take up the arms of Our Lord against the devils of hell lest these prevent them from fulfillling their duty in this noble service for which Our Lord has given them the power to consecrate His own body in their hands, which is then shown to us by them through God's grace every day in the Holy Church. Such men, who are ordained to perform this holy service, should lead pure and saintly lives. And they can and ought to do so in holiness and in security, for if they have the will to have a clear conscience and to be free from sin, they need fear nothing, for as long as they are in that state, they have no need to be afraid of devils, who are the most powerful enemies they have to deal with, for they should not have to fear enemies of this world, nor should they deserve to have any enemies, nor would one expect any men to be hostile to them or harm them. And they can perform their office in security, for in that situation God is with them visibly. In holding this glorious service in the churches, where they perform it, they are secure. And all those who come there should come devoutly and obediently to hear and see the service and to obey the holy commandments of our faith and to remember them and to act according to them, and to honor those by whom such services are performed and such great and good truth announced. Now you can see that such good priests have the opportunity, if they avail themselves of it, to take up the arms of Our Lord to perform this glorious service in a holy way, in security and without fear if they do not hesitate. But of the good knights and good men-at-arms

35 et les bonnes genz d'armes, qui pour touz les biens qui par avant sont dit se veulent armer et souvent, bien pourroit l'en tenir que leurs vies souverainement devroient estre honestes autant ou plus comme il pourroit appartenir a nul prestre; car il sont en peril touz les jours, et la ou il cuident estre le plus asseur, c'est adont que soudainement les convient armer et prendre
40 pluseurs foiz de dures et perilleuses aventures. Et n'est ce dont de grant neccessité a teles bonnes genz d'armes que quant il veulent prendre et vestir leurs armeures, qui se peuent et doivent bien appeller les armes de Nostre Seigneur, quant l'en les pourte pour soustenir raison et droiture, que l'on les doye prendre et vestir vrais confez et repentans de touz ses pechiez et les
45 prendre et vestir en vraye et pure devocion, et prier a Nostre Seigneur qu'il leur pardoint leurs meffaiz et qu'i leur veille estre en aide? Et trop bien leur appartient a requerir devotement l'aide de Nostre Seigneur a si perilleuse service comme il appartient a faire a eulz en tel mestier d'armes, que a celi service n'ap(f.128v)partient mie que il se face es eglises qui sont belles et
50 fors, ne raison n'est de le faire, ne es lieus seurs, mais convient que tieux services se facent et doivent estre faiz enmi les champs si perilleusement comme a tel estat peut et doit appartenir et quant a ytel service faire que il appartient de faire, pour quoy teles genz s'arment; et ceulx qui viennent a telx services contre ceulx qui le font, n'y viennent point pour honorer ceulz
55 qui sont chiefs de telz services faire, mais y viennent pour eulz tuer et desheriter ou deshonorer, s'il pouoient, et pour prendre touz leurs biens, s'il en ont la poissance. Et par ainsi peut l'on trop bien cognoistre et savoir que telx services et ytelx mestiers, et lequel l'en peut trop bien faire et selon Dieu, est trop plus doubteux, perilleux et penibles a faire pour les corps et
60 pour les ames que nulles autres genz qui soient ordenez a servir Nostre Seigneur en Sainte Eglise n'ont a faire; car il ont et doivent avoir leur regle et ordenance de leur estaz et de leurs vies et de leurs services faire, ainsi comme il doivent et il sont tenus et seurement faire. Et ycelles bonnes genz d'armes ne peuent tenir nulle regle ne ordenance, ne de leurs vies ne de leurs
65 estaz, fors que de touzjours amer et doubter Dieu et garder de lui courroucier et d'eulz estre en telz estaz come touz les jours sont en teles aventures plus que nul autre gent. Et pour ce pourroit l'en bien dire et par verité que entre toutes les genz qui en ce monde peuent estre et de quelque (f.129r) estat qu'il soient, ne religieux ne autres, n'ont tant de besoing d'estre bon
70 crestien entierement, ne de si tres bonne devocion en leurs cuers et de tres honeste vie de leurs corps et de touz leurs ouvraiges faire loyaument et raisonablement, comme ont celle bonne gent d'armes qui ce mestier veulent faire et mener, ainsi comme dessus est dit,*° raisonnablement et selon Dieu;

who, in pursuit of all the benefits mentioned earlier, desire often to take up arms, it might well be considered that they should be of as great or even greater integrity than might be required of a priest, for they are in danger every day, and at the moment when they think themselves to be the most secure, it is then that they may suddenly have to take up arms and often to undertake demanding and dangerous adventures. And is it not essential for such good men-at-arms that when they want to take up and don their armor, which can and should be called the armor of Our Lord, when donned to defend right and justice, that they should put it on in true and pure devoutness, having confessed all their sins and repented of them, praying to Our Lord that He forgive their misdeeds and that it may please Him to come to their aid? And it behooves them to seek in humble devotion for the help of Our Lord in such a perilous service as is required of them in the vocation of arms, for this service may not fittingly be performed in churches, which are beautiful and strong, nor can it by its nature be carried out there nor in safe places, but such services must perforce be performed on the field and in such danger as can and should pertain to such a calling and to the performance of the service for which such men take up arms. And those who come to encounter the men who perform such service do not come to honor those who are the leaders in such a service, but they come there to kill, disinherit, or dishonor them, if they can, and to take everything from them if they have the power. And through this one can know and fully understand that such a service and calling, which can well be performed according to God's will, is very dangerous and perilous, and its practice makes greater physical and spiritual demands than those required of any of the men who are ordained to serve Our Lord in the Holy Church, for they have and ought to have their rule and ordinance and position for the conduct of both their lives and the service it is their duty to perform; but these good men-at-arms have no rule or ordinance to observe in relation to their their way of life and their position except to love and fear God always and to take care not to anger Him, and to be themselves always in such a situation that they are all the time more engaged in such dangerous enterprises than any other men. Hence one could well say truly that of all the men in the world, of whatever estate, whether religious or lay, none have as great a need to be a good Christian to the highest degree nor to have such true devoutness in their hearts nor to lead a life of such integrity and to carry out all their undertakings loyally and with good judgment as do these good men-at-arms who have the will to pursue this calling, as has been set out above, wisely and according to God's will. For

car en teles gens n'a nulle fermeté de vivre, mais plus se doit l'on tenir fermes
de mourir et sanz grant pourveance, que moult de foiz avient que ycelles
gens meurent sanz avoir loisir d'avoir fivres ne autres maladies de corps, de
quoy l'en pourroit gesir longuement et avoir avis sur leurs faiz. Car qui bien
voudroit considerer toutes les perilleuses aventures et brieves qui peuent
avenir a ycelles bonnes genz d'armes qui veulent ainsi deuement travaillier
leurs corps pour venir et acquerir ce tres haut nom de vaillance qui tant vault
et selon Dieu et tant est prisiez, loez et honorez que bien peut l'on dire
fermement que, entre touz les estaz de ce siecle, c'est celi la ou l'on devroit
miex vivre en tel estat comme de cuidier mourir toutes heures et touz les
jours, car entre touz estaz c'est celi en qui l'on peut avoir moins de seurté
de leurs vies, car leurs vies sont en grans paines et travaulz et perilleuses
aventures et hayneuses et envieuses et pluseurs qui voudroient leur mort
avancier. Et pour ce est il que souverainement leurs estaz et leurs vies doivent estre come pour (f.129v) servir et deservir de touz leurs cuers a Nostre
Seigneur et a la glorieuse Virge Marie de bons confors et des tres honorables eschapemens que Nostre Sires leur a faiz et fait de jour [en jour]. Et
certes, se ainsi ne le faisoient, toutes leurs euvres vendroient a chetive fin;
et moult de foiz en a l'on veu et voit on les exemples, comme de perdre
honnour ou corps ou chevance et aucune foiz perdre le tout ensemble, l'ame
encores avecques, pour deffaute de non avoir cognoissance a Nostre Seigneur des biens que il donne et fait moult de foiz a pluseurs qui ne li en
rendent graces, dont puis leur vient a tart du repentir, que l'on ne pourroit
mie avoir le temps. Et n'est ce bien raison que, ce aucuns reçoit et a bien
d'autrui, qu'il ne soit tenuz du deservir? Et moult de foiz a l'on veu avenir
que entre touz ceulz de plus mauvaise vie qui en cest siecle regnent se tiennent de mal faire a ceulz de qui il ont receu aucuns biens, comme de larrons
et robeurs, qui moult de foiz se sont delaissiez d'embler et de rober a ceulz
qui leur avoient fait biens en aucune maniere, et de aucuns murdriers qui
tuent genz pour avoir le leur, qui par ceste mesmes maniere s'en sont retraiz
de le faire a ceulx dont il ont et avoient receu aucuns biens, et de aucuns
traitours qui n'ont voulu trahir ou ont fait assavoir a ceulz de qui il avoient
eu aucun bien. Et quant ycelles genz et de si mauvaises condicions et qui
tant ont volenté de mal faire, et en ce mal veulent (f.130r) il reguerredonner
les biens qu'il ont euz d'autrui en eulz retraiant de leur malfaire, et n'est ce
dont mieulx raison que ceulz qui n'ont nulle volenté de faire telz maulx ne
de mener teles mauvaises vies, que il ne doivent miex deservir les biens,
proffiz, honnour ou services qu'il ont euz de autrui et en pluseurs meilleurs
manieres que celle malvaise gent dessus dite ne le devroient faire? Certes oïl.

there is in such men no firm purpose to cling to life; they should rather show firmness in the face of death and be prepared to meet it at any time, for it often happens that these people die without the leisure to fall ill of fever or other physical ailments from which a person might suffer for a long time and reflect on his past deeds. Indeed, let anyone consider all these perilous adventures which may in a brief span be encountered by these men-at-arms who choose to make the appropriate personal and physical effort to achieve the high reputation for valor which is of such great worth and is in accord with the will of God. It is indeed so prized, praised, and honored that one can say in all certainty that of all the conditions of this world, it is the one above all others in which one would be required to live with the constant thought of facing death at any hour on any day; for of all conditions it is the one in which one's life is least secure, for it is a life spent in great effort and endurance and perilous adventure arising from others' hate and envy, where many would like to cause one's death. Therefore the position and way of life of these men-at-arms should above all be devoted to serving with all their hearts Our Lord and the glorious Virgin Mary in return for the good comfort and honorable escape from death which Our Lord has granted them from day to day. And indeed, if they did not act in this way, all their undertakings would come to a miserable end, and examples of this are often to be seen, such as losing one's honor or one's life or one's fortune, and sometimes all of them together and one's soul as well, through lack of gratitude to Our Lord for the gifts He has bestowed on many who do not give Him thanks for them and repent too late of this, for there might be no time left. And is it not right that if some one receives a gift from another, he should be required to give something in return? And it has often been seen to happen that men of the most evil way of life, of whom there are many to be found in this world, refrain from harming those from whom they have received some benefits, like thieves and robbers, who often stop stealing from those who have in some way done them favors, and like some murderers, who kill people to get their possessions and in the same way hold back from murdering those from whom they have received some favors, and like some traitors, who have chosen not to betray or have given information to those from whom they have received some benefit. These people of such bad character and who are so intent on evil doing, in this evil doing want to give something in return for those benefits they have received from others by not practicing their evil doing on them. Is there not, therefore, even greater reason that those who have no intention of committing such misdeeds or leading such wicked lives, ought to give more

Et ou pourroit l'on trouver nul qui tant de biens, de graces, de misericordes, d'onnours, de toutes perfeccions, de touz biens peut faire ne face touz les jours, come fait et peut faire cilz tres glorieux Sires qui est lasus et sa tres glorieuse Virge Mere a touz ceulz qui les requierent ainsi comme il doivent et par tele devocion comme l'on doit requerir tel Seigneur et tele Dame, qui si tres habundanment donnent tant de biens a ceulz qui les veulent servir de tres bon cuer et deservir les biens a qui il les font? Et pour ce que c'est le souverain Seigne[u]r en qui sont touz les biens et dont touz les biens viennent et pour qui touz les biens sont faiz et qui est trestout poissans de les donner si tost comme il veult et les faire durer si longuement comme il li plaist, et poissans de les oster et a ceulz qui ne le recognoissent ainsi comme il doivent, si tost comme il li plaist, pour ce est il que nul ne doit tenir en soy que biens qu'il leur soit faiz d'autrui, ne honnours qui leur viengne d'autrui, ne services qu'il aient eu d'autrui, ne proffiz qu'il aient eu d'autrui, (f.130v) viengne tant seulement d'iceulz mais de la grace de Dieu a qui il plaist ainsi qu'il soit fait; que l'on doit savoir que nulz n'a rienz en ce monde seur qui sien soit, fors tant seulement comme il plaist a Dieu qui tout preste et tout peut reprendre comme drois sires souverains qu'Il en est et tout a sa volenté. Et quant ceulz doivent deservir et sont tenuz de servir a ceulz de* qui il reçoivent aucuns biens, bien doivent dont servir et deservir, loer et doubter, honorer et aorer a cent doubles et sanz nombre de tout leur cuer entierement, humblement et devotement ce tres glorieux Seigneur et sa tres glorieuse Vierge Mere, que par son prest et par sa volenté a baillié les biens et les graces a ceulz qui les font a autrui; car il n'ont rienz en tels graces ne en telx biens fors tant comme Dieu leur laisse et preste de sa grace et non plus. Mais moult en y a qui po se prennent garde dont les biens, les graces, les honnours, les hautesces et les seigneuries leur viennent, mais les prennent si deshordeneement comme l'en peut veoir ou temps de maintenant, que quant Nostre Sires veult, sueffre que li aucun aient biens [et] honnours dont il ont fait qu'il ont aucune bonne renommee, si leur semble que celle renomme[e] leur doie touzjours durer et sanz faillir et que leur doie touzjours avenir ainsi. Et se autrefoiz leur avient ainsi qu'il aient fait de quoy leur bonne renomme[e] leur croist, si se pourpensent li aucuns comment il la pourront faire durer, si se delaissent a souvenir de (f.131r) Nostre Seigneur et se prennent a souvenir du tout de la plaisance de cest siecle, si se font de manieres et de contenance meilleur qu'il ne sont ne que l'on ne les tient. Et se il ont aucune poissance de mise, il n'endureroient a mettre du leur la quarte partie ou nient en honnourer Nostre Seigneur ne sa douce Mere ne sains ne saintes ne Sainte Eglise ne donner aus povres ne en au-

in return for the benefits, profits, honors, or services they have received from another, and in many better ways than should those above-mentioned evil men? Indeed yes. And where could one find anyone who can and does always bestow so many benefits, favors, mercies, honors, and every kind of perfection and good other than that very glorious Lord who is up above and His glorious Virgin Mother? They give to all those who ask in the right way and with such devoutness as is fitting for requests made to such a Lord and such a Lady, who have bestowed so great an abundance of benefits on those who have the will to serve them with all their hearts and to give something in return for these benefits to those who grant them. It is indeed the Sovereign Lord in whom all that is good is to be found and from whom all that is good comes and for whom all good is done and who has the power to give all good things, whenever it is His will, and to make them last as long as it pleases Him, and who also has the power to take them away, whenever it pleases Him, from those who do not acknowledge Him. Therefore no one should consider that the good done them by others, or honors bestowed on them by others, or service done them by others, or any profit deriving from others, that any of these come only from other people. These benefits come rather from the grace of God whom it pleases that these things should be done, for it should be known that no one has anything in the world which is certainly his except in so far as it pleases God who lends everything and can take back everything as the true Sovereign Lord that He is, with everything dependent on His will. And when it is the duty of these men to acknowledge and they are required to serve those from whom they receive some benefit, they ought then indeed to serve and acknowledge, praise and be in awe of, honor and worship a hundredfold and infinitely more with all their hearts, totally, humbly, and devoutly this glorious Lord and His glorious Virgin Mother, For those who pass on to others these benefits and favors have themselves been granted them by God as a loan and dependent on His will: they have nothing of these favors and benefits except what God allows them and lends them of His grace, and they have nothing more. But there are many who pay little heed to the source of these benefits, favors, honors, high positions, and lordships which come to them, but grab them in such an unseemly fashion as is to be seen today; and when Our Lord by His will allows some to have benefits and honors from which they gain some kind of renown, it seems to them that this renown should last for ever without coming to an end, and that it should always happen to them like this. And if in the past they happen to have achieved something which increased their good name,

mosnes ne a paier ce qu'il doivent ne satisfier a autrui, que il veulent mettre
en leurs povres corps aourner et parer* de pierres, de perles, d'ouvrages et
de brodure qui tant coustent cher et si po valent, et les aneaus en leurs dois
155 et les grosses courroies d'or ou d'argent, dont li ouvraiges coustent plus
moult de foiz que ne fait l'or ou l'argent de quoy elles sont faites. Et miex
leur vausist ores mettre celle mission en autres meilleurs usaiges, dont Nostre Seigneur leur en sceust trop plus grant gré et miex leur en rendist tel
guerredon et si grant et meilleur qu'il ne li sceussent requerir. Mais ainsi
160 comme il mettent Dieu en oublie pour teles chetivetez, et Dieux les y met
autresi, si en perdent a venir et parfornir es grans biens et honnours qu'il
ont euz et ont encomenciez de faire, que touz ces riches aournemens
qu'il mettent sur leurs chetiz corps qui n'ont heure ne terme de durer et
n'est fors que de leur remirer en eulz ce qui tantost s'en peut aler, mesmes
165 en pensant que d'eulz doient un chascun tenir grant compte. Et encores si
tres deshonestement (f.131v) sont il vestus que ce dont uns chascuns doit et
devroit avoir plus grant honte de le monstrer, c'est ce qu'il monstrent touz
les jours a touz ceulz qui le veulent veoir, car il ne peuent laissier qu'il ne
monstrent leurs dos a qui qui le veille veoir. Et se il se veulent seoir, il
170 ne s'ont de quoy couvrir ne devant ne derrieres, et de ce n'ont il nulle honte,
qui doit estre si honteuse chose a le monstrer. Et c'est bien raison que les
outrages des ornemens dessus diz qu'il* mettent sur eulz leur font oublier
moult de biens a faire, et maintes en y a qui oublient toutes hontez; et ainsi
comme il oublient toutes hontes, ainsi sont obliez toutes honnours, et bien
175 peut apparoir en pluseurs manieres, dont c'est pitiez et domages. Et encor
ne leur souffist il mie de estre telx comme Diex les a faiz, mais se tiennent
mal a paiez de telz comme il sont, si se varainglent et se estraingnent par le
ventre tant et si fort que le ventre que Dieu leur avoit donné il veulent
mettre a ny qu'il n'en ont point, n'onques ne l'eurent autre, et scet chascuns
180 le contraire. Et de ceulz ainsi estrains a l'on veu maintes [fois] que en
l'armeure les en a convenu desarmer a grant haste, qu'il ne pouoient plus
souffrir leur harnois, et d'autres qui en sont enz pris hastivement, qu'il ne
pouoient faire ce qu'il deussent pour deffaut de pouoir pour cause d'estre
ainsi estrains. Et moult en sont enz mors armez pour celle mesmes cause a
185 petite defense, et desarmez sont il si estrains et si athachiez qu'il ne (f.132r)
se peuent de rienz entremettre, car il ne se peuent ploier bas ne il ne peuent
courre ne saillir ne gester pierre ne autres gieus de force ou aucune apper-
teté, et envis se peuent seoir et ausi po redrecier que tout a grant poine. Et
d'aucuns en y pourroit bien avoir qui miex ameroient resembler estre bons
190 que le estre, mais n'en doubtoit° nul, tant soit desguisé, ou autres tant soit

some reflect on how they might make it last, and they no longer remember Our Lord and begin to think only of the pleasures of this world, and they present themselves in their ways of behavior and bearing as better than they either are or are held to be by others. And if they have any financial resources, they cannot bring themselves to devote a fourth part to honoring Our Lord or His gentle Mother or the Saints or the Holy Church, or to giving alms to the poor or paying what they owe or settling their debts to others, for they want to spend it all on adorning their wretched bodies and on decking themselves out with precious stones, pearls, fine work, and embroidery, which cost so much and are worth so little, and on buying the rings on their fingers and great bands of gold and silver of which the workmanship costs many times more than the gold or silver of which they are made. And it would be better for them now to put this expenditure to better use, for which Our Lord would look more favorably upon them and would give them so much in return that they could not ask for a greater or better reward. But just as they forget God for the sake of such paltry trifles, so God too will forget them. And because of this they will no longer win the great benefits and honors they won at the outset, for they deck out with rich adornments their wretched bodies, destined to endure for so short a time,° and all that is left to contemplate in these men is that which at any time may vanish away, even while they think everyone should hold them to be of great account. And they are dressed in such an indecent way that that which everyone ought to be most ashamed to show is what they show all the time to those who want to look, for they cannot refrain from showing their backsides to whoever wants to see them. And if they want to sit down, they do not have enough to cover themselves neither in front nor behind, and they feel no shame about showing what should cause them such great shame. And it is to be expected that the excessive adornments with which they deck themselves out make them neglect to perform many great deeds; and there are many who forget all shame, and just as they forget all shame, so is all honor forgotten; this can be seen in various forms of behavior, which is a great pity. What is more, it is not enough for them to be as God made them; they are not content with themselves as they are, but they gird themselves up and so rein themselves in round the middle of their bodies that they seek to deny the existence of the stomachs which God has given them: they want to pretend that they have not and never have had one, and everyone knows that the opposite is true. And one has seen many of those thus constricted who have to take off their armor in a great hurry, for they could no longer bear to wear their equipment; and there are others

simples, que es besoignes faire, tant en l'armeure comme dehors, que ceulz qui plus y font de bien, et plus en est parlé et plus sont honorez entre touz autres. Et ainsi le veult Dieux, car Nostre Sires assiet et met ses biens la ou il voit qu'il est miex emploié, et aussi les hontes et les maulz sur yceulz qui cuident avoir les biens et les honnours d'eulz meismes sanz souvenir de lui, et ce doit l'on tenir et par verité. Mes pour ce n'est ce mie que trop bien n'appartiengne et peut appartenir es joennes gens qu'il soient en touz estaz a l'ostel et es champs honestement, faitissement et joliement sanz grant outrage et de jolieses choses de po de coust et souvent renouvelees; car raisons est que l'on se gouverne selon les ages, mes que l'on ne mette mie tant sur le corps de li que li plus demoure a faire, c'est a entendre le bien. Et s'il est ainsi que l'on soit jolis ainsi et en bonne maniere comme il affiert a joennes gens, si ne le doit l'en mie faire pour orgueil ne oublier Nostre Seigneur, mais garder de tant cointir que Dieux vous face oublier, que, se Dieu mettez en oubli, Dieux vous y mettra (f. 132v) autresi. Mais le doit l'en faire pour estre avecques les autre joennes et pour avoir maniere d'estre avecques eulz, et belle chose et vertueuse est de passer joennesce honestement, et ceuls doivent bien loer Dieu toute leur vie qui ainsi la passent.

43 Et quant a parler de la joennesce des dames, damiselles et autres fames d'estat, qui le peuent faire, peut l'on bien dire que a elles appartient de porter belles couronnes, cercles, chapiaux, perles, pierres, aneaulx, brodures, bien vestues et bien ornees de leurs testes et de leurs corps selon ce que chascune le a d[r]oit*° peut faire et peut appartenir de le faire miex assez qu'il n'appartient de les porter aus hommes, que les jeunes damiselles si s'en

who have been quickly seized, for they could not do what they should have done because they were handicapped by being thus constricted; and many have died inside their armor for the same reason, that they could put up little defense. And even without their armor they are so constricted and strapped up that they cannot undertake anything, for they cannot bend down, nor can they run nor jump nor throw stones nor engage in any other sports requiring strength or agility; indeed they can hardly sit down, and it demands just as great an effort to struggle to their feet again. There might be some who would prefer to give the appearance of being a good man-at-arms rather than the reality, but no one, however devious or simple, would doubt that when it comes to achieving something, whether in or out of armor, it is those who perform the greatest deeds whose names are on everyone's lips and who are most honored. It is God's will that it should be so, for Our Lord bestows his benefits where he sees they will be best used, and from Him come also the disgrace and ill fortune which he bestows on those who think they can have the benefits and honors by their own efforts without remembering Him; and this should be accepted as the truth. But there is no reason why it should not and cannot be fitting for young men in all circumstances, whether at home or on the field, to be dressed decently, neatly, elegantly, with due restraint and with attractive things of low cost and often replaced; for it is right that people should behave, each according to their years, provided so much be not devoted to adornment of the body that the more important things remain undone, that is to say, great and good deeds. And if anyone is thus elegantly dressed and in good fashion, as befits a young man, it should not be done through pride nor should Our Lord be forgotten; but be careful not to spruce yourself up so much that you do not remember God, for if you do not remember God, God will not remember you. But one should dress well when in company with other young people and to fit in with them; and it is a fine and good thing to spend one's youth in honest fashion, and those who spend it thus should praise God all their lives.

What Young Ladies Should Wear

43 As for the youth of noble ladies, damsels, and other women of high rank, it can indeed be said that for those of them who are in a position to do so, it is fitting to wear fine circlets, coronetals, pearls, precious stones, rings, embroidery, to be beautifully dressed, their heads and bodies well adorned according to what is right and fitting for each person to do; it is much more suitable for them to wear fine adornments than for men, for

marient aucune foiz miex quant l'on les voit en bon estat et qui bien leur avient. Et celles qui sont mariees si se doivent mettre et tenir ou meilleur estat que elles peuent pour miex plair[e] a leurs maris et pour estre plus convenablement entre les autres dames et damiselles. Et a fames d'estat appartient trop bien de estre es meilleurs estaz de riches aornemens* sur elles et miex qu'il n'appartient aus hommes, que les biens des hommes et la cognoissance sont trop plus tost cogneuz et sceuz et en plus de manieres que la cognoissance des fames ne leurs biens* ne peuent estre sceuz, car les hommes vont ou il veulent entre les gens et en pluseurs pays: ce ne font mie les fa(f.133r)mes. Et si peuent les homes jouster et tournoier: ce ne peuent mie les fames. Et si se arment les hommes pour la guerre: ce ne font mie les fames. Et vont et sont* en plus de compaignies que les fames ne peuent estre. Si appartient aus fames, quer, pour ce qu'elles se tiennent plus es hostiex que les hommes ne font et po s'en partent et tant ne peuent avoir de cognoissance, que elles soient en meilleur estaz de leurs corps et miex aournees de joyaus et d'atours et de vesteures que il n'affiert aus hommes qui en tant de manieres peuent avoir la cognoissance des biens quant l'en les a faiz. Si doit l'en laissier aus dames et aus damiselles ces riches aornemens qui bien et trop miex leur sieent a porter sus elles que ne font aus hommes, car pour leur bonté et beauté et bonne maniere qui en elles sont, avecques tels aournemens comme desus est dit et qui bien leur avient et leur siet, a l'on cognoissance de elles. Si leur doit on laissier les riches aournemens pour elles. Dont yceulz qui ont volenté de bien faire, de quoy se peuent il miex parer et aourner que d'estre bien condicionés de toutes bonnes taches comme d'estre preudommes sages, loyaux, humbles, liez, larges, courtois, appers, hardiz et bien travaillans et [de bonne] maniere entre touz, sanz soy loer ne mal dire d'autrui? Et se de telle robe vous voulez vestir et enveloper et qu'elle soit brodee et [de] tel ouvraige comme dessus est dit (f.133v) et enjouellee et aournee de telz joyaus comme dit est dessus et de y mettre et adjoindre les autres biens et enseignemens qui par avant sont diz, bien pourront*° dire qu'il n'est robe tant soit courte ne estroite, ne astaches tant les y sceut on mettre fors, ne pierres ne perles ne courroies d'or ne d'argent ne touz autres joyaux ne les pourroit si bien vestir, ne si bien athacher pour garder de faire mal, ne dont il peussent estre miex parez, aournez, enjoyllez, loez, amez, prisiez et honorez selon Dieu et de tout le monde comme il seroient d'estre vestuz et aournez de toutes ycelles bonnes condicions ci dessus escriptes, et ceulz qui plus en avront, plus loez et amez en seront. Et se vous voulez estre armez cointement et joliement et que voz armes soient bien ramenteues, recogneues et aournees entre les autres, si

young damsels sometimes achieve better marriages when they are seen in rich apparel which suits them. And those who are married ought to maintain as high a standard of dress as they can, the better to please their husbands and to appear in appropriate fashion among other noble ladies and damsels. And it behooves women of high rank to present themselves in the most stately apparel, wearing the richest adornments, and it befits them better than it does men, for the qualities and reputation of men are more quickly known and recognized and in more ways than the qualities and reputation of women can be known, for men go where they want among people and in different lands, but women cannot do this. Men can joust and tourney: women cannot do this. Men take up arms for war: women cannot do this. Men go out more widely in society than women can. It is appropriate for women, because they spend more time at home than do men and do not often leave it and cannot get the same recognition, that they should pay more attention to their physical appearance and be more splendidly adorned with jewels, rich ornaments, and apparel than would be suitable for men, who can in so many different ways win recognition for their achievements. One should leave to noble ladies and damsels these rich adornments, the wearing of which suits them so much better than it does men, for by the goodness and beauty and fine behavior to be found in them, together with such adornments as are mentioned above, which suit them well, they receive recognition. These rich ornaments should be left to them. Therefore, for those who have the will to rise to great achievement, how can they better adorn themselves than by being equipped for it by all the good qualities? They can do so by being men of worth, wise, loyal, without arrogance, joyful, generous, courteous, expert, bold, and active, and of good conduct toward all others, without indulging in self praise or speaking ill of others. And if you want to wear such a garment as this, embroidered and richly worked with the qualities described above, and encrusted and decorated with those kinds of jewels, and to add to these the other qualities and precepts set out earlier, it could well be said that there is no garment, however short or tight, nor however well adorned with bands, precious stones, pearls, gold and silver straps, and all the other jewels, that could provide so great a protection against doing wrong, nor by which one could be better dressed, adorned, bejeweled, praised, loved, esteemed, and honored in the sight of God and all the world, as one would be through being invested and adorned with all those good qualities set out above. And those who have the greater amount of these qualities will be the more greatly praised and loved. And if you want to be armed elegantly and styl-

querez les faiz d'armes souvent et diligenment. Et quant Dieu vous donra si bon eur de les trouver, si faites bien vostre devoir sagement et hardiement, sanz rien redoubter fors que honte, en besoignant de la main et du travail de vostre corps tant et si avant comme la puissance s'i pourra esten-
50 dre au domage de ceulz a qui vous avrez a faire et touzjours des premiers. Si avront plus cognoissance voz amis et voz anemis de vostre bienfait, et ainsi seront voz armes belles a regarder partout, et en serez trop plus cointement et joliement armez que se elles estoient (f.134r) toutes semees de perles et de pierres precieuses, ne n'est broderie qui a ceste beauté se
55 prengne. Si devez cointir voz armeures de tel ouvrage, et qui plus en fait, plus en est muez et parez. Et se vous voulez estre fort et seurement armez a l'encontre de touz perilz d'arme et de honte et moult de foiz de perilz de corps, si soiez bien avisiez de mener teles vies et si plaisans a Nostre Seigneur que par raison il li doie souvenir de vous quant vous l'appellerez
60 a voz tres grans neccessitez a perilz de corps. Et ne vous armez ne ne mettez voz corps en peril en nulle maniere, se vous ne vous mettez en si bon estat envers Dieu que il vous doie oïr en voz prieres a requeste que vous li voudrez faire de raison et que vous ne doiez trop doubter la mort. Et se ai[n]si le voulez faire bien continuelment et souvent, travaillez vous, armez vous,
65 combatez vous, ainsi comme vous devrez, alez partout et par mer et par terre et en pluseurs paÿs, sanz doubter nulz perilz ne sanz espargne de voz chetiz corps, dont vous ne devez tenir nul compte, fors que de l'ame et vivre honoreement, si serez partout sauvez, amez, prisiez et honorez, cogneuz et ramenteuz pour voz grans biens et travaulz et bons faiz entre voz amis et
70 ennemis et en pluseurs paÿs et marches et de ceulz qui onques ne vous virent ne jamais ne vous verront, ne lonc aprés voz mors, dont l'en priera pour vous et en vostre vie et (134v) aprés vostre mort, et vostre hoirs et lignages en seront aprés honorez.

44 Or peut on assez veoir et cognoistre quel tres noble tresor est a amasser touz ces biens dessus diz et en mettre assez ensemble; et qui plus en amasse et met entour lui, si est souverainement* riches, aornez et prisiez et amez et doubtez et plaisans a Dieu et toutes gens, et belle grace et grans ver-

ishly and desire that your arms be remembered, recognized, and adorned above others, seek constantly and diligently opportunities to perform deeds of arms. And when God grants you the good fortune to find them, do your duty wisely and boldly, fearing nothing except shame, striving with the skill of your hand and the effort of your body to as great a degree as your powers can extend in order to inflict damage on your opponents, always being among the first in battle. By so doing you will receive greater recognition for your achievements from your friends and enemies, and your arms will be splendid to behold, and you will through this appear more elegant and stylish under arms than you would if your equipment were strewn with pearls and precious stones, nor is there any embroidery which can be compared to this beauty. You should make your armor more elegant with such work; and whoever achieves the most is the most transformed and adorned. And if you want to be strong and securely armed against all the perils of the soul and against shame, and on many occasions against physical dangers, be careful to lead a life that will be pleasing to Our Lord, that He might have reason to remember you when you call upon Him in your times of great need, when in physical danger. And do not take up arms nor in any way put your life in danger without first seeking to be in such a good state in relation to God that He will listen to any entreaties and requests that you might with reason make to Him in your prayers, so that you should not fear death too much. And if you want to continue to achieve great deeds, exert yourself, take up arms, fight as you should, go everywhere across both land and sea and through many different countries, without fearing any peril and without sparing your wretched body, which you should hold to be of little account, caring only for your soul and for living an honorable life. If you do this, you will be everywhere safeguarded, loved, esteemed, and honored, recognized and remembered for your fine achievements and efforts and great feats among your friends and enemies and throughout many lands and marches, and even by those who never saw you and never will see you, and long after your death. Because of all this people will pray for you both during your lifetime and after your death, and your heirs and descendants will be honored afterward.

A Good Man-at-Arms Can Be Pleasing to God
44 Now one can see and know what a noble treasure it is to amass and gather together all these above-mentioned good achievements; and he who amasses and gathers together the most is supremely rich, adorned, valued, loved, feared, and pleasing to God and to all people. And fine grace and

tuz est en ceulz qui seculierement peuent mener teles vies dont les corps peuent honoreement en cest siecle conduire leurs ames en paradis en l'autre avecques celle g[l]orieuse compagnie qui durera touz temps en si tres grant joie et sanz fin. Hé Dieux! coment ont les cuers de faire maulz ceuls qui les font, quant il voient et ont cognoissance de ceuls qui les biens font, qui font ycels biens si seurement et si joyeusement, si honoreement et si plaisanmant et sanz doubte de nul et finer bonnement? Et les mauls a faire sont si perilleux, si merencolieux, si deshonorables, si mal* gracieux° et sanz nulle seurté et pour venir a tres mauvaise [fin]*. Et que pourroit on dire autre chose que mal de ceuls qui ont le chois et qui le savroient et pourroient bien faire, quant il laissent les biens a faire, qui sont si seur et si honorables, pour faire les mauls, qui sont si perilleux a faire et si tres hontables? Et se vous voulez savoir coment vous serez confortez en faisant et en multipliant (f.135r) touz ces biens et en delaissant la volenté de faire touz ces maulz, si vous mettez de touz vos cuers a prier a celle tres glorieuse Vierge Marie que de sa benigne et humble grace et par la sainte puissance qu'elle a envers son tres precieus et glorieus et souverain Seigneur et Pere et Filz que de sa tres digne, humble, piteuse misericorde il ait son tres glorieux regart sus voz cuers, sus voz corps, sus voz oeuvres et sus vos armes, car° il vous veille garder, maintenir et soustenir en touz voz bons estaz en sa sainte, benigne grace, et laquelle grace vous devez desirer souverainement de* touz voz cuers de y venir de voz encommancemens jusques a voz definemens. Or est il bien chetiz qui laisse telle tres douce fontaine ou chascuns se puet resasier et saouler de touz ses bons desirs, car il n'y peut avoir fors que bon encomencement, plus bon moyen et tres bonne fin. Et si est celle fontaine et tuit si ruissel abandonnee a touz ceulz qui par bien faire en veulent avoir et demander. Et se vous voulez boire de celle fontaine et estre lavez et nettoiez de ses ruissiaus, et venir et acomplir touz vos bons desirs, si vous souviengne de la droite doys dont celle fontaine vient: c'est a parler proprement Dieux nostre createur qui voult aombrer a passer par celle glorieuse fontaine de netteté et de virginité, la tres douce glorieuse Vierge Marie. Adont de ceste glorieuse fontaine s'estendent tant de ses ruissiaux sus (f.135v) nous autres povres pecheurs dont elle prie et qui nous ravoie et enseigne touz les jours pour nous et ramaine par ses douces prieres a bonnes voies et a bonne fin envers celle glorieuse doys, son tres benoist cher filz. Or bien devez po resongnier et redobter voz chetiz corps entre vous qui avez volenté de acquerir ces grans biens et honnours de les mettre en peril, en poine et en travail de quelque estat qu'il soient, un chascun endroit de son estat, car il n'y a ne viel ne jeune ne fort ne foible ne sain ne malade ne riche ne povre

great worth are to be found in those who can live in secular terms the kind of lives through which mortal men can with honor in this world lead their souls into paradise in the next and take their place in that glorious company which will continue for ever in bliss without end. Ah God! how do those who commit evil deeds have the heart to do so when they see and know those who perform great deeds and do so with such confidence and joy, so honorably and pleasantly, and without fear of anyone, and coming to a good end; and wrongdoing is so perilous, so grievous, so dishonorable, so disgraceful,° so unsure, and leading to a bad end? And how can one say anything but ill of those who have the choice and who have the skill and strength to perform worthy deeds, when they give up doing those things which are so assuredly honorable in order to do bad deeds which are so perilous to carry out and so shameful? And if you want to know how you will be encouraged in performing and multiplying all these great deeds and in abandoning any desire to commit all these evil deeds, pray with all your hearts to the glorious Virgin Mary that with her benign and humble grace and by the holy influence she has over her precious, glorious and sovereign Lord, Father and Son, that of His noble gentle tender mercy He may, in his glory, look upon your hearts, bodies, and actions, and upon your souls, that He may preserve you,° maintain and sustain you in a good state within His holy, benign grace, this grace which you should desire above all else and with all your hearts to participate in from your beginnings until your ends. Now he is indeed a poor wretch who leaves this sweet spring at which everyone can quench his thirst and satisfy all his good desires, for he can only find there a good beginning, a better middle and a very good end. And this spring and all its streams are accessible to all those who have done worthy deeds and want to partake of it. And if you want to drink from this spring, to be washed and purified by its streams, and to attain and fulfill all your good desires, remember the true source from which this spring comes: that is, to speak plainly, God our Creator, who chose to become incarnate by passing through this glorious spring of purity and virginity, the gentle and glorious Virgin Mary. Therefore, from this glorious spring, so many streams spread out over us other poor sinners, as she prays for us and guides and teaches us, and brings us back by her gentle entreaties to the paths of righteousness and to a good end in relation to this glorious source, her dear and blessed Son. Now you who have the will to attain these great achievements and honors should not hesitate nor fear to subject your feeble bodies to danger, pain, and effort, of whatever rank you may be, each one according to his station in life, for there is no one, whether old or young, strong

qui sache liquel doit morir le premier. Si doit l'en mener bonne vie, s'avra l'on moins freeur de la mort, et doit l'on bien vivre aise et nient redoubter, qui ainsi bien vit et en tele esperance de bien comme vous devez avoir en ce tres glorieus Seigneur et sa tresdouce glorieuse Vierge Mere. Et quant l'en cognoist ou l'on doit prendre son fondement de tout ces biens dont l'en doit avoir si tres grant envie et volente d'y venir et de les avoir, pourquoy ne les fait l'en? Que vous devez estre certains et tenir fermement que vous n'avez nulle autre chose a faire, fors tant que, se vous amez Dieu, que Dieu vous amera. Servez le bien: miex le vous deservira. Doubtez le: il vous asseurera. Honorez le: il vous honorera. Requerez le, et assez vous donra. Priez li merci: il vous pardonra. Reclamez le en voz perilz: il vous en getera. Appellez (f.136r) le en voz doubtes, et il vous gardera. Priez li qu'il vous conforte, et il vous confortera. Creés le parfaitement, et il vous sauvera en sa glorieuse compaignie et en son tres dous paradis qui touzjours mais durera, ne ja ne finera. Qui ainsi faire le voudra, le corps et l'arme sauvera, et qui le contraire fera, d'arme et de corps dampnez sera. Priez a Dieu pour celui qui ce livre fait a.

EXPLICIT CHARNI: CHARNY:

or weak, healthy or ill, rich or poor, who knows who is to die first. So one should lead a good life, and then one will be less afraid of death, and one should indeed live at ease and fear nothing if one dwells in such good hope as one should have in the glorious Lord and His gentle and glorious Virgin Mother. And when one knows where one could find the foundation for all these good things which one should have such a great desire and will to attain, why does one not do what is required? For you should be certain of and hold firmly to the belief that you have no other course of action to take except to remember that if you love God, God will love you. Serve Him well: He will reward you for it. Fear Him: He will make you feel secure. Honor Him: He will honor you. Ask of Him and you will receive much from Him. Pray to Him for mercy: He will pardon you. Call on Him when you are in danger: He will save you from it. Turn to Him when you are afraid, and He will protect you. Pray to Him for comfort, and He will comfort you. Believe totally in Him and He will bring you to salvation in His glorious company and His sweet paradise which will last for ever without end. He who is willing to act thus will save his body and his soul, and he who does the opposite will be damned in soul and body. Pray to God for him who is the author of this book.

                Explicit Charni, Charny.

Notes to the Text and Translation

Variants

B = Brussels, Bibliothèque Royale de Belgique, MS 11124–26, the base manuscript.
P = Paris, Bibliothèque Nationale, MS, nouvelles acquisitions françaises 4736.
L = Kervyn de Lettenhove's edition of the text in *Oeuvres complètes de Froissart,*, Brussels 1877.

Full variants from *P* are given except for minor variations in orthography. From *L*, where the spellings and constructions of the Brussels manuscript seems to have been modified quite freely, only significant variants affecting meaning or sentence structure are given. The reading which has been adopted in the text is always given first, followed by a square bracket. All divisions in the text correspond to divisions in the base manuscript marked by decorated initials, with only two exceptions. Section 30 is marked in *B* by spacing in the form of a paragraph but has only a small, plain initial; however, it is clearly marked in *P* by spacing and a decorated initial. Section 31 is marked in *B* only by a small plain initial and no paragraph, but is again clearly marked in *P* by a decorated initial and paragraph.

    1.2   en voeil] *BP*   voeil *L*

    3.6   si appert] *BP*]   appert *L*
    3.14   font bien] *BP*   sont bien *L*

    4.3   font bien] *BP*   sont bien *L*
    4.5   que bon] *BP*   qui bon *L*
    4.10   faictes] *BP*   faittes *L*

    5.1   pays] *B*   pais *PL*
    5.2   que] *BP*   car *L*

5.5	font a] *BP*	sont a *L*
5.9	et heritage de leurs amis] *BL*	et leur heritage *P*
5.13	li servir] *BP*	le servir *L*
6.5	itele] *B* telle *P*	icelle *L*
6.6	deussent] *BP*	seussent *L*
7.20	des bonnes] *BP*	de bonnes *L*
7.21	que par] *BP*	car par *L*
9.14	grant mise] *BL*	grant misere *P*
9.16	entre ceulx] *BP*	outre ceulx *L*
9.18	arrestent et ne p.] *BP*	arrestent ne p. *L*
9.18	mie trouver] *B* mie se trouver *L*	mie estre trouuez *P*
9.22	en tout plain de pais] *B* en tout plain de pays *L* en pluseurs pays *P*	
10.2	font a] *BP*	sont a *L*
10.2	font a] *B*	sont a *PL*
10.17	font a] *BP*	sont a *L*
10.19	de legier] *BP*	do legier *L*
10.20	que quant] *BL*	car q. *P*
11.4	aient bien] *BL*	eussent bien *P*
12.9–10	avoient eu nulle] *BP*	avoient nulle *L*
12.16	font les] *L*	sont les *BP*
13.1	font a] *BP*	sont a *L*
13.9	attendre et de trouver les] *BL*	attendre les *P*
13.18	jusques au temps] *BP*	jusques un temps *L*
14.2	font a] *BP*	sont a *L*
14.8	font il] *BP*	sont il *L*
15.1–2	font a] *BP*	sont a *L*
15.12	foiz comment une] *BL*	foiz de quoy comme une *P*
15.14	au gaing] *BP*	aux grans gaings *L*
15.23	cuer et] *BPL* In B que *is crossed out after* cuer

16.1	ces estas] *BL*	ces cas et estas *P*
16.16–17	et tant] *BL*	et de tant *P*
16.18	manieres de tous] *BL*	maniere et de *P*
16.22	il] *PL*	ilz *B*
16.24	mouvement et bonne volenté] *BL*	m. et de leur propre v. *P*
16.25	ni avoir] *B*	ne avoir *PL*
16.27	mestier d'armes] *BL*	m. de or mais *P*
16.32	si leur semble] *LP*	si leur semblent *B*
16.33	honorables qui] *BL*	h. a ceux qui *P*
17.1	veulent] *BL*	vouloient *P*
17.8	faire ce] *BP*	f. et ce *L*
17.15	se font] *BL*	se sont *P*
17.16	en autres] *BP*	et autres *L*
17.17	baffrois] *BP*	beffrois *L*
17.19	et prendre] *LP*	et et p. *B*
17.25	les bons] *BL*	ilz *P*
17.29–30	tres hautes besoignes] *BL*	nobles b. *P*
17.30	et grant grace] *BL*	*not in P*
17.31–32	et servir] *BP*	et le s. *L*
17.42	sceu, fait, esté] *BL*	s. sont este *P*
17.51	font bien a] *BP*	sont bien a *L*
17.59–60	que leur] *BP*	car leur *L*
19.5	a chargier] *BP*	a chargiet *L*
19.6	cheoir] *BP*	chevir *L*
19.25	de bons faiz] *BP*	des bons f. *L*
19.25	de bonnes paroles] *BP*	des bonnes p. *L*
19.37	jennes] *B*	joennes *P* jeunes *L*
19.50	t'entremettes] *P*	trentremettes *B* t'entremettre *L*
19.58–59	hommes pou se] *L*	h. qui pou se *BP*
19.60	se peuent] *BL*	sen p. *P*
19.61	quar qui pour] *BL*	car quant p. *P*
19.62	dens toute] *B*	dens toutes *PL*
19.64	dont d'eulz . . .] *BPL*	Hole in MS B. Neither *P* nor *L* fills lacuna.
19.84	Et] *BPL*	Very small initial in B and paragraph. No paragraph in P.
19.85	l'ou] *B*	la ou *P* d'ou *L*

19.88   Si] *Very small initial and paragraph in B. No paragraph in P.*
19.91   Ne des] *Very small initial and paragraph in B. No paragraph in P*
19.98   gardant] *BP*   querant *L*
19.98   en fait] *L*   et fait *BP*
19.100 en telx gieux] *BP*   et telx gieux *L*
19.103–04 l'encommencement et de l'encommencier a ceulx] *BP*   et de l'encommencier *not in L.*
19.114 que moult] *BP*   car m. *L*
19.115 creuz] *BP*   receus *L*
19.116 achaitivez] *BP*   achattivés *L*
19.130 certes qui] *BP*   certes celui qui *L*
19.134 sanz essoine de] *P*   se essoine de *B*   se essonié de *L*
19.140 qu'i vaut] *B*   quil v. *P*   que v. *L*
19.142 que ceulx] *BP*   car c. *L*
19.145 c'est bele] *BP*   c'est se b. *L*
19.146 saouler] *B*   souler *P*   s'avaler *L*
19.150 l'en, et semble] *BL*   len en s. *P*
19.156 ne pourroit estre] *BL*   ne pourroient estre *P*
19.161 firtee] *B*   frotee *P*   frutee? *L*
19.168 doubte a] *BP*   d. de *L*
19.168 que li bien] *BP*   car li b. *L*
19.185 que c'est le] *BP*   car l'est li *L*
19.189 venter] *B*   vanter *PL*
19.191 que nul] *BP*   car nul *L*
19.200 que plus] *BP*   car p. *L*
19.206 l'onnour] *BP*   l'amour *L*
19.210 doie tenir] *BP*   doit t. *L*
19.216 que ainsi] *B*   qui a. *PL*
19.217 temps a un] *P*   temps un *B*   temps en un *L*

20.1   Laquelles des] *B*   Laquelle *PL*
20.15   on le] *BL*   on ne le *P*
20.39   d'armes] *PL*   darme *B*

21.6   et li trop] *BL*   et aussi trop *P*
21.8   ces chetifs corps] *PL*   ces chetifs ces chetifs corps *B*
21.11   trouver savoir et d'aprendre] *BL*   tr. et aprendre *P*
21.14   et ainsi] *BL*   et se ainsi *P*

21.14 si leur en est de miex] *BL*   si ne leur en est que m. *P*
21.18 attraient] *BL*   attrait *P*
21.19 ouir] *B*   oir *P*   ores *L*
21.24 pehu] *BL*   precheux *P*
21.27 gloutonnies] *P*   gloutnnies *B*   gloutines *L*
21.28 honour] *BPL*   ho *expunctuated before* honor *in B*
21.30 et le po et l'auques tout] *B*   et le po et le grant t. *P*   et le pain et l'eau t. *L*
21.31 l'onnour] *BL*   lamour *P*

22.3 il seuffrent] *BPL*   il seuffre *crossed out after*   il seuffrent *in B*
22.7 avient encore] *B*   ament encore *L*   aiment *P*
22.17 quoy qu'il demeure] *BL*   *not in P*
22.19 maisons que il] *BL*   m. et ilz *P*
22.21 qu'elle leur doie cheoir] *BL*   quelles leur doient cheoir *P*
22.24 encores] *BPL*   enco *crossed out before* encores *in B*
22.25 fonde] *PL*   fondent *B*
22.26–27 pour trouver le dur] *BL*   *not in P*
22.29 leurs avoirs] *BL*   leur auoir *P*
22.31 et encores cilz treschaitis] *BL*   *not in P*
22.32 maison, car] *BL*   m. que *P*
22.34 pour ce que] *BL*   *not in P which omits* pour ce que . . . ont
22.35 cheoir, que] *BL*   ch. et que *P*
22.36 Or] *Very small initial with no decoration at beginning of line in B; no paragraph in P*
22.36 que ycelles] *BLP*   n *expunctuated after* que *in B*

23.9 Si devez] *BL*   Or devez *L*
23.11 vous ennemis] *B*   voz e. *P*   vos e. *L*
23.12 vous amis] *B*   voz a. *P*   vos a. *L*
23.12–13 vous ennemis] *B*   voz e. *P*   vos e. *L*
23.15 trop a.] *BLP*   e *expunctuated after* trop *in B*
23.19–20 ne pour avoir l'autruy] *BL*   ne penre lautrui *P*
23.22 envie] *PL*   ennuie *B*
23.24 haut] *BL*   grant *P*
23.25 et tres laide chose est de tencier a fol et a yvre] *BL*   *not in P*
23.26 asseignent] *B*   enseignent *PL*
23.27 vous paroles] *B*   voz p. *P*   vos p. *L*

23.27 profectables] *B*   proufitables *P*   perfectables *L*
23.28 loez vostre] *BL*   loez trop v. *P*
23.29 souverainement] *BL*   songneusement *P*
23.30 despit nulles povres] *BL*   despit p. *P*
23.30 ne nulz mendre] *BL*   ne m. *P*
23.31 a des povres] *BL*   a de p. *P*
23.32 parler convient que l'en die] *BL*   p. ne poeut on que on ne d. *P*
23.38 folz, que] *B*   f. car *PL*
23.39 sages qui vous] *BL*   s. car ilz v. *P*
23.43 les amis] *BL*   ses amis *P*
23.49 d'escharceté] *BL*   descarsete *P*
23.50 que quant] *B*   car q. *PL*
23.52 que mieulx] *BP*   car m. *L*
23.54–55 qu'il ne deviengnent] *BL*   quil d. *P*
23.64 ou au dessus] *BP*   soit au dessus *L*
23.69 perde] *B*   perte *PL*
23.69 touzjours] *BL*   *not in P*
23.70 droite, ferme] *BP*   droite et f. *L*
23.74 vaincu] *PL*   vainscu *B*
23.76–77 que de vous] *BP*   que se vous *L*
23.83 anmoine] *BP*   ameine *L*
23.93 les males et] *BL*   les maulz et *P*
23.93 bonnes. Et] *BL*   bonnes choses et *P*
23.96 mauvaise garde] *BPL*   m *crossed out before* garde *in B*
23.99 que vous devez] *BP*   car vous d. *L*
23.102 qu'il fust jusques] *BL*   quil venist j. *P*
23.104 naist] *B*   naissent *PL*
23.109 que ce] *BP*   car ce *L*
23.110 que la mort] *BP*   car la m. *L*
23.111 remiser] *BL*   (*not clear in B*)   remirer *P*

24.2 sont, les convient il un po plus d'esclarcir] *B*   sont, les convient il un po plus esclarcir *L*   s. et pour ce les convient il aucunement e. *P*
24.3 les estaz] *BL*   lestat *P*
24.6–7 par vostre travaille] *BL*   pour vostre trauail *P*
24.15 bons homs] *B*   bons homes *L*   bon home *P*
24.16 travaille] *BL*   trauail *P*

Variants

24.23 bon ordenance] *BL*   bonne o. *P*
24.25–26 ycelles journees]   journees *not in BPL*
24.34 et longue] *BP*   et de longue *P*
24.41 gardez, mettez et] *BL*   g. nettes et *P*
24.53–54 a perde et a nient] *B*   a perte et a nient *L*   *not in P*
24.54 de la descendue] *B*   de le descendre *P*   de la descendre *L*
24.54–55 que ce qu'il y fussent onques euz montez] *BL*   que se ilz ni fussent oncques montez *P*
24.57–58 comparez] *BL*   achettez *P*
24.60 en prennent] *BP*   en y prennent *L*
24.68 que quant] *BP*   car quant *L*
24.70 monde ou] *BP*   m. il en sera plus ou *L*
24.73 eslevez] *BL*   esleu *P*
24.78 premiers] *PL*   premieres *B*
24.79 delites] *B*   delices *PL*   (c *and* t *are sometimes difficult to distinguish in B but it looks more like* t *here*)
24.83–84 enrichir sanz autre bonne cause. Certes nennil. Furent] *BL*   enrichir. Certes nennil sans aucune bonne cause f. *P*
24.88–89 mengier] *BPL*   certes *crossed out after* mengier *in B*
24.89–90 fait qu'il] *BP*   fait pour qu'il *L*
24.95 et en mal] *BL*   et le mal *P*
24.97 alongier] *BL*   eslongier *P*
24.101 nulz mauvais fait] *B*   nul mauuais fait *PL*
24.102–03 furent] *PL*   fuerent *B*
24.103–04 chaitis jeux] *BL*   chetiz geus *P*
24.105 fait que quant] *B*   fait pour que quant *L*   fais quant *P*
24.107 leur servans] *P*   leur desseur *BL*
24.114 sceussent ou] *BL*   *not in P*

25.3 eslevez] *BL*   esleus *P*
25.5 travaillier ou] *BPL*   a *expuncuated before* ou *in B*
25.6 tant en temps de] *BL*   tant en gouuernement de *P*
25.11 li peuple] *B*   le p. *PL*
25.13 leurs cuers] *BPL*   a *expuncuated after* leurs *in B*
25.14 charge qu'il] *BPL*   que *crossed out before* qu'il *in B*
25.23 faire] *PL*   fair *B*
25.39 leur] *PL*   leurs *B*
25.48 consaintement] *BL*   consentement *P*
25.54 faiz que pour leur noblece ne devoient] *B*   f. que par leur

	noblesce ne doiuent *P*	f. pour ce que leur noblece ne devoit *L*
25.56	faiz que quant] *BP*	f. pour que quant *L*
25.58	faiz, quant] *BPL*	pour *expunctuated in B between* faiz *and* quant
25.60	ennemis, que] *BP*	ennemis pour que *L*
25.61	et estre misericors] *P*	estre *not in BL*
25.67	faiz que] *BP*	f. pour que *L*
25.72	l'exemplaire] *BL*	lexemple *P*
25.72–73	faiz que] *BP*	f. pour que *L*
25.74	le plus riches] *B*	le plus riche *P* les plus riches *L*
25.75	le dequoy] *BL*	le pourquoy *P*
25.75	poursuigre] *B*	poursieure *P* poursuivre *L*
25.76–77	perdu a avoir leur raison] *BL*	a avoir *not in P*
25.77	de mise] *BL*	de mire *P*
26.17	et a mener] *BL*	*not in P*
26.20	plainement] *BL*	seurement *P*
27.1	meurs] *PL*	uieures *B*
27.5	en vivront] *BLP*	viront *expunctuated before* vivront *in B*
27.10	escharciz] *B*	escharciz *P* esclarciz *L*
27.12	comment ainsi] *BL*	tout ainsi *P*
29.1	Se y sont] *P*	Le y s. *B* Qui sont *L*
29.7	Et ainsi pourroit] *BL*	et aussi p. *P*
29.12	tel veus] *BL*	tels biens *P*
30.1	Se] *Decorated initial in P; very small initial and paragraph in B*	
30.1	Se en y a] *P*	se y en y a *BL*
30.2–3	destournent] *PL*	destourent *B*
31.1	Se] *Decorated initial and paragraph in P; small initial and no paragraph in B*	
31.6	s'il] *BPL*	l *added above line in B without change in ink*
31.9	euvrent] *BL*	eussent *P*
32.1	vient] *BP*	viens *L*
32.3	touzjours tele]	touzjours eue tele] *BP* tousjours veue tele *L*
32.9	estat ne] *BPL*	*something erased between* estat *and* ne *in B*

Variants

34.1	qui souverainement] *BP*	que s. *L*
34.4	mise] *BL*	*not in P where a blank is left*
34.7	l'onneur] *PL*	lonner *B*
34.18	des faiz] *BL*	de f. *P*
34.22	contenances] *BL*	conuenances *P*
34.29	ceulz] *BLP*	ceulz *added in B above the line without change of ink*
34.32	qui y deviennent] *BL*	qui d. *P*
34.34	font] *BL*	fait *P*
35.4	villanz] *B* villains *P*	vaillans *L*
35.4	villans] *B* villaines *P*	vaillans *L*
35.6	villans] *B* villains *P*	vaillans *L*
35.9	cilz deust se convertir] cilz deus se conuertist *B* si se deuust conuertir *P* cils dons se convertist *L*
35.9	du tout] *BPL*	de *expunctuated and* du *added above line in B*
35.14	personne ait] *BPL*	e *expunctuated in B before* ait
35.15	de trois] *BP*	des trois *L*
35.17	preudommie] *P*	preudomme *BL*
35.18	manieres et de preudommie] *B* m. est de p. *P* m. de p. *L*
35.18	ci dessur] *BP*	ci dessus *L*
35.20	manieres et de preuesce] *B* m. est de p. *P* m. de p. *L*
35.21	sont enz et sont] *P* sous eus et sont *B* sous eus sont *L*
35.23	genz a v.] *L*	g. et v. *BP*
35.23	villanz] *B* villans *P*	vaillans *L*
35.23–24	valent et que] *BP*	v. si que *L*
35.25	villans] *BP*	vaillans *L*
35.25	fait] *PL*	fail *B*
35.30	villans] *BP*	vaillans *L*
35.35	Nennil voir, que] *B* n. voir car *P* Nennil. Voir que *L*
35.37	li met sur, tout] *B* li met sur tout *L* li met sur ly t. *P*
35.40–41	leur soit] *BP*	leur sont *L*
35.43	ytels] *B* yceulx *P*	ycels *L*
35.45	endurent] *L*	en disent *BP*
35.50	effaciee] *BPL* efficaciee *expunctuated in B before* effaciee
35.55	celle] *BL*	tele *P*
35.55	fole] *PL*	fol *B*
35.56	cheoir] *BP*	chevir *L*
35.57	grace, mais] *PL*	grace grace m. *B*
35.58	les donne] *BP*	le d. *L*

35.58	les doit] *B*	le doit *PL*
35.58	regracier et requerir] *BL*	regracier et *not in P*
35.61	et en] *BP*	en *L*
35.61	une seule] *LP*	un seule *B*
35.62–63	recognoissance] *BL*	congnoissance *P*
35.64	n'y fait] *BL*	nen fait *P*
35.65	mettent paine de acquerir] *BL*	m. leur entente a a. *P*
35.68	et faiz] *BL*	*not in P*
35.70	dessus dites] *BP*	dessus devisees *L*
35.72	par exemple] *BP*	pour e. *L*
35.73	fu] *B*	fut *P* fust *L*
35.74–75	coulonme] *B*	coulonne *PL*
35.76	fu] *B*	fut *P* fust *L*
35.78	post] *BL*	poeut *P*
35.80	fu] *B*	fut *P* fust *L*
35.93	et tant fist] *BP*	*not in L*
35.95	Romme, et pour] *BP*	R., pour *L*
35.105	Si avint] *BP*	Or avint *L*
35.108	Si avint] *BP*	Or avint *L*
35.108	a l'eure] *P*	a lentree *BL*
35.109	qui savoit] *BP*	qui savoient *L*
35.125	ferme] *B*	fermes *PL*
35.128	recelez, et qu'il ne] *BP*	r. quil ne *L*
35.142	et de acquerir] *BP*	et a. *P*
35.145	onques] *BP*	*not in L*
35.152–53	et par les] *PL*	et par les et par les *B*
35.159	avoit en li, le] *BL*	auoit il le *P*
35.159	gouverna] *BL*	*not in P*
35.161	tesmoigne, qui est] *BL*	t. et est *P*
35.161	furent] *BL*	sont *P*
35.166	tres beaus] *BP*	tieus beaus *L*
35.172	qui ainsi] *BPL*	en *crossed out in B before* ainsi
35.175	que moult] *BP*	car q. *L*
35.184	mais quant es] *BL*	mais es *P*
35.186	que quant] *BP*	car q. *L*
35.186–87	des guerres] *BL*	de guerres *P*
35.187	guerres deuement encommanciees] *BP*	g. sont deuement e. *L*
35.190	que se l'en] *BP*	car se l'en *L*
35.191	les en destournent] *BL*	les encombre *P*

Variants

35.192 l'on vouloit] *BL*   len v. *P*
35.200 entrer en] *PL*   entroir *B*
35.203 maintenir] *BL*   soubstenir *P*
35.203 espargnier a y] *BL*   e. et y *P*
35.208 que les] *BP*   car les *L*
35.210 que l'on] *BP*   car l'on *L*
35.215 eschever] *BL*   esquieuer *P*
35.215 a ces mestiers] *BL*   a cest mestier *P*
35.218 de quoy] *PL*   do quoy *B*
35.218 se doient ne puissent] *BL*   se doie ou puist *P*
35.220 que qui] *B*   car qui *PL*
35.225 que vous] *BP*   car vous *L*
35.230 ordené] *B*   ordonnez *P*   ordenés *L*
35.237 veritablement que c'est] *BP*   v. c'est *L*
35.238 appartient plus et mieux gouverner nettement c.] *BL*
appartient lui gouverner sagement et nettement de c. *P*
35.238–39 ceste ordre] *BP*   c'est o. *L*

36.1 quoy, et les bonnes raysons] *BP*   q. et par quelles bonnes r. *L*
36.2 l'orde] *B*   lordre *PL*
36.3 veult faire chevalier] *L*   veult c. *B*   fait c. *P*
36.4 convient tout premierement que] *BL*   c. de commencement q. *P*
36.12 ceulz] *BLP*   cu *ex punctuated before* ceulz *in B*
36.12–13 sont issu] *L*   *not in BP*
36.13 du grant] *BL*   de grant *P*
36.14 repos comme repos] *BP*   comme repos *not in L*
36.16 au lit] *PL*   aut lit *B*
36.19 pechié, le] *BL*   p. et pour ce le *P*
36.20 lors en la] *BL*   lors en auant *P*
36.23 dessus dites] *BP*   d. devisees *L*
36.27 tout orgueil] *PL*   toute o. *B*
36.29 et l'en seignent et mettent entour de] *BL*   et lenseigne mettent entour lui *P*
36.31 les chevaliers un manteu vermeil] *BL*   *not in P*
36.32 que mantiaus] *BL*   car m. *L*
36.32 ainsi faiz furent faiz] *BL*   ainsi fait et furent faiz *P*
36.36 ou temps] *BPL*   faiz *expunctuated after* ou *in B*
36.41 dite, dont les] *BL*   dite les *P*

36.43   deux esperons dorez a deux chevaliers] *BPL*   *underlined in B*
36.45   qu'il oste] *BP*   pour qu'il o. *L*
36.46   de son cuer]*PL*   de soy c. *B*
36.49–50   et les droiz] *BP*   et est drois *L*
36.52   recevoient] *BP*   reçoivent *L*
36.54   donner la colee] *BPL*   *underlined in B*
36.66   des droiz] *BL*   de droiz *P*
36.66   de chevalerie] *BL*   de cheualiers *P*
36.72   et doivent] *BLP*   doie *expunctuated after* et *in B*
36.72   car il doivent] *BP*   mes il d. *L*

37.1   l'orde] *B*   lordre *PL*
37.12   et leur aaige] *BL*   ne leur a. *P*

38.10   voies] *PL*   *not in B*
38.14–15   telz tres desordenez] *BPL*   trois *crossed out after* telz *in B*

39.5   que moult] *BP*   car m. *L*
39.5   qu'il ne] *P*   et ne *L*   *not in B*
39.8   moult mal] *BL*   moult de mal *P*
39.22   boire] *PL*   boir *B*
39.23   vivre en paiz en leurs cuers de] *BP*   v. en leurs cuers en pais de *L*

40.2   qui entre] *BP*   que e. *L*
40.8   n'est ce mie] *BL*   ce nest mie *P*
40.14   dit] *PL*   dite *B*
40.24–25   et a tresnuitier] *BP*   et atremucier *L*
40.27   et en la paine] *L*   et la p. *BP*
40.28   tel fait] *BL*   telz faiz *P*
40.33–34   honorer. Toutesvoies qui fait les faiz d'armes plus pour la gloire de ce monde que] h. Toutes voies, qui fait plus pour la gloire de ce monde que *L*   h. que *BP*
40.41–42   que maintes . . . li chevalier] *BL*   *not in P*
40.41   ainsi bon] *B*   aussi bon *L*
40.42   ausi d'aucuns] *B*   et ainsi d. *P*   et ensi d. *L*

41.2   deshonestes] *BPL*   et desh *crossed out after* deshonestes *in B*
41.7   ne autrement] *BL*   autrement *P*

Variants

41.17–18	Il n'ont nulle volenté . . . faire a autrui] *BL* *not in P*
41.22–23	Il n'ont nulle raison . . . faire a autrui] *BL* *not in P*
41.30	ordenez] ordenz *B* ordenés *L* ordonnez *P*
41.33	mettent leur temps] *BL* m. leurs corps et leurs temps *P*
41.34	deshonnoree fame et] *BL* tel deshonneur et tele fame et *P*
41.34–35	certes ne plus] *BL* c. neant plus *P*
41.39	d'armer] *BP* d'armes *L*
41.39	tresnuitier] *B* tresmucier *L* tresmuchier *P*
41.40	boire, mout] *BP* boire estre moult *L*
42.3	nulz chetiz faiz] *BL* nul chetif cas *P*
42.3	fors que pour] *BL* fors p. *P*
42.8	les armes] *BL* les armeures *P*
42.13	tres pure et devote] *BL* t. et nette *P*
42.13	conscience] *BPL* cognoissance *expunctuated before* conscience *in B*
42.16	consecrer] *B* consacrer *LP*
42.17	lequel] *PL* lequele *B*
42.21	que tant] *BP* car t. *L*
42.23	que des] *BP* car des *L*
42.25	vouloir] *BL* faire *P*
42.29–30	conmandemens] *PL* conmandens *B*
42.32	armer] *BPL* amer *with* r *inserted above in same ink in B*
42.44	vrais confez] *BP* vrais et c. *L*
42.46	qu'i] *B* quil *P* que *L*
42.48	armes, que] *BP* a. qui *L*
42.50	raison n'est] *BPL* est *expunctuated before* nest *in B*
42.52	a ytel service] *B* a ycel s. *PL*
42.63	tenus et seurement] *BP* t. de s. *L*
42.70	et de tres] *BL* et de si tr. *P*
42.73	est dit] *P* est dist *BL*
42.74	fermes] *B* ferme *PL*
42.76	fivres] *BL* fieures *P*
42.86	et pluseurs] *BP* et sont p. *L*
42.90	en jour] *P* *not in BL*
42.95	et fait] *BL* et fait donner *P*
42.97	ce aucuns] *B* se a. *PL*
42.100–101	aucuns biens . . . robeurs] *BL not in P*
42.108	malfaire, et n'est] *BP* f. n'est *L*
42.119–120	le souverain] *BPL* leur *expunctuated before* le *in B*

42.120   seigneur] *PL*   seigner *B*
42.123   et a ceulz] *BP*   a c. *L*
42.124   nul ne] *BPL*   a *expunctuated between* nul *and* ne *in B*
42.125   soit] *BL*   soient *P*
42.130   est et tout] *BL*   est tout *P*
42.131–32   de qui] *L*   a qui *B*   *not in P which omits* a ceulz . . . deservir
42.134   ce tres] *BP*   le tres *L*
42.135   que par] *BP*   qui par *L*
42.141   biens et honnours] *L*   biens honnours *BP*
42.142–43   si leur semble que celle renommee] *BL*   *not in P*
42.145   renommee] *PL*   renomme *B*
42.148   meilleur] *BL*   meilleurs *P*
42.152   que il veulent] *BP*   car il v. *L*
42.153   parer de] *PL*   paier de *B*
42.153   pierres, de perles, d'ouvrages] *BPL*   *underlined in B*
42.154–55   et les aneaux en leurs dois et les grosses courroies d'or ou d'argent] *BPL*   *underlined in B*
42.157   celle mission] *BP*   celle mise *L*
42.160   en oublie] *B*   en oubli *PL*
42.160   chetivetez, et Dieux] *BP*   ch. Dieux *L*
42.163   corps qui n'ont] *B*   c. quilz nont *P*   c. n'ont *L*
42.168   car il ne] *BL*   ou il ne *P*
42.169–70   il ne s'ont de quoy] *BP*   il ne se sevent de quoy *L*
42.172   qu'il] *L*   quil quil *B*   quilz *P*
42.173–74   et ainsi comme . . . hontes] *BL*   *not in P*
42.179   mettre a ny qu'il] *BL*   mettre a neant quilz *P*
42.180   maintes fois que] *P*   maintes que *B*   maints que *L*
42.182   sont enz pris] *BP*   sont suspris *L*
42.184   sont enz mors] *BP*   sont ceus mors *L*
42.190   doubtoit] *BP*   doubte *L*
42.199   jolieses] *B*   jolietes *P*   jolies *L*
42.204   oublier] *BPL*   ob *expunctuated before* oublier *in B*
42.206   avecques] *BPL*   e *expunctuated before* avecques *in B*

43.3   belles couronnes . . . brodures] *BPL*   *underlined in B*
43.3–4   brodures, bien vestues] *BP*   brodures et d'estre bien v. *L*
43.5   a droit peut] *L*   a doit peut *B*   a doit et peut *P*
43.6   que les] *BP*   Car les *L*
43.9   plaire] *PL*   plair *B*

43.11   aornemens] *L*   aornrnemens *B*   aournemens *P*
43.12   que les biens] *BP*   car les b. *L*
43.14   biens] *PL*   biens biens *B*
43.18   sont en] *PL*   font en *B*
43.19   fames, quer, pour] *B* (in which querre *is expunctuated before* quer)   f. que pour *P*   f. pour *L*
43.32   appers] *BPL*   appres *crossed out before* appers *in B*
43.32   et de bonne maniere] *L*   et maniere *BP*
43.34   brodee et de tel] *P*   b. et tel *B*   b. de tel *L*
43.37   bien pourront dire] *P*   bien pourront bien dire *BL*
43.37   ne astaches] *BP*   en a. *L*
43.51   Si avront] *BP* (Si *quite clear in P*)   Or *L*
43.59   que par raison il li doie souvenir de vous] *BL*   *not in P*
43.60   a perilz de] *BP*   en perils de *L*
43.62   prieres a requeste] *BP*   p. et requestes *L*
43.63   ainsi] *PL*   aisi *B*
43.71   voz mors] *B*   vo mort *P*   vos mors *L*

44.1   Or peut] *BP*   (peuet *with second* e *expunctuated in B*) peuet *L*
44.3   souverainement] *PL*   souuerainnent *B*
44.7   glorieuse] *PL*   gorieuse *B*
44.12   merencolieux] *BL*   melancolieux *P*
44.12   si mal gracieux] si male fin gracieux *BP*   si disgracieux *L*
44.13   tres mauvaise fin. Et] tres mauuaise Et *BL*   tres-male fin. Et *L*
44.18   biens et en delaissant] *B*   b. et d. *P*   b. en d. *L*
44.21   Seigneur et Pere] *B*   Seigneur Pere *LP*
44.23   armes, car il] *B*   a. quar il *P*   a. que il *L*
44.25   grace, et laquelle] *B*   g. laquelle *PL*
44.25   de touz] *PL*   do t. *B*
44.26   definemens] *BPL*   *P ends at this point.*
44.32–33 souviengne] *BL*   souuei *expunctuated before* souuiengne *in B*
44.34   aombrer a passer] *B*   a. et passer *L*
44.36   s'estendent tant] *B*   se scindent tant *L*
44.48   ces biens] *BL*   tes *expunctuated and* ces *added above in same ink in B*
44.50   Que] *B*   Car *L*
44.53   et assez] *B*   il assés *L*

Notes

Abbreviations used in the notes

Cotgrave: Randle Cotgrave, *A Dictionarie of the French and English Tongues*. London, 1632.
FEW: W. von Wartburg, *Französiches etymologisches Wörterbuch*. Bonn, 1922–8, Leipzig, 1932–40, Basel, 1955–68.
Godefroy: Frédéric Godefroy, *Dictionnaire de l'ancienne langue française*. Paris, 1880–1901.
L : Kervyn de Lettenhove's edition of the text in *Oeuvres complètes de Froissart*. Brussels, 1877.
LK: *Lancelot do Lac: The Non-Cyclic Old French Prose Romance*, ed. Elspeth Kennedy. 2 vols. Oxford, 1980.
LM: *Lancelot: roman en prose du XIIIe siècle*, ed. Alexandre Micha. 9 vols. Paris-Geneva, 1978–83.
LOC: *Livre de l'ordre de chevallerie*, the medieval French translation of Ramon Llull, *Le Libre del orde de cavallería*, in *Obres de Ramon Lull*, ed. Antoni M. Alcover, Mateu Obrador, Bennassar. Palma de Mallorca: Comissio Editora Lulliana, 1906, vol. I, 249–291.
OC: *L'Ordene de chevalerie*, in *Le Roman des eles, by Raoul de Hodenc and L'Ordene de chevalerie*, ed. Keith Busby. Utrecht Publications in General and Comparative Literature 17, Amsterdam, 1983.
Perceforest 1: *Le Roman de Perceforest, première partie*, ed. Jane Taylor. Geneva, 1979.
Perceforest 3: *Perceforest, troisième partie*, ed. Gilles Roussineau. 2 vols. Geneva, 1988.
Perceforest 4: *Perceforest, quatrième partie*, ed. Gilles Roussineau. 2 vols. Geneva, 1987.
TL: A. Tobler and E. Lommatzsch, *Altfranzösisches Wörterbuch*. Berlin, from 1925.

Except where otherwise stated, all the translations of quotations from other works are by Elspeth Kennedy.

Text, 5.8–11; Trans., 5.9–12
honneur/honor, coupled as it is here with *heritage*/inheritance, may well still have the meaning of land held as a fief.

Text, 7.7–8; Trans., 7.8–10
glaive can mean "lance" (as it does in *fer de glaive*, 7.7) or sword; in the fourteenth century it can also mean "infantry weapon," presumably inappropriate here.

Text, 12.4; Trans., 12.4

amer par amours (cf. *LK*, 30.32, 30.36, 296.21, 303.3) is the medieval French term used to denote the practice of *fin' amour* (another medieval expression) or "courtly love," a term invented in the nineteenth century to describe the idealized form of love service celebrated in lyric and romance. The true love of a knight for a noble lady as a source of inspiration for great deeds is a theme explored in the Arthurian romances, especially the Prose *Lancelot*. See, for example, the message sent by the Lady of the Lake to the young Lancelot that he must devote himself to a love which will increase his honor, not diminish it (*LK*, 205–6).

Text, 12.14–17; Trans., 12.15–18

For the honor a lady can win through her love for a great knight, see the Lady of the Lake's words to Guinevere: "Se vos poez de ce vanter que onques mais dame no pot faire, car vos iestes compaigne au plus preudome do monde et dame au meillor chevalier do monde" (*LK*, 557.5–7). (And you can boast of that which no lady could ever boast of before, for you are the companion of the most worthy man in the world and the lady of the best knight in the world) (*Lancelot of the Lake*, trans. Corin Corley, Oxford, 1989). For the lady's duty toward the good knight who loves her, see also Text, 20.35–41; Trans., 20.37–42.

Text, 17.2; Trans., 17.3

coureurs: light horsemen used as scouts or foragers.

Text, 17.15; Trans., 17.16

battifol is not in *TL*; it is glossed as *moulin*/mill in Godefroy. The meaning of the term in this context is obscure.

Text, 17.16–17; Trans., 17.18–19

truyes, "sows," and *chas*, "cats," are roofed mobile structures often used to cover mining operations. The *baffroi*, "belfry," a siege tower, could also be used for this. We can find no reference to *buyre* as an item of siege equipment; the term usually means "vase;" it seems likely that within this context it is used to denote a mobile protective structure, possibly vase-shaped, which served the same purpose as cats and sows, as these devices were called by many names. See Jim Bradbury, *The Medieval Siege* (Woodbridge, 1992), 271.

Text, 17.37–38; Trans., 17.44

The phrase *es honorables* is unusual; the translation given represents the probable meaning of the sentence.

Text, 19.6
ces for *ses* (possessive): see "The Language of Manuscript B," *Consonants*, 4.

Text, 19.64; Trans., 19.69
There is a lacuna in the text: see variants.

Text, 19.134; Trans., 19.140
sanz essoine de, the reading of *P*, has been accepted as an emendation of *se essoine de*, the reading of *B*, as it makes sense as the standard expression in this context, rather than the *L* reading, *se essoinié de*.

Text, 19.140
qu'i vaut: for *i* for *il*, see "The Language of Manuscript B," *Consonants*, 2.

Text, 19.161; Trans., 19.171
firtee is an unusual and obscure word. A possible explanation is that it is a form of the verb *ferter* (listed in *TL*) from Latin *firmitare*, "bound with metal etc.," with a figurative meaning: "firm," "secure," "well established."

Text, 19.166; Trans., 19.176
quoy qu'il demeure: The one example of this phrase recorded in Giuseppe di Stefano, *Dictionnaire des locutions en Moyen Français* (Québec, 1991), is in the fifteenth-century farce, *Maistre Pierre Pathelin*, line 658, where different editors of the text have interpreted the phrase in a variety of ways (for a list of some of these, see edition of R. Holbrook, Paris, 1967), including "whatever the delay," which seems to be the probable meaning here. Pierre Aubailly and Jean Dufournet translate the phrase in *Pathelin* as "quoi qu'il arrive," "whatever happens," which does not seem to fit this passage.

Text, 19.183; Trans., 19.193–94
mais que bien soit quant il le doivent faire: The translation given, "provided there are honorable deeds to be done when they should do them," provides one possible interpretation of an obscure phrase.

Text, 19.183–85; Trans., 19.195–97
To be compared with *LK*, 30.32–31.9, where Claudas explains why he has given up love: he wants to live for a long time and therefore does not want to love (*amer par amors*), for this would make him want to surpass the whole world and thus put his life in danger; but he admits: "il ne puet estre tres preuz d'armes se il n'aimme tres leialment" (no one can achieve worth in the pursuit of arms if he does not love loyally).

Text, 19.186–204; Trans., 19.197–216
The need for secrecy in love receives great emphasis in the medieval lyric and romance. For example, in a short thirteenth-century romance, *La chastelaine de Vergi*, a knight is granted the love of the *chastelaine* on condition that the love remains secret; he is forced to reveal the love to his lord, and as a result both he and his lady die. The reference by Geoffroi de Charny to Guinevere in this passage would link up with the Prose *Lancelot*, where the hero always remains silent about his love for the Queen. For example, when imprisoned by the Lady of Malehaut, he refuses to name the one he loves *par amors*, although by doing so he would have obtained his freedom (*LK*, 303).

Text, 19.216–17; Trans., 19.228–29
dame que ainsi aimeroit: This could be interpreted in two ways: a) "the lady whom he would so love," or b) "the lady who would so love," as *que* sometimes represents the subject of a clause in *B* (see "The Language of Manuscript B," Morphology, 7). The reading of *P* might appear to support interpretation b), although in *P* as in *B* the form *qui* can represent the direct object (**34.1**, where *P* has the same reading as B).

Text, 20.1
Laquelles des deux dames doit avoir: see "The Language of Manuscript B," Syntax, 1.

Text, 20.15–16; Trans., 20.17
ne on le festie: For the absence of the negative *ne* after the coordinating conjunction *ne*, see "The Language of Manuscript B," Syntax, 5.

Text, 20.35–41; Trans., 20.37–42
For the honor to be gained and the duty owed by the lady to the good knight who loves her, see also **12.15**–20 and note.

Text, 22.17; Trans., 22.18
quoy qu'il demeure: see note to **19.166**.

Text, 23.11
The form *vous* is used as a possessive four times on one folio. See "The Language of Manuscript B," Morphology, 6.

Text, 23.26
asseignent for *enseignent*: see "The Language of Manuscript B," *Consonants*, 7.

Text, 23.111; Trans., 23.115
remise can mean "the act of putting off until later "(*FEW*, X, 242), but *remiser en soy* is obscure and the translation is tentative.

Text, 24.23
bon ordenance: For hesitation over gender in nouns beginning with a vowel, see "The Language of Manuscript B," Morphology, 1.

Text, 24.54–55
fussent onques euz montez: See "The Language of Manuscript B," Morphology, 13.

Text, 24.56–57; Trans., 24.58–59
"He that climbs higher than he should, falls lower than he would" is Cotgrave's version of the proverb.

Text, 24.71–78; Trans., 24.75–81
For the sources for this account of the origin of emperors, kings, and princes, see note to 25.1–6.

Text, 25.1–6; Trans., 25.1–6
The explanation of the origin of emperors, kings and princes appears to have been drawn from Ramon Llull's account of the origin of knights. According to Llull, after the Fall of Man those with the greatest physical and moral qualities were chosen and set apart from other men as defenders of justice and of the Holy Church. Charny would also have found a similar account in another text he knew well, the Prose *Lancelot*, itself the main source for Llull's version of the origin of knights. See *LOC*, p. 254, where the people are divided into thousands and from each thousand one man is elected, he who is "plus loyal, plus fort et de plus noble courage et mieulz enseigné que tous les autres" (the most loyal, the strongest and the noblest in heart and the best educated of all men). See also *LK*, 142, where, as in Charny, there is no division into thousands, but the men are chosen for the same types of qualities: "Ce furent li grant et li fort et li bel et li legier et li leial et li hardi, cil qui des bontez del cuer et del cors estoient plain" (These were the big and the strong and the handsome and the nimble and the loyal and the courageous, those who were full of the qualities of the heart and of the body).

Text, 25.11
gouverner li peuple: see "The Language of Manuscript B," Morphology, 2.

Text, 25.6–15; Trans., 25.6–16
The heavy responsibility resting on the shoulders of the men chosen to be emperors, kings and princes recalls the following passage from the Lady of the Lake's explanation of chivalry in the Prose *Lancelot*, LK, 142: "Mais la chevalerie ne lor fu pas donee an bades ne por neiant, ençois lor en fu mis desor les cox mout granz faissiaus" (but knighthood was not given to them frivolously and for no good reason; on the contrary, a heavy burden was put on their shoulders). The obligations of those chosen for high office, the charges put upon them and the moral qualities and behavior expected of them in Charny and traditionally required of kings are similar to those demanded of the men chosen to be knights in *LK*. Indeed, in medieval literature in general, the advice given to kings on their duties and that given to knights on theirs frequently overlap.

Text, 25.16–17; Trans., 25.17–18
"Si estoient esleuz et faiz pour amer, doubter et servir Dieu et toutes ses oevres." To be compared with Llull, *LOC*, 268, IV, 2: "Car sans amer et doubter Dieu nul homme n'est digne d'entrer en l'ordre de chevallerie (For no man who does not love and fear God is worthy to enter the order of knighthood.) Llull and the Prose *Lancelot* both emphasize the duty of the knight to protect the Holy Church, which cannot use arms to defend itself, *LOC*, 257–58, III, §2; *LK*, 143–45.

Text, 25, 23–24; Trans., 25, 25–27
For the duty of rulers to see that justice is upheld, cf. Llull (*LOC*, 259, III, 8), and *LK*, 142. However, both these texts also emphasize the duty of the knight to help the King in the maintenance of justice. In *LK*, the adventures which the Knights of the Round Table undertake often concern the maintenance of justice in the lands over which Arthur is lord (see Kennedy, *Lancelot and the Grail*, 79–80, 102–7). Arthur is told that it is his duty to see that justice is done (*LK*, 283), but that he needs the help of *li bas gentil homme* to maintain his land (*LK*, 285).

Text, 25.26–7; Trans., 25.29–30
For the need to be prepared to journey constantly, cf. *LK*, 286–87, where Arthur is told by a holy man that he must travel round all his *boenes viles* so that the great and the humble can seek justice at his court. Knights errant also are constantly promising not to spend more than one night in a place until they have completed the object of their quest. See, for example, Gauvain's oath (*LK*, 220) and the Lady of the Lake's instructions to the young

Lancelot before he leaves for Arthur's court (*LK*, 154). See also Perceval's oath in *Le Roman de Perceval ou le Conte du Graal,* ed. William Roach (Geneva, 1956), ll. 4728–40.

Text, 25.31–33; Trans., 25.34–37
To be *large* (generous) is a traditional quality demanded of both knight and king. In the Prose *Lancelot* it is made clear that generosity is expected of knights and kings (*LK*, 34, 71, 287–89). See also *Le Roman des Eles,* by Raoul de Hodenc, ll. 150–266.

Text, 25.74
le plus riches: For other examples in *B* of hesitation over the use of flexional *s,* see "The Language of Manuscript B," Morphology, 2.

Text, 27.10; Trans., 27.10
escharciz appears to be an alternative form for *esclarciz* explain, clarify. An example of *escharcir* is listed in the *Anglo-Norman Dictionary,* ed. Louise W. Stone, William Rothwell, and T. B. W. Reid (London 1992).

Text, 29.1
Se y sont ceulz: I have based the emendation on the reading of *P*. For examples in *B* of *se* for the coordinating conjunction *si,* see "The Language of Manuscript B," Morphology, 14.

Text, 34.1
qui here represents the direct object of the verb. See "The Language of Manuscript B," Morphology, 7.

Text, 35.4
villanz, villans: For other examples of this unusual variant form of *vaillanz,* see "The Language of Manuscript B," Vowels, 9. *P* uses similar forms in *vill-*.

Text, 35.18 *manieres et de preudommie*: For this unusual construction with *de,* see "The Language of Manuscript B," Syntax, 6.

Text, 35.20
manieres et de preuesce: For this unusual construction with *de,* see "The Language of Manuscript B," Syntax, 6.

Text, 35.73–76; Trans., 35.75–79
Note that the blind Samson's action in pulling down the pillars is here condemned as a misuse of strength, although in the biblical account there is no

such condemnation: Samson prays to God to give him strength to pull down the pillars so that he might avenge himself on the Philistines. See Judges xvii: 25–30.

Text, 35.76–80; Trans., 35.79–83
For Absalom hanging by his hair from a tree, see 2 Samuel xviii: 9

Text, 35.78
post This form might possibly be explained as a *passé simple* in which an *s* has been added by analogy with strong perfect forms such as *dist*. .

Text, 35.80–84; Trans., 35.83–87
For Solomon's worship of idols, see 1 Kings, ii.

Text, 35.84–89; Trans., 35.87–92
For Peter's threefold denial of Christ, see Matthew, xxvii; Mark, xiv; Luke, xxii.

Text, 35.93–120; Trans., 35.96–123
Caesar's assassination: Dr. Jane Taylor has drawn our attention to a similar account of Caesar's death to be found in the fourteenth-century romance *Perceforest*, and has kindly provided a transcription of the relevant passages in MS Bibliothèque Nationale, fond français 348, ff. 35v, 41r, 42r. According to the *Perceforest*, the leader behind the plot had special *greffes* made from metal (*greffes* are styles, pointed instruments used for writing on wax tablets). Caesar was given a warning letter on his way to the Senate; he took it in his hand, but did not read it. Before the conspirators entered the Senate House, they were given these styles under the pretense that they could use them to record Caesar's pronouncement: "Seigneurs, dist Ursus, selon la coustume rommaine prenez voz greffes et escripsiez en voz tables le jugement. Atant il se leva et a presenté aux douse plus notables les douse greffes que Oursel son oncle avoit apportees de la Grant Bretaigne" (MS 348, f. 41r).

The chief conspirator plunged his style into Caesar's chest and the others followed his example. According to Suetonius, *De vita Caesarum*, Book I, LXXXI–LDDDIII, Caesar tried to defend himself with a style (*graphio*), but was surrounded by drawn daggers and stabbed many times. Gilles Roussineau (*Perceforest*, 4, vol. 2, p. 1098) has drawn attention to similarities between the version of the death in Suetonius and that in *Perceforest*: doors or windows opening by themselves on the night before the assassination; the unread letter still clutched in Caesar's left hand as he dies. However, as far as Charny's account is concerned, the close resemblances

are with *Perceforest*, not Suetonius, and it would seem very probable that he was using the French romance as a source. Jane Taylor, in her edition (*Perceforest* 1, 24–29), gives as a probable date for the romance 1330–1350. G. Roussineau (*Perceforest* 4, pp. ix-xiv) concludes that the work was finished between 1337 and 1344.

Text, 35.148; Trans., 35.152
Judas Maccabeus is cited as one who benefited from divine assistance in a prayer for the recipient of the knightly sword in the late thirteenth-century pontifical of Guillaume Durand. See Jean Flori, "Chevalerie et liturgie: remise des armes et vocabulaire "chevaleresque" dans les sources liturgiques du IXe au XIVe siècle," *Le Moyen Age* 84 (1978), pp. 247–78 and 409–42 (438). There are many allusions to him in medieval literature as one of the first of the great knights; they culminate in his promotion to the rank of one of the Nine Worthies in the *Voeux du Paon* of Jacques de Longuyon (1312). See D. A. Trotter, "Judas Maccabeus, Charlemagne and the oriflamme," *Medium Aevum* 54 (1985): 127–31. There are allusions to Judas Maccabeus in *LK*, 146, and *LOC*, 283 (not, according to the editor, in the Catalan source), but none of these present close verbal similarities with the reference in Charny.

Text, 35.176–77
armes here is a variant form of *ames* ("souls"). See "The Language of Manuscript B," *Consonants*, 8.

Text, 36.2
orde: For other examples of this variant form of *ordre*, see 37.1, 39.17.

Text and Trans., 36.4–57
This account of the knighting ceremony follows very closely that to be found in *OC*, 108–12.

Text 36.27
mettre tout orgueil: For a discussion of the reading of *B*, *toute orgueil*, see "The Language of Manuscript B," *Vowels*, 18.

Text, 37.1
orde: See note to 36.2.

Text, 40.33–34; Trans., 40.35–36
The text of *B* and *P* does not make sense as it stands. *L*'s reading is presumably an attempt at emendation. I have based my emendation on the pattern of the following sentence in *B: Et qui fait les faiz d'armes plus pour avoir la*

grace de Dieu et pour les ames sauver que pour la gloire de ce monde. However, it is possible that the omission in *B* and in *P* derives ultimately from a source rather like the following, where the hypothetical reading is italicized: "Certes en ceste ordre de chevalerie peut l'on tres bien les aumes sauver et les corps tres bien honorer. *Toutesvoies qui fait les faiz d'armes plus pour le corps tres bien honorer* que pour l'ame sauver . . ." The eye of the scribe in *B* or that of the manuscript he was copying would then have jumped from *corps tres bien honorer* to *corps tres bien honorer*.

Text, 41.15; Trans., 41. 14–15
bien escorche qui le pié tient, translated as "he does mischief enough who helps mischief." The literal translation would be "he who holds the foot also takes part in the flaying." Cotgrave's rendering of the proverb has been used.

Text, 42.73
est dit: This is an emendation based on *P* for the reading in *B* and *L: est dist*. As *B* never elsewhere uses the form *dist* as a past participle, I have interpreted its reading as an example of a common type of mechanical error in which the scribe repeats the ending of the previous word; the disappearance from the pronunciation of [s] before a consonant, which had already taken place by the thirteenth century, would be a contributory factor.

Text, 42.162–63; Trans., 42.170–71
It is not quite clear from the readings of *B* and *P* whether it is the *riches aournemens* or the *chetiz corps* which are the subject of the clause *qui n'ont heure ne terme de durer*.

Text, 42.190
doubtoit: For this Burgundian form of the present subjunctive, see "The Language of Manuscript B," Morphology, 10.

Text, 43.5; Trans., 43.5
a d[r]oit peut faire: Another possible emendation, *le doit et peut faire*, is suggested by the reading of *P*, but this is somewhat undermined by the fact that *P (le a doit et peut faire)* keeps the *a* present in *B*.

Text, 43.37
The reading of *B, bien pourront bien dire,* is an example of a common form of scribal error arising from a tendency to repeat words which can occur in more than one position in the sentence. Cf. *LK*, vol. 2, 57.

Text, 44.12–13; Trans., 44.12–13
si mal gracieux. The reading of *BP*, *si male fin gracieux*, is very odd; it may derive from a scribe, copying a reading *si mal gracieux et sanz nulle seurté et pour venir a tres male fin*, whose eye jumped from *mal* to *male fin* and who then made a rather unsuccessful attempt to incorporate the words he had omitted.

Text, 44.23–24; Trans., 44.24
car il vous veille garder: car is here used to reinforce a wish.

Bibliography

DESCRIPTIONS OF MANUSCRIPTS AND EDITION OF THE *Livre de Chevalerie*

Dogaer, Georges and Marguerite Debae. *La Librairie de Philippe le Bon: Exposition organisée à l'occasion du 500ᵉ anniversaire de la mort du duc. Catalogue rédigé par Georges Dogaer et Marguerite Debae.* Brussels, 1967.
Gaspar, Camille, and Frédéric Lyna. *Les principaux manuscrits à peintures de la Bibliothèque Royale de Belgique.* Paris, 1937; reprinted Brussels, 1984, pp. 410–12.
Geoffroy de Charny. *Le livre de chevalerie.* In Froissart, *Oeuvres complètes de Froissart*, ed. Kervyn de Lettenhove, 11 vols. Brussels, 1867–77. vol. I, part iii, 463–533.

EDITIONS AND TRANSLATIONS OF OTHER TEXTS

Adam Murimuth. *Adae Murimuth, continuatio Chronicarum Robertus de Avesbury, De Gestis Mirabilibus Regis Edwardi Tertii*, ed. Edward M. Thompson, Rolls Series 93. London, 1889.
Bernard of Clairvaux. *Treatises III: On Grace and Free Choice: Praise of the New Knighthood*, trans. Daniel O'Donovan and Conrad Greenia. In *The Works of Bernard of Clairvaux*, vol. 7. Christian Fathers Series 19. Kalamazoo, MI, 1977.
Chandos Herald. *Life of the Black Prince, by the Herald of Sir John Chandos*, ed. Mildred K. Pope and Eleanor C. Lodge. Oxford, 1910, reprint New York, 1974.
La Chastelaine de Vergi, ed. F. Whitehead. 2nd ed. Manchester, 1952.
Chrétien de Troyes. *Le roman de Perceval ou le conte du Graal*, ed. William Roach. Geneva, 1956.
Chronique des quatre premiers Valois, ed. Siméon Luce. Paris, 1862.
Chronique normande du XIVe siècle, ed. August Molinier and Emile Molinier. Paris, 1882.
Complainte sur la Bataille de Poitiers, ed. Charles de Beaurepaire. Bibliothèque de l'Ecole des Chartes 12. Paris, 1850.
Documents parisiens du règne de Philippe VI de Valois, ed. Jules Viard. Vol. I *(1328–1338)*. Paris, 1899; Vol. II *(1339–1350)*, Paris, 1920.
François de Monte Belluna. "Le tragicum argumentum de miserabili statu regni

Francie de François de Monte Belluna (1357)," ed. A. O. Vernet. In *Annuaire-Bulletin de la Société de l'Histoire de France*. Paris, 1962–63.
Froissart, Jean. *Oeuvres complètes de Froissart*, ed. Kervyn de Lettenhove. 25 vols. Brussels, 1867–77.
———. *Chroniques de Jean Froissart*, ed. Siméon Luce. 4 vols. Paris, 1869–99.
Genet, Jean-Philippe. *Four English Political Tracts of the Later Middle Ages*. Camden Fourth Series 18. London, 1977.
Geoffrey de Vinsauf. *Poetria Nova of Geoffrey de Vinsauf*, trans. Margaret F. Nims. Toronto, 1967.
Geoffrey le Baker. *Chronicon Galfridi le Baker de Swynbroke*, ed. Edward M. Thompson. Oxford, 1889.
Geoffroy de Charny. "Les Demandes pour la joute, le tournoi, et la guerre de Geoffroy de Charny (XIVème siècle)," ed. Jean Rossbach. Unpublished dissertation, University of Brussels, 1961–62, deposited in the Bibliothèque Royale.
———. "A Critical Edition of Geoffroy de Charny's 'Livre Charny' and the 'Demandes pour la joute, les tournois, et la guerre,'" ed. Michael Anthony Taylor. Unpublished PhD dissertation, University of North Carolina, 1977.
Grandes Chroniques de France, ed. Jules Viard. Société de l'Histoire de France IX. Paris, 1937.
Guillaume de Lorris and Jean de Meun. *The Romance of the Rose by Guillaume de Lorris and Jean de Meun*, trans. Charles Dahlberg. Princeton, NJ, 1971.
Henry of Lancaster. *Le livre de sayntz medecines: The Unpublished Devotional Treatise of Henry of Lancaster*, ed. E. J. Arnould. Anglo-Norman Text Society. Oxford, 1940.
L'Histoire de Guillaume le Marechal, ed. Paul Meyer. 3 vols. Paris, 1891–1901.
Jean de Bueil. *Le Jouvencel*, ed. Camille Favre and Léon Lecestre. 2 vols. Paris, 1887–89.
Jean de Venette. *The Chronicle of Jean de Venette*, trans. Jean Birdsall, ed. Richard Newhall. New York, 1953.
Jean le Bel. *Chronique*, ed. Jules Viard and E. Deprez. Paris, 1905.
John of Salisbury. *Policraticus*, ed. C.C.J. Webb. Oxford, 1909.
Les Journaux du trésor de Philippe VI de Valois, suivis de l'Ordinarium thesaurii de 1338–1339, ed. Jules Viard. Collection des Documents Inédits de l'Histoire de France. Paris, 1899.
Knyghthode and Bataile, ed. Roman Dyboski and Zygfryd M. Arend. London, 1935.
Lancelot do Lac: The Non-Cyclic Old French Prose Romance, ed. Elspeth Kennedy. 2 vols. Oxford, 1980.
Lancelot: roman en prose du XIII siècle, ed. Alexandre Micha. 9 vols. Paris-Geneva, 1978–83.
Lancelot of the Lake, trans. Corin Corley. Oxford, 1989.
Llull, Ramon. *The Book of the Ordre of Chyvalry*, trans. William Caxton, ed. Alfred T. P. Byles. Early English Text Society, London, 1926.
———. *Libre que es de l'ordre de cavallería*, in *Obres essencials*, ed. Pere Bohigas, vol. 1. Barcelona, 1957.
———. *Livre de l'ordre de chevallerie*, medieval French translation of *Le Libre del orde de cavallería*, in *Obres de Ramon Lull*, ed. Antoni M. Alcover, Mateu Obrador,

and Bartolome Bennassar. Palma de Mallorca, Comission Editora Llulliana, 1906, Vol. I, 249–91.
———. *Livre de l'ordre de chevalerie*, ed. Vincenzo Minervini. Bari, 1972.
———. *Selected Works of Ramon Llull (1232–1316)*, trans. Anthony Bonner. 2 vols. Princeton, NJ, 1985.
Maistre Pierre Pathelin, ed. Richard T. Holbrook. 2nd ed. Paris, 1967.
Malory, Sir Thomas. *Works*, ed. Eugene Vinaver, rev. P.J.C. Field, 3rd ed. 3 vols. Oxford, 1990.
La Mort le Roi Artu, ed. Jean Frappier. 3rd ed. Paris, 1964.
Olivier de la Marche. *Mémoires*, ed. Henri Beaune and J. d'Arbaument. 4 vols. Paris, 1883–88.
Ordonnances des rois de France, ed. E.-J. Laurière et al. 22 vols. Paris, 1723–1849.
Perceforest: Le roman de Perceforest, première parte, ed. Jane Taylor. Geneva, 1979. *Perceforest, troisième partie*, ed. Gilles Roussineau. 2 vols. Geneva, 1988. *Perceforest, quatrième partie*, ed. Gilles Roussineau. 2 vols. Geneva, 1987.
Perlesvaus. Le Haut Livre du Graal: Perlesvaus, ed. William A. Nitze and T. Jenkins. Chicago, 1932–37.
Perlesvaus. The High Book of the Grail: A Translation of the Thirteenth-Century Romance of Perslesvaus, trans. Nigel Bryant. Cambridge, 1978.
Philippe de Beaumanoir. *Les Coutumes de Beauvaisis*, ed. Amédée Salmon. 2 vols. SATF. Paris, 1884–85, reprinted 1976.
———. *The* Coutumes de Beauvaisis *de Philippe de Beaumanoir*, trans. F.R.P. Akehurst. Philadelphia, 1992.
Philippe de Novare. *Les quatre âges de l'homme: traité moral de Philippe de Navarre, publié pour la première fois d'après les manuscrits de Paris, de Londres, et de Metz*, ed. Marcel de Fréville. SATF. Paris, 1888.
La Queste del Saint Graal, ed. Albert Pauphilet. Paris, 1923.
The Quest of the Holy Grail, trans. Pauline M. Matarasso. Harmondsworth, 1969.
Raoul de Houdenc. *Le Roman des eles, by Raoul de Houdenc and The Anonymous Ordene de la chevalerie*, ed. Keith Busby. Utrecht Publications in General and Comparative Literature 17. Amsterdam, 1983.
Rule of the Templars: The French Text of the Rule of the Order of the Knights Templar. Trans. J. M. Upton-Ward. Woodbridge, 1992.
Rymer, Thomas. *Foedera, Conventiones, Literae*, ed. Adam Clarke and Frederick Holbrooke. 2 vols. London, 1856.
Vulgate Version of the Arthurian Romances, ed. H. Oskar Sommer. Washington, D.C., 1909–13.

SECONDARY WORKS

Allmand, C. T., ed. *War, Literature and Politics in the Later Middle Ages*. Liverpool, 1976.
Anselme, Père F. *Histoire généalogique de la maison royale de France*. 1733. VIII.
Arnould, S. J. "Henry of Lancaster and His Livre de Seyntz Medicines." *Bulletin of the John Rylands Library* 21 (1937), 352–86.

Atiya, Aziz S. *The Crusade in the Later Middle Ages*. London, 1938.
Barber, Malcolm. *The New Knighthood: A History of the Order of the Temple*. Cambridge, 1994.
Barber, Richard and Juliet Barker. *Tournaments, Jousts, Chivalry, and Pageants in the Middle Ages*. New York, 1989.
Benson, Larry D. "The Tournament in the Romances of Chretien de Troyes and *L'Histoire de Guillaume le Marechal*." *Chivalric Literature*, ed. Larry D. Benson and John Leyerle. Toronto, 1980. 1–25.
Boulton, D'Arcy Dacre Jonathan. *The Knights of the Crown: The Monarchical Orders of Knighthood in Later Medieval Europe, 1325–1520*. New York, 1987.
Bradbury, Jim. *The Medieval Siege*. Woodbridge, 1992.
Brundage, James A. *Medieval Canon Law and the Crusader*. Madison, WI, 1969.
Cazelles, Raymond. "La Réglementation royale de la guerre privée de Saint Louis à Charles V et la précarité des ordonnances." *Revue Historique de Droit Française* 4th ser. 38 (1960), 530–48.
———. *Société politique, noblesse et couronne sous Jean le Bon et Charles V*. Paris, 1982.
Chevalier, Ulysse. "Etude critique sur l'origine du Saint Suaire de Lirey-Chambery-Turin" and "Autour des origines du Suaire de Lirey." Parts 2, 4 of *Bibliothèque Liturgique* 5 (1900).
Clanchy, Michael, *From Memory to Written Record: England, 1066–1307*. 2nd ed. London, 1993.
Coleman, Janet. *Medieval Readers and Writers, 1350–1400*. New York, 1981.
Contamine, Philippe. "Froissart: art militaire, pratique et conception de la guerre." *Froissart: Historian*, ed. J. J. N. Palmer. Bury St. Edmunds, 1981.
———. "Geoffroy de Charny (début de XIVe siècle–1356), 'Le plus prudhomme et le plus vaillant de tous les autres.'" *Histoire et société: Mélanges Georges Duby, II, Le tenancier, le fidèle et le citoyen*. Aix-en-Provence, 1992. 107–21.
———. *Guerre, état, et société à la fin du Moyen Age*. Paris, 1972.
———. "L'Oriflamme de Saint Denis aux XIVe et XVe siècles." *Annales de l'Est* 7 (1973), 179–244.
Coville, Alfred. *Les premiers Valois et la Guerre de cent ans (1328–1422)*. Vol. 4 of E. Lavisse, gen. ed., *Histoire de France depuis les origines jusqu'à la Revolution*. 9 vols. Paris, 1901–1910. Reprint New York, 1969.
Dale, W.S.A. "The Shroud of Turin: Relic or Icon?" *Nuclear Instruments and Methods in Physics Research* B29 (1987), 187–92.
Damon, P.E. et al. "Radiocarbon Dating of the Shroud of Turin," *Nature* 337 (1989), 511–615.
Delachenal, R. *Histoire de Charles V*. 3 vols. Paris, 1909.
Devon, Frederick, ed. *Issues of the Exchequer*. London, 1837.
Denholm-Young, Noel. "The Tournament in the Thirteenth Century." *Studies in Medieval History Presented to Frederick Maurice Powicke*, ed. R. W. Hunt, W. H. Pantin, and R. W. Southern. Oxford, 1948.
Duby, Georges, *Les trois ordres: ou, l'imaginaire du féodalisme*. Paris, 1978.
———. *William Marshal: The Flower of Chivalry*, trans. Richard Howard. New York, 1985.

Erdmann, Carl. *The Origin of the Idea of Crusade*, trans. Marshal W. Baldwin and Walter Goffart. Princeton, NJ 1977.
Favier, Jean. *La Guerre de Cent ans*. Paris, 1980.
Flori, Jean. "Chevalerie et liturgie: Rémise des armes et vocabulaire 'chevaleresque' dans les sources liturgiques du IXe au XIVe siècle," *Le Moyen Age* 84 (1978), 247–78, 409–42.
———. *L'Essor de la chevalerie: XI–XII siècles*. Paris, 1986.
———. "Pour une histoire de la chevalerie: L'adoubement dans les romans de Chretien de Troyes." *Romania* 100 (1979).
Forgeais, Arthur. *Collection de plombs historiés trouvés dans la Seine*. Paris, 1865.
Frappier, Jean. *Etude sur le mort le Roi Artu*. 2nd ed. Paris, 1961.
Gillingham, John. "War and Chivalry in the *History of William the Marshal*." *Proceedings of the Newcastle Upon Tyne Conference, 1987*, ed. P. R. Coss and S. D. Lloyd. Thirteenth-Century England 2. Bury St. Edmunds, 1988. 1–15.
———. "Richard I and the Science of War in the Middle Ages." *War and Government in the Middle Ages: Essays in Honour of J. O. Prestwich*, ed. John Gillingham and J. C. Holt. Bury St. Edmunds, 1984. 78–92.
Godefroy, Fréderic. *Dictionnaire de l'ancienne langue française*. Paris, 1880–1901.
Gove, H. E. "Dating the Turin Shroud—An Assessment." *Radiocarbon* 32 (1990), 87–92.
———. "Progress in Radiocarbon Dating the Shroud of Turin," *Radiocarbon* 31 (1989), 965–69.
Guenée, Bernard. "La culture historique des nobles: le success des *Faits des Romains* (XIIIe–XVe siècles)." *La Noblesse au Moyen Age*, ed. Philippe Contamine. Paris, 1976.
Hazard, Harry W., ed. *The Fourteenth and Fifteenth Centuries*. Vol. 3 of *A History of the Crusades*, gen. ed. Kenneth M. Setton. 4 vols. Madison, WI, 1969–89.
Henneman, John Bell. *Royal Taxation in Medieval France: the development of War Financing (1322–1356)*. Princeton, NJ, 1971.
Hewitt, H. J. *The Black Prince's Expedition of 1355–57*. Manchester, 1958.
———. *The Organization of War Under Edward III, 1338–1362*. Manchester, 1966.
Kaeuper, Richard W. *War, Justice and Public Order: England and France in the Later Middle Ages*. Oxford, 1988.
Keen, Maurice. *Chivalry*. New Haven, CT, 1984.
———. "Chivalry, Nobility, and the Man-at-Arms." *War, Literature and Politics in the Later Middle Ages*, ed. C. T. Allmand. Liverpool, 1976.
Kennedy, Beverly. *Knighthood in the Morte Darthur*. Bury St. Edmunds, 1985.
Kennedy, Elspeth, "The Knight as Reader of Arthurian Romance." *Culture and the King: The Social Implications of the Arthurian Legend, Essays in Honor of Valerie M. Lagorio*, ed. Martin B. Schichtman and James P. Carley. New York, 1995. 70–90.
———. *Lancelot and the Grail: A Study of the Prose Lancelot*. Oxford, 1980.
———. "The Quest for Identity and the Importance of Lineage in Thirteenth-Century Prose Romance." In *The Ideals and Practices of Medieval Knight-*

hood, II, ed. Christopher Harper-Bill and Ruth Harvey. Woodbridge, 1988.

——. "Social and Political Ideas in the French Prose *Lancelot*." *Medium Aevum* 36 (1957).

LeClercq. "Saint Bernard's Attitude Toward War." *Studies in Medieval Cistercian History II*, ed. John Sommerfeldt. Kalamazoo, MI, 1976.

Lizerand, Georges. *Le Dossier de l'affaire des Templiers*. 2nd ed. Paris, 1964.

McFarlane, K.B. "The Education of the Nobility in Later Medieval England." *The English Nobility in the Later Middle Ages*. Oxford, 1973.

Menestrier, Claude François. *De la Chevalerie ancienne et moderne*. Paris, 1683.

Mollat, Guillaume. "Clement VII et le Suaire de Lirey." *Le Correspondant* 210 (1903), 254–59.

Newton, Stella Mary. *Fashion in the Age of the Black Prince—A Study of the Years 1340–1365*. Bury St. Edmunds, 1980.

Painter, Sidney. *William Marshal: Knight-Errant, Baron, and Regent of England*. Baltimore, 1933.

Pantin, W. A. *The English Church in the Fourteenth Century*. Notre Dame, IN, 1962.

Parkes, Malcolm. "The Literacy of the Laity." *The Medieval World*. London, 1973.

Perrett, André. "Essai sur l'histoire du Saint Suaire du XIVe au XVIe siècle." *Académie des Sciences, Belles-lettres, et Arts de Savoie, Mémoires* ser. 6, IV (1960).

Perroy, Edouard. *The Hundred Years War*. New York, 1965.

Piaget, Arthur. "Le Livre Messire Geoffroi de Charny." *Romania* 26 (1897).

Pope, Mildred K. *From Latin to Modern French with Especial Consideration of Anglo-Norman: Phonology and Morphology*. 2nd ed. Manchester, 1952.

Richardson, H. G. and G. O. Sayles. *The Governance of Medieval England from the Conquest to Magna Carta*. Edinburgh, 1963.

Riley-Smith, Jonathan. *The Atlas of the Crusades*. New York, 1991.

Runciman, Steven. *A History of the Crusades* 3 vols. Cambridge, 1951–54.

Salch, Charles-Laurent, Joelle Burnouf, and J.-F. Fino, eds. *L'Atlas des châteaux forts en France*. Strasbourg, 1977.

Savio, P. "Ricerche sopra la Santa Sindone." *Pontificium Athenaeum Salesianum* 1 (1955), 120–55.

Saxer, Victor. "Le Suaire de Turin aux prises avec l'histoire." *Revue d'Histoire de l'Eglise de France* 76 (1990), 21–55.

Stefano, Giuseppe di. *Dictionnaire des locutions en Moyen Français*. Quebec, 1991.

Stone, Louise W., William Rothwell, and T. B. W. Reid, eds. *Anglo-Norman Dictionary*. London, 1977–92.

Strayer, Joseph R. *The Reign of Philip the Fair*. Princeton, NJ, 1980.

Sumption, Jonathan. *The Hundred Years War: Trial by Battle* Philadelphia, 1991.

Thurston, Henry. "The Holy Shroud and the Verdict of History." *The Month* 1 (1903), 17–29.

Tobler, Adolf and Erhard Lommatzsch. *Altfranzösisches Wörterbuch*. Berlin, from 1925.

Trotter, D. A. "Judas Maccabeus, Charlemagne and the Oriflamme." *Medium Aevum* 54 (1985), 127–31.

Turner, Ralph V. "The *Miles Literatus* in Twelfth-Century England: How Rare a Phenomenon?" *American Historical Review* 83 (1978).

Vale, Malcolm. *War and Chivalry: Warfare and Aristocratic Culture in England, France, and Burgundy at the End of the Middle Ages*. Norwich, 1981.

Wartburg, W. von. *Französiches etymologisches Wörterbuch*. Bonn, 1922–28; Leipzig, 1932–40; Basle, 1955–68.

Wilson, Ian. *The Shroud of Turin*. New York, 1978.

Index

Absalom, 58
Aiguillon, 8
d'Arcis, Pierre de, bishop of Troyes, 40
Ardres, battle of, 13

Baker, Geoffrey le, 3
Beaumont, Francis, 51
Bel, Jean le, 67–69
Belconroy, Hugues de, 14
Béthune, siege of, 8
Blois, Charles de, 5
Bohun, William de, earl of Northampton, 6

Caesar, Julius, 58, 74
Calais, 8, 10–13
Castiel-Villain, Sire de, 6
Charny, Geoffroi de
　captured: (1342), 5–6; (1350), 11–12
　children, 4
　councilor to Philippe VI, 9
　on crusade, 7–8
　death and burial, 4, 17–18
　early military career, 4–5
　lands, 4
　origins, 3–4
　wives. *See* Toucy, Jeanne de; Vergy, Jeanne de
　written works, 19–23, 28–38, 41–64, 67–83
Charny, Jean de, father of Geoffroi, 3
chivalry: and kingship, 61–63; and love, 69–74
Clairvaux, Bernard of, 44–45, 47
clothing styles, changes in, 34–35, 50 and n., 51, 55
Company of the Star, 13–15, 20–22, 29, 34, 43, 47 n., 52, 59–61, 63
Coutumes de Beauvaisis, by Philippe de Beaumanoir, 61–62
Crécy, battle of, 8, 52
crusade, Charny's participation in, 7–8, 22

Edward the Black Prince, son of Edward III, 11, 16–18
Edward III, king of England (1327–77), 5, 8, 10–12
Epitre d'Othea à Hector, by Christine de Pisan, 64

Froissart, Jean, 3, 10, 12, 13, 17, 32

Goodrich castle, 6
Grandes Chroniques de France, 51
Guinevere, 69–70, 72–73

Henry II, king of England (1154–89), 56
Humbert II, Dauphin of Viennois, 7–9, 22
Hundred Years War, 4–18, 49–50

Jean II, king of France (1350–64), 4, 13–15, 17, 20–22, 34, 51–54, 59, 60–63
Joinville, Jean, Sire de, 3–4
Joinville, Marguerite de, mother of Geoffroi de Charny, 3–4
Le Jouvencel, by Jean de Beuil, 64

kingship, 53–54
Knights Templar, 39 n., 49
Knyghthode and Bataile, 64

Lancaster, Henry of, author of *Le Livre de seyntz medicines*, 18, 46
Lancelot do Lac, 21, 23, 28, 32, 34, 67, 69, 70–74
Lirey, Charny's church at, 38, 39–41
literacy, among medieval layfolk, 18
Llull, Ramon, 19 n., 23–31, 34, 37, 46, 55, 63, 67, 69, 70

Maccabeus, Judas, 36, 58
Marigny, Jean de, archbishop of Rouen, 54
Marshal, William, and the *Histoire de Guillaume le Marechal*, 23, 27, 32, 46, 48, 55 n.

Mauron, battle of, 15
Montfort, Jean de, 5
Morlaix, battle at, 5–6
La Mort le Roi Artu, 22

Nogent, Guibert de, 42, 45

Ordene de chevalerie, 21, 24, 28–32, 42, 67, 70
oriflamme, 15–17, 29, 41

Pavia, Aimery de, 10–14, 22
Philippe IV, king of France (1285–1314), 63
Philippe VI, king of France (1328–1350), 4–5, 10, 13, 38
Poitiers, battle at, 3, 16, 59
Poitiers, Henri de, bishop of Troyes, 40
Potenhale, John de, 11–12

Queste del Sainte Graal, 31–32

Raoul, count of Eu, constable of France, 5, 49
Richard I, king of England (1189–1199), 56

Roman des eles by Raoul de Hodenc, 23–24, 28, 30, 32, 48, 55
Roman de Perceforest, 74

Saladin, 24, 29
St. Denis, monastery at, 15–16
St. Peter, 58
Samson, 58
Shroud of Turin, 29, 39–41
Smyrna, 7

Tabarie, Hue de, 24, 29
Talbot, Richard, 6
Toucy, Jeanne de, first wife of Geoffroi de Charny, 4
Tournai, siege of, 5
tournament 9 n., 19–21,, 33, 45–46, 48 n.

Vannes, siege of, 6
Venette, Jean de, 50–51
Vergy, Jeanne de, second wife of Geoffroi de Charny, 4, 40
Veronica (holy cloth), 41

CR 4513 .K34 1996

Kaeuper, Richard W.

The book of chivalry of
  Geoffroi de Charny

DISCARDED

AUG 6 2025